The Mobile Nation:
España cambia de piel (1954-1964)

The Mobile Nation:
España cambia de piel (1954-1964)

by Tatjana Pavlović

intellect Bristol, UK / Chicago, USA

First published in the UK in 2011 by Intellect,
The Mill, Parnall Road, Fishponds, Bristol, BS16 3JG, UK

First published in the USA in 2011 by Intellect, The University of Chicago Press,
1427 E. 60th Street, Chicago, IL 60637, USA

A catalogue record for this book is available from the British Library.

Cover design: Holly Rose
Typesetting: John Teehan

ISBN 978-1-84150-534-3

Printed and bound in Great Britain by 4edge Limited, Hockley.

MIX
Paper from
responsible sources
FSC
www.fsc.org
FSC® C020822

Contents

Acknowledgements

Several individuals and institutions have contributed to the making of *The Mobile Nation: España cambia de piel (1954–1964)*. Many ideas incorporated into this book have resulted directly or indirectly from discussions with friends over the several past years. It could not have been written without intense conversations, theoretical debates and the friendship of Anthony Leo Geist, Isolina Ballesteros, John Charles, Marline Otte, Ari Zighelboim, Laura Bass and Henry Sullivan. Henry gets my extra-special thanks for helping to smooth out some rough spots in the manuscript, far-ranging insights and careful judgement. He read the entire manuscript and thoughtfully engaged its arguments. My sense of his personal and intellectual support goes well beyond the pages of this book. I am also grateful to Camillo Penna and Suna Ertugrul for their friendship and for bringing my attention to certain key theoretical texts. Their own relationship to theory and writing has been very important to me during the composition of this book. Above all, I pay tribute to my mother Biljana Pavlović, who originally instilled in me the love of books and reading.

At Tulane University, I am fortunate to be surrounded by talented and generous colleagues who are also true friends. My deepest thanks go to them and to our Chair Marilyn Miller for her consistent support. I also wish to thank my students at Tulane University in a wide range of courses on Spanish cinema, film history and film theory who have listened to early versions of the manuscript and raised many excellent questions. Several scholars working on contemporary Spanish culture have read earlier versions of various chapters and given me valuable critical feedback. Special thanks also go to my colleagues in Spanish Film Studies from the United States, Spain and the United Kingdom who have been remarkably generous in sharing their work and expertise: Marvin D'Lugo, Katy Vernon, Eva Woods, Susan Martin-Márquez, Steven Marsh, and Josetxo Cerdán. Since my student days I have always been inspired by Jo Labanyi and Paul Julian Smith, two outstanding scholars of Spanish literature, film and visual culture. Their work continues to be essential to my own understanding of Spain and its cinema.

This book could not have been written without the help of various institutions in Spain and the United States. The Dean's Office of the School of Liberal Arts and Sciences at Tulane University provided me a Research Grant in the summers of 2007 and 2009 and a Junior Research Leave during the 2003–2004 academic year. That same office was also generous in aiding Intellect Publishing of Bristol, United Kingdom, with publication costs. Funding from The Program for Cultural Cooperation between Spain's Ministry of Culture and United States' Universities allowed me to spend two summers (2005 and 2006) viewing many films discussed in the book. I am also indebted to Margarita Lobo and other personnel of the Filmoteca Española who have been tremendously helpful in providing me access to the Filmoteca's collection. At Intellect Publishing, I would like to thank the Associate Publisher, May Yao, for her efficiency, patience and commitment to the project. I am also indebted to Integra Software Services for their diligent copy-editing and to the typesetter, John Teehan. In addition, I also thank Holly Rose for the design of the cover, which uncannily captures the spirit of the book and period studied.

Sections from the Introduction appeared in an earlier version as '*España cambia de piel*: The Mobile Nation (1954–1964),' *Journal of Spanish Cultural Studies*, Vol. 5, Issue 2, July 2004: (213–226). A condensed portion of Chapter 2 was published as 'Television (Hi)stories: "*Un escaparate en cada hogar*,"' *Journal of Spanish Cultural Studies*, Vol. 8, Issue 1, March 2007: (5–21). I gratefully acknowledge the publishers of these articles for permission to reproduce parts of them in this book.

This book is dedicated to my two great loves: my life-partner Rachel and our son Constantin. Rachel's keen critical acumen and understanding of the project shaped the way I look at Spanish cinema. Above all, she was my companion in the pleasures of film-going and film-viewing. Our shared love of cinema and literature was a main impetus in writing *The Mobile Nation*. But while this project is now over, she continues to inspire me into an unlimited future.

Introduction

The Mobile Nation: España cambia de piel (1954–1964) focuses on a period of transition in the history of Spanish culture that has not received sufficient critical attention.[1] Several forces converged in the early 1950s to put Spain on a path of integration with the more developed countries of Europe. Autarkic Spain abandoned its outdated and sluggish economic model developed mostly as a response to Spain's international isolation following the Spanish Civil War.[2] It gradually curbed the state interventionism that had been an integral part of autarkic economic principles. Autarky, a type of economic nationalism, had formed part of Franco's stock rhetoric by which the post-war ostracism of Spain was modified, even eulogized as a self-sufficient, autonomous cultural polity sustained, among other strategies, by an insistence on the superiority of Spain's 'blessèd backwardness' (*bendito atraso*).[3] With this easing of autarkist principles, the government needed to reframe its political tactics, visible in a revision of nationalist rhetoric that now defined 'progress' as a technocratic mutation of the prevailing ideology. The regime's self-justification ceased to be metaphysical and became more frankly material. The insistence on an Eternal Spain with its religious essence and God-chosen destiny was no longer desirable or optimal and was replaced by the language of efficiency, rational thinking and a belief in high living standards. The triumphalist, bellicose discourse of the post-war period now centred on a rhetoric of prosperity and an ever-broadening horizon of expectations. Franco's regime ceased to be providential and became technocratic. Spaniards would no longer be preparing for the heavenly paradise, but enjoying an earthly one. A discourse sustained by the old-fashioned values salvaged from the Civil War now morphed and became compatible with the siren call of hedonism. A society of sacrifice become a society of leisure, much more in line with emergent global consumerism.

The period studied in this book includes three overlapping stages of development: (1) the moribund autarky of the post-war era; (2) the technocratic period initiated by the restructuring of the cabinet in February of 1957; and (3) a so-called *fraguismo* during Manuel Fraga Iribarne's all-important tenure as Minister of Information and Tourism from 1962 till 1969. The transition from autarky to technocracy was aptly named by those economists who dubbed it the 'hinge decade' (*decenio bisagra*).[4] The term captures the shift from post-war insistence on moderation, restrictions, hoarding or rationing to the wave of new commodities and, hence, concepts that now entered the market—apartments (*apartamentos* instead of *pisos*), televisions (*televisores*), washing machines (*lavadoras*), financing (*financiación*), parking (aparcamiento)—neologisms that were just then being admitted to the Dictionary of the Spanish Royal Academy (Sánchez Vidal 1990: 156). The impact of consumer durables on everyday life was remarkable, and the percentage of urban households that owned a refrigerator, television set, car, telephone, electric food-mixer or record player soared exponentially.[5] By 1954, per capita income was approaching pre-war levels, but overall growth still encountered stubborn problems. As Tortella observed:

> An economy as backward and capital-hungry as was the Spanish had an inordinately strong propensity for import; in addition, market pressures for both capital and consumer goods, combined with an archaic fiscal structure and a policy of state investment virtually free of orthodox financing norms, provoked price increases that were very soon evident in labor market. The result was a rapid and powerful inflationary spiral. (2000: 450)

Inflation had become so rampant by 1959 that urgent measures were needed. The Franco regime proved reactive rather than forward-looking, and it was the inflation crisis pinpointed by Tortella—rather than any premeditated design—that determined the radical change in economic policy which became the 1959 stabilization plan. A year of unavoidable but salutary recession in 1960 was followed by dramatic economic growth. The whole ethos of the nation began to shift: 'The new slogans of the sixties were rationality, efficiency, the maxims of the world of the impersonal, competitive business corporation rather than of the comfortable world of family connection and personal favour' (Carr and Fusi 1981: 80). During Fraga's tenure, the country was well on its way to a full-scale Spanish 'economic miracle,' adopting Western European economic models, modes of material consumption and lifestyles.

The nation was becoming what I am terming more 'mobile' and the social consequences of this mobility began to affect all aspects of society. Once more, as in earlier demographic shifts, the countryside suffered a steady depletion as the peasantry abandoned low-paid agriculture and fled seeking new forms of employment or opportunity available in the relatively affluent cities.[6] An expanding educational system enabled increased social and class mobility, creating a deeper and broader middle class (what has been well called a 'mesocratization' of the population), as well as inflated armies of civil servants—even if underemployed in a make-work jobs –crucial to the regime's capture of human capital and its consequent prosperity. There was also a rapidly expanding white-collar class, related to jobs in the growing service sector (travel agents, tourist guides, new hotels, banks) and blue-collar construction jobs along the coastline (the development of fishing villages into international playgrounds such as Benidorm or Torremolinos) or in burgeoning urban belts of well-established cities (Madrid or Barcelona). Huge foreign investment and massive industrialization testified to a diverse mobility of resources, while the modernization of the antiquated roadways altered transportation patterns, especially once the network of peripheral coastal highways reached completion. Coastal highways provided a necessary solution to the drastically increasing volume of tourists, a European boom that became synonymous with Fraga himself and that was of inestimable importance for Spain's economic miracle. Mobility exploded as a geographical phenomenon: from depopulated villages to cities (the rural exodus previously referenced, urbanization, etc.), from Spain itself to Germany, Switzerland and France (worker migration) or from centre to periphery (coastal tourism).[7] As Tortella stated, all these changes were inseparably tied to the post-war European socio-economic trends: 'The convulsions of Spain's recent history, although presenting characteristics that are particular and original to this country, plainly fall within the framework of the social transformations that capitalist economic development has introduced into Western Europe' (2000: 441).[8] Spain was becoming an industrialized, technological, consumer society. By our *terminus ad quem* date of 1964, Spain, styling itself a 'society of well-being' (*sociedad del bienestar*), entered an era interpreted by some cultural historians as a *franquismo sociológico*.[9] The enforced peace and new prosperity led to a mood of acceptance that carried over to today's arguably apolitical democracy and a postmodern blend of amnesty and social amnesia gelled in the 'pact of oblivion' (*pacto de olvido*) (1975–78).

The Mobile Nation is divided into five chapters that examine the following aspects of Spanish consumer society as described above: (1) the connections between literature and the publishing industry; (2) the expansion of Spain's television network; (3) popular cinema and the making of a child-star system; (4) the development of mass tourism; and (5) the national automobile-manufacturing industry. The study, essentially a socio-cultural history of consumerism, uses a strong theoretical gantry to undergird my detailed survey of the massive expansion of consumer industries in mid-century, several of which have never before been studied systematically.[10] The choices of cultural figures, literary works, films and television shows studied undoubtedly bear traces of my own taste and emotional investments, and I do not claim either that they are exhaustive or exclusively representative of mid-twentieth-century Spanish culture.

The study also explores the relationship between mass-culture industries and the political and economic systems under which they emerged, a dimension that has been theorized since the days of the Frankfurt School.[11] However, this study does not propose a direct ratio between Spanish mass-cultural tendencies and Spain's political system. To quote Tortella once more: 'The interrelationships between economics and politics are almost always complex and torturous, and especially so in the Spanish case' (2000: 445).

The study therefore examines the imbrication, refractive rather then reflective, between the two phenomena. My approach neither demonizes consumer culture as a harbinger of apathy nor celebrates it as a force of liberation, but looks dispassionately at the ways consumerism impacted Spanish society during the era studied. It examines the co-opting of the benefits of the new mass-culture by the regime, presented now as an outgrow of Franco's political stability and looks into the intricate capitalist reorganization of leisure time in the Spain of the 1950s. I also pay attention to audiences' 'resignification' of popular and mass forms of entertainment.[12] Examining the formation of the *sociedad de consumo*, my aim is to show how the conflicts expressive of Spanish culture are inscribed and contested in Spanish popular, mass-cultural and industrial forms.[13]

My first chapter '*La hora del lector*: Literature and the publishing industry' centres on the disengagement of the publishing industry from the literary model of neo-Realism which ran *pari passu* with a process of critical self-reflection on the part of social-realist novelists and critics themselves. In particular, the chapter examines the intersections in the literary careers of Juan Goytisolo the novelist, José María Castellet the critic, and Carlos Barral the publisher. The Seix Barral publishing house (that unites them) joined the vanguard of the editorial world and became an active force in the global circulation of cultural capital in the 1960s, thereby altering the course of Spanish literary history. The imbrication of art and market-forces in the creation of Seix Barral would call forth an anxiety produced by this demeaning proximity of culture and economic return. The chapter focuses attention more on the production and distribution systems, therefore, than on sales statistics or 'reception aesthetics' (that is, the readers' reaction and response to the trends described above).[14] It also looks at the emergence of Latin America as a literary world power, such that '…the reception of the Latin-American novel was the "burning question" (*la cuestión palpitante*) of contemporary Spanish literature' (Santana 2000: 17).[15]

The second chapter 'Television (Hi)stories: *Un escaparate en cada hogar*' analyses the tumultuous politics of television's implementation in Spain. In 1956, the Minister of Information and Tourism Gabriel Arias Salgado inaugurated Spanish national television, invoking Christ and his powers across heaven and earth and insisting that Spanish television would became an instrument of the National Movement's advocacy of religious orthodoxy. However, a change of government in February of 1957 soon altered the moralizing tone that accompanied television's start. Television (alongside other novel mass-produced goods) was inscribed in a new discourse of progress mirroring a society oriented increasingly towards consumer values. Though TV was born under the reactionary Arias Salgado, the subsequent development of the medium reflected the influence of the more liberal Fraga Iribarne. The massive spread of TV from 1956 on went hand in hand with a strategic and uninhibited embrace of consumer capitalism. This chapter also explores the connections between daily experience and media experience and traces how the implementation of television modified Spaniards' experience of time and space.

Chapter III '*Voces de oro*: Spain, modernity, and the child-star system' explicates the institutionalization of a child-star system in its relation to Spain's turn to consumerism. Central to this story are the film careers of Joselito and Marisol, figures inescapably associated with Spain's children's cinema of the 1960s (in ways similar to the earlier impact Shirley-Temple cinema had on English-speaking audiences). Joselito and Marisol were the first two child actors produced by the making-of-a-star system.[16] This system demanded exclusive contracts, the morphing of personal life into their star personae and the multiple marketing ploys aimed at promoting their image, such as fan clubs, franchises, merchandise endorsements and carefully scheduled 'impromptu' appearances. Joselito's and Marisol's early films span from the last year of the Falangist grip on power and the technocrats' entry into the cabinet (*El pequeño ruiseñor*, 1956; *Saeta del ruiseñor*, 1957) to the so-called *Plan de estabilización* and subsequent *Plan de desarrollo* (*Escucha mi canción*, *El pequeño coronel*, 1959; *Un rayo de luz*, 1960; *Ha llegado un ángel*, 1961; *Tómbola*, 1962). The chapter examines the various ways in which the films reflected a crisis of meaning and search for new parameters, given the vacuum left after the decline of Nationalist-Catholic discourse and its vacuous rhetoric of Spanish essence and destiny.

The last two chapters 'Spain's Mass Tourism: *Condenada belleza del mundo*' and 'Mobile Subjects: *La vida sobre ruedas*' centre on two aspects of the ample mobility of human resources into and out of Spain that began in the late 1950s: the rapidly rising tourism industry and Spanish emigration to northern Europe, both which left profound traces on Spanish culture of the time.[17] The emergence of the tourism industry was simultaneous with Spain's signing of bilateral emigration agreements with Switzerland, Germany and France. On the one hand, tourism, as Dean MacCannel has suggested, 'is the cutting edge of the workdwide expansion of modernity' (1999: 184). It was an emblem of the global flows of capital and border crossing, traits which were intrinsically counter to the dictatorial model. On the other hand, during the 1960s 'tourism became the linchpin of the Franco's dictatorship's symbolic structure, not only facilitating the normalization of diplomatic relations with Western liberal democracies, but also affording the regime a previously unthinkable level of political stability at home' (Crumbaugh 2009: 4). Mass tourism manifested into a form of international relations: from dissemination of information and strengthening alliances to promoting tolerance and even bringing political change. Tourism created a vital impact on the political dynamics and 'was a form of engagement with democratic Europe, where political pressures prevented close high-level ties to the Franco regime.' Furthermore, 'as Spain's doors opened to millions of foreign tourists, its hospitality industry became an increasingly useful auxiliary to the regime's formal diplomacy' (Pack 2006: 11). Tourism proved to be one of the key instruments of socio-economic and political change in Spain of the 1960s.

'Mobile Subjects: *La vida sobre ruedas*' ties emigration and tourism to one of the most significant artefacts of modernity: the automobile, a machine that guaranteed unlimited personal and familial mobility, a dream-turned-commodity of personal freedom.

Introduction of the car, a mass phenomenon by the mid-1950s, marked Spanish culture deeply. SEAT (la Sociedad Española de Automóviles de Turismo) showcased its affordable model, the 'seiscientos' (Fiat 600) in June of 1957. Cars were inseparably tied to 'progress' and modernization. Waldo de Mier, the author of the original *España cambia de piel*, proclaimed that 'una población con automóviles sin rasponazos ni abolladuras es una población subdesarrollada' (1964: 14) and that '[ahora que] los españoles han descubierto el placer de ir sobre ruedas caminar se hace como dura obligación o deporte' (1964: 122). In a similar vein, the 1959 motto of Spanish television was 'la vida sobre ruedas' ('Easy Street,' or literally 'life on wheels'). Combining analysis of Spain's rapid motorization together with tourism and emigration, this chapter highlights a turbulent moment in Spanish modernity that attests to space defined more by mobility than by fixed dwelling.

In terms of theory, this study inhabits different disciplinary frameworks: literature, film and television studies, cultural studies, tourism studies, economics and the broader historical background. Many scholars have influenced me, but I draw particularly on Slavoj Žižek's radical re-envisioning of mass culture, Michel Chion's work on voice in cinema, Cathy Caruth's reading of trauma and history, and John Corner, Anna McCarthy and Lynn Spigel's individual contributions in television studies. The book is also indebted to Paul Preston, Raymond Carr, Juan Pablo Fusi, Stanley Payne, Carolyn Boyd, and the discriminating editors, David Gies' and Santos Juliá, for their work on Spanish history, especially the research that focuses on the Franco era. Manuel Palacio's history of Spanish televison and Gabriel Tortella's study on Spanish economy proved indispensable.[18] *The Mobile Nation* also complements and dialogues with several crucial texts in the field of Spanish cultural studies such as Jo Labanyi's numerous insights on the cultural history of Francoism, Paul Julian Smith's writings on film and television and Stephanie Sieburth's book on modernity and mass-culture. Pioneer scholars of Spanish tourism studies, such as Justin Crumbaugh, Sasha Pack, Eugenia Afinoguénova and Jaume Marti-Olivella, have contributed significantly to my own understanding of this key service-industry phenomenon of the 1960s.

The ultimate question my study poses is this: to what extent did the staggered decade 1954–64 constitute a radical departure from the dictatorial past? Or was it, rather, a decisive moment in the reinvention of the dictatorship? My doubts on this whole problematic were first triggered by an eccentric text entitled *España cambia de piel* by an unknown Falangist journalist Waldo de Mier, whose happy title I borrowed for my own manuscript. The interval between Waldo de Mier's two books, both entitled *España cambia de piel*, the first published in 1954 and the second in 1964, marks the time span of this book.[19] De Mier remained so wrapped up in his metaphor that, ten years after the publication of the first version, 'with his cripple's orthopaedic leg,' he revisited the places described in it and entitled his new epiphany—once more—*España cambia de piel* (but now subtitled *Nuevo viaje por la 'España del Milagro'*). His physical impairment had not dampened his enthusiasm for recording and participating in the optimism of incipient development. The dates that frame the study may seem somewhat arbitrary, but they do correspond to crucial moments in cultural transition, dating from the wholesale recruitment of technocrats into the power structure to the unmistakable lignament of late Francoist culture.

Waldo de Mier's texts perfectly match my own interests in Spanish culture of the mid-twentieth-century. De Mier's writing was so intensely caught up in the transformation of Spanish society and entirely symptomatic of the drastic changes the country was experiencing. Though a Falangist, De Mier swapped the party's rhetoric of militarism for a rhetoric of progress celebrating Spain's entry into the modern European economy. His gradual abandonment of the Falange and embrace of new economic ideals paralleled the technocratic Spanish government's decisive break with its own autarkist rhetoric and Falangist ideology. Nevertheless, De Mier's texts are imbued with contradictions and remain intriguing precisely because they lie trapped between these two epistemes (the Falangist/autarkic and the technocratic) and hence epitomize the spirit of the times, while proving incongruously faithful to Spain's national trajectory.

Significantly, the implausible and high-flown encomium of Rafael García Serrano, a well-known Falangist writer, furnished the Prologue to *España cambia de piel*:

> Toda la vida de Waldo de Mier está relacionada con una honda pasión española, con el afán de salvar a España, de mejorar a España, de hermosear a España, de conseguir una España justa, de trabajar para España, de ver a España, de adivinar España, de cantar España; de criticar lo malo de España; de comer, beber, vivir y dormir con España; de llevar a España en los pulsos y en los pies, en la cabeza, [y] en el corazón. (1964: xii)

García Serrano's encomium can be actually taken quite literally: very rarely does one see such a complete symbiosis or merging of an individual's life into the nation or a political narrative such as this.[20] Waldo de Mier's life was so fused with the trajectory of Spain, the country that he figuratively drank, lived and slept with. Above all, García Serrano's prologue to *España cambia de piel* is really a testimony to his Falangist comradeship with Waldo de Mier. Laín Entralgo, a Falangist intellectual, described fascism precisely as 'a "style" appropriate to "poets writing a vast communal poem" ' (Labanyi 1989: 38, 39).[21] García Serrano's style, like that of several other of his comrades, is laced with virulent rhetoric, emphasizing courage, honour, strength and heroism and exalting themes of militarism, patriotism and nationalism: 'Yo sirvo en la literatura como serviría en una escuadra. Con la misma intensidad y el mismo objetivo. Cualquier otra cosa me parecería una traición'...'Nada nos importa pasar por el Mundo sin dejar otra huella que la de las botas de clavos' (Rodríguez-Puértolas 1987 (Vol I): 237, 508).

In *España cambia de piel* Waldo de Mier swaps the Falangist rhetoric of imprinting the world with military boots and embraces a rhetoric of progress. Members of the Falange felt increasingly discontent due to the ideological disarmament of their party and the domestication of José Antonio Primo de Rivera's vocabulary that then became one of the pillars of Franco's post-war rhetoric. The party was gradually being reduced to external symbols and paraphernalia. Hence, while Waldo de Mier embarked on a path of progress 'the radical Falangists turned back to the roots of Falangist ideology in the 1898 writers and Ortega in order to vindicate the anti-capitalist platform of their founder, José Antonio, which they felt Franco had betrayed' (Labanyi 1989: 55). While discontented and nostalgic Falangists were trying to reclaim their place in a Spain that had 'betrayed' them, autarkic Spain was irrevocably becoming technocratic.

The tensions in Waldo de Mier's writing are symptomatic of all the drastic changes that the country itself was experiencing. His texts are caught between promoting the movement of modernity and thwarting threats to the moral traits so long cherished by the autarky. A technocratic articulation of progress is ideologically grafted onto Falangist rhetoric. Despite Waldo de Mier's 'evolution,' *España cambia de piel* is at times still reminiscent of the old Falangist rhetoric. Witold Gombrowicz explains such historical transitions well when he says: 'when certain customs are about to be finished, they become afflicted with a kind of sclerosis—the living content escapes from them and only the rigidity of 'pure form' remains.'[22]

Departing from the concepts of essential destiny, organic wholness, mythical returns, and tragic, mournful and sick national spirit Waldo de Mier describes the Spain that is like Klee's 'Angelus Novus' 'irresistibly propeled toward the future...by the storm that we call progress' (Benjamin 1969: 257, 258).[23] Waldo de Mier even envisions the Spanish landscape as 'el Far-West de todos los españoles, la Tierra Prometida, el Nuevo Mundo para nosotros mismos' (1964: 77). It is also the Spain, as García Serrano observes, 'que ya huele a petróleo' (1964: xiii). In that spirit of optimism and faith in modernization *España cambia de piel* covers the incipient signs of economic development, ranging from market integration, foreign direct investment and the changing trade relations with Europe and the United States to massive industrialization, development of the car industry and increasing mobility.

Traveling through Spain with an American couple, Denis and Alice Moore, Waldo de Mier boasts, 'si sumara sus Wonderful, What a nice thing y Marvelous, los contaría por centenares' (1954: 34). Thus the 1954 'edition' of *España cambia de piel* also points to the rapidly changing relationship to the United States and its adoption as a model of development and industrialization. The titles of the sections alone bear witness to this change: Vigo is the 'San Francisco de California español,' El Castro is 'The little Manhattan;' la Playa de San Lorenzo is baptized Miami, Barcelona is 'la Detroit española,' and Lugo's slaughterhouse is 'de proporciones chicaguescas.'

The publication of *España cambia de piel* corresponds to the opening up of the Spanish economy. Cold War politics very much contributed to ending the country's isolation and eased Spain's entry into various international alliances. The dictatorial regime was futher legitimated internationally in the early to mid-1950s as Spain was admitted to UNESCO (November 1952), signed a Concordat with the Vatican (August 1953), and was shortly thereafter admitted to the United Nations (December 1955) and the OEEC (Organization for European Economic Co-operation) (January 1958).

The cabinet restructuring of February 1957 with the inclusion of the technocrats—the new Minister of Finance, Mariano Navarro Rubio, the new Minister of Commerce, Alberto Ullastres Calvo, and Laureano López Rodó who held the key post as head of the Technical Secretariat of the Presidency of the Government—'was to be one of the great watersheds of Franco's political career. It marked the beginning of his transition from active politician to symbolic figurehead' (Preston 1994: 665).[24] Laureano López Rodó (the Catalan monarchist and professor of administrative law) was 'a deeply religious member of Opus Dei,' and the very model of its values: 'militant, quietly confident, hard-working and efficient' (Preston 1994: 657). According to López Rodó 'the National Programme for Regulating Investment (March 1959) was the first step that led to the later Development Plans, the first use of the new administrative machinery to act on the economy as a whole, 'a vast programme that would affect all sectors of national life' (Carr and Fusi 1981: 54, 55).[25]

As in the immediate post-war period, Franco continued to blame Spain's economic woes on communists as well as on Masonic elements. Franco was becoming anachronistic even vis-à-vis his own regime, which was profoundly changing, modernizing and leaving him behind. The appointment of a new technocratic cabinet had meant the uninhibited embrace of late consumer capitalism that in its aftermath brought 'huge foreign investment, massive industrialization, population migration, urbanization, educational expansion, the social consequences of which were to turn Franco and Falangism into historical anachronisms' (Preston 1994: 666). The technocrats played a key role in this transformation because they offered an apparent compromise to the contradictory demands between autarky and capitalist liberalization. Several technocrats were members of Opus Dei (like López Rodó), an organization committed to

> the sanctification of the secular world. As conceived by its founder and leaders, the labor of disseminating spiritual values could be most effectively prosecuted through the key professions of late industrial society such as university teaching, business, finance, and the higher levels of management. (Payne 1987: 437, 438)

López Rodó considered that the integration of Spain into the dynamic European economy would necessarily have political consequences in Spain and 'his views were summed up in a phrase, erroneously attributed to him, that only when per capita income in Spain reached $1000.00 per annum could there be democratization' (Preston 1994: 699). This claim that ties increasing purchasing power and the rise of consumer society to political change was obviously erroneous since there was no democratization of Spain until the end of dictatorship, and Spain's political structures were not changed until Franco's death. However, López Rodó's assertion is interesting because it fits into a larger European trend of unwavering faith in modernization in the post-Second World War period (this phenomenon is also noticable in Waldo de Mier's optimism regarding *España del milagro*). This fervour of development and modernization was backed up by 'the post-1945 "modernization theory" emerging from the unexpectedly successful western capitalist reconstruction and expansion in the post-Second World War period' (Graham and Labanyi 1995b: 10). López Rodó's technocratic embrace of modernization theory is a part of the trend of other ideologues of this period. For example, Gonzalo Fernández de la Mora claimed, as the title of his 1965 book *El crepúsculo de ideologías* suggests, that progress will nullify all political tensions and that all ideologies will become obsolete and substituted by technical and economic government plans. López Rodó's democratization through increased purchasing power is close to Fernández de la Mora's anouncement of the twilight of ideology: 'De la política como arte y como retórica vamos a la política como ciencia y como técnica. Y cuanto no se inserte en esta línea, que es la del progreso y la de la vida, será rémora y anacronismo. Se acerca la jubilación del ideólogo retoricista. Se imponen los expertos' (1965: 120). Thus the figure of the politician becames superfluous since 'el político se ha despojado de su 'attrezzo' altisonante y enfático, para tratar de convertirse en un gerente modesto y eficaz' (Fernández de la Mora 1965: 52).[26]

The technocrats envisioned Spain as an administered post-ideological society. An efficient administration—the regime's new ideologues claimed—was redirecting the task of state politics. Political decisions, argued Fernández de la Mora, should be left to 'ideocrats' who would 'superintellectualize' politics: 'La solución propuesta no es la tecnocracia, sino la ideocracia. No es una desintelectualización, sino una superintelectualización de la vida social' (1965: 23, 24). The new mode of governance became contingent on a technical management of the economy. The task of guiding economic progress and development replaced politics proper: that is, the idea of voting or an electorate. Elections became superfluous: '…el voto no es un deber, sino un derecho renunciable' (Fernández de la Mora 1965: 56) and the resulted degree of apathy became construed as a sign of political and social health or index of popular content: 'La salud de los Estados libres puede medirse por el grado de apatía política. El fenómeno no es inquietante, sino esperanzador' (Fernández de la Mora 1965: 59).[27]

Like López Rodó and Fraga Iribarne, Fernández de la Mora was a law university professor and professional civil servant.[28] As Carr and Fusi have written: '…the regime's capacity to absorb ambitious professionals was one of the secrets of its political survival' (1981: 36). The post-war structure of Francoism that had been established on the three main pillars of the Regime –the Nationalist army, the Falange and the Church –was now expanding in consequence. Franco's 'political families' included technocrats and the professional cadres who had faith in statistics and rates of productivity rather than Spain's divine mission.[29] 'Scientific' governance with its host of technocrats required a new vocabulary, a switch from a militaristic and Providential lexicon to one of stock charts and percentages. In the words of Carr and Fusi, Spain was experiencing a bloodless revolution of a different kind:

> The new era was reflected in a new style, a semantic revolution with the language of international business (López Rodó was fond of comparing government with an efficient firm) replacing that of economic nationalism *à outrance*; rationalization was to take precedence over tradition –though they must be reconciled if possible. (1981: 54)

The 'statistical triumphalism' of the regime, however, and the claim to economic and political expertise did not correspond to reality, a disconnect that often showed a disastrous lack of aptitude by this technocratic elite.[30] The economic competence that these technocrats laid claim to was partly a matter of words, and their success was due in large part to the steadily ascending curve of European economic prosperity. It was all the more remarkable in Spain, since the country had only just emerged from widespread famine in the 1940s to the precarious economic conditions of post-war poverty and unremediated destruction. In *The Development of Modern Spain*, Gabriel Tortella points to an ongoing governmental incompetence and lack of any comprehensive long-term economic planning:

> The broad masterstrokes of the pro-development, liberalist policy of the 1960s and 1970s—a plan that was loudly touted as the shining glory of the regime—in fact was drawn up and presented in the aftermath of the total failure of the fascist-autarkist policy of the previous twenty years. And in both these fundamental phases, the minor modifications in policy were general responses to emergencies caused by serious failures in the system. (2000: 449, 450)

In a similar vein, Carr and Fusi observe:

> [The regime's] triumphs were fictitious and fragile, a mere bonus handed to Franco and his technocrats by the European boom of the sixties, a bonus which they were incapable of managing in the interests of sound

> development. Dependent on these windfall gains, it would wither with a European recession as tourist revenues, emigrants' remittances and foreign loans dropped off. (1981: 59)

The economic crises of the 1970s showed that the realization of some technocratic de-ideologized Utopia was a mirage. Ramón Tamames, one of the most influential Marxist critics of the regime, had already prefigured this mismanagement of the economy in the 1960s by terming the technocratic period a 'neo-autarky.'[31]

Besides, the zeal for technocratization and modernization was highly problematic since, to quote Graham and Labanyi,

> ...rather than being seen as a conceptual framework for investigating a specific period of Western development, modernization is projected as something that will transform the non-European world in the image of contemporary Western European and North American society (far-from-homogeneous societies and cultures in themselves), whereupon history will implicitly 'end'. (1995b: 10)[32]

Such insistence on the supremacy of technocracy and the prophecy of the end of ideology, in a dictatorship that officially did not allow any political parties to start with, was ironically 'redundant.' It also points to a major contradiction at the heart of dictatorship: the attempt at modernization without modernity and democratization.

The publication of the second *España cambia de piel* in 1964 can be phased in a wider cultural context too. At about the same time the new version appeared, the cabinet of 1962 implemented the 'Plan for Economic and Social Development, 1964–67' (*Plan de Desarrollo*).[33] The freshly shuffled cabinet 'was distinguished from its predecessors by a largely forward-looking orientation, motivated not least by the dictator's advancing age' (Pack 2006: 106). Serendipitously, the second *España cambia de piel* was concurrent with the celebration of 'Twenty-Five Years of Peace.' Also indicative of how far his personal life was symbiotic with national life, Waldo de Mier dedicated *España cambia de piel* to his wife 'con la que también este año cumplo XXV AÑOS DE PAZ y de felicidad matrimonial' (author's emphasis). 'Twenty-Five Years of Peace' marked 25 years from the end of Spanish Civil War and Franco's victory in it. But Franco's triumph was no longer emblazoned in the slogans of crusade, but in the more conciliatory discourse of peace and prosperity brought about by the 'Spanish miracle' (*la 'España del Milagro'*).

Significantly, Manuel Fraga Iribarne was the architect of this slogan and the celebration of 'Twenty-Five Years of Peace' confirmed his rising stardom on Spain's political scene. The giant 'multimedia' propaganda campaign that accompanied the celebration demonstrated Fraga's capacity for a slick modus operandi in the rapidly changing political scene of a nascent 'age of the image' (Fraga 1965: 315). As Preston has written, 'With his short-cropped hair and natty suits, the can-do style and appearance of a busy American entrepreneur, [Fraga] was seen as someone capable of resolving the intractable problems…in a vertiginously changing society' (1994: 705). Fraga's capacity for innovation was evident from the very beginning of his stellar academic and political career. His first post was at the Complutense law school as Professor of Constitutional Law and Theory of the State; next he became a Secretary General in the Instituto de Cultura Hispana (1951); and, finally, Director of the Instituto de Estudios Políticos (1956). His intellectual engagement in those years, as seen from one of his earlier texts *How Spain is Governed*, ranged from the legitimization of the state and dictatorship to normalizing relationships with Western Europe and the 'democratic' West.

These posts prepared him well for what would become his major impact on Spain's political scene, his rise to power as Minister of Information and Tourism (1962–69). This appointment signaled yet another radical step towards Spain's political opening and economic liberalization, and Fraga became almost singlehandedly equated with this politics of *apertura*. Fraga's posture was in sync with some aspects of technocratic models, but his relationship with López Rodó and the latter's self-styled technocratic team was fraught with tensions. There was a certain degree of continuity between the politics of autarkists and the technocrats since

> apart from a general concern among the *Opus Dei* clique over the negative social impacts of tourism, these ministers maintained close connections with large industrialists and remained attached to the conviction that industrialization was more reliable as a basis for long-term economic growth than an 'invisible' revenue source such as tourism. (Pack 2006: 107)

The technocrats' clash with Fraga was not solely economic in nature, as it had been for their autarkist predecesors. In the 1960s, the struggle with Fraga's politics of development was implicated in a larger struggle for political leadership and the question of the regime's future: 'Fraga's belief in the primacy of politics positioned him in natural opposition to the technical-bureaucratic elite'…'he conceived of the tourism industry as a significant component of his reformist agenda' (Pack 2006: 107). The tourist boom and Spain's broader political and economic path were inseparable from speculation about the country's aging dictator and the inevitable political strategizing over his succession.

According to Preston, the entry of the technocrats into Spain's economic sphere 'meant the abandonment of every economic idea that the Caudillo had ever held dear and the uninhibited embrace of modern capitalism' (1994: 666). The technocratic break from post-war falangism was followed by Fraga's ascendance to power which, according to Preston, earned him epithet of 'a grave-digger of the regime' (1994: 705). But things were more complex than Preston seems to suggest. Rather than digging the regime's grave, Fraga modernized and revolutionized stale dictatorial structures. Fraga's period in office could be conceived as a third phase of Spain's 'defascistization' (Payne's terminology), the first one being an obliteration of the fascist past after 1945 as a gesture of disassociation from the Axis powers, and the second one a technocratic de-ideologization and refashioning of the mechanism of state power in the 1950s.[34] Crumbaugh, borrowing from Deleuze and Guattari, sees this passage, very perceptively, as a 'shift from "macrofascism" to "microfascisms"' (2009: 8). He adds: 'It seemed the less "totalitarian" the regime managed to be, the more deeply ingrained and insidious it became' (2009: 7).

Fraga's key impact on Franco's 1960s Spain was a liberal refashioning of the military dictatorship, within the limits of its inner structure. Fraga was concerned with the legitimacy of the state and he was rethinking the bases of its continued legitimacy. The rhetoric of 'Spanish miracle' or economic prosperity functioned as a euphemism for democratization.[35] This rationale was strengthened through a seemingly linear line of political development that erroneously seemed to suggest a natural progression from (1) defascistization to (2) de-ideologization, and finally (3) to democratization. Fraga was the perfect ideologue of the Spanish miracle since he successfully elaborated a complex vision of a modernized form of Francoism, seamlessly melding the right-wing ethos with 1960s neo-liberal political and economic models.[36] Fraga's intricate politics of *apertura* was designed both to strengthen the Franco regime and to assimilate Spain into a Western democratic 'normality.'

Shlomó Ben-Amí called this phenomenon 'a revolution from above.'[37] Spain's 'revolution from above' can be seen in various aspects of Fraga's legal and political moves, a good example of which was Fraga's call for political reform (the draft programme for a political association) and the draft for a press law, the latter promulgated on 23 January 1964. Ben-Amí writes:

> Al igual que todo el sistema de Fraga, este paso [la Ley de Prensa] fue un ingenioso ejercicio de tolerancia restringida con el objeto de desvirtuar los argumentos acerca de una presunta falta de libertad, a la vez que complacer a Occidente y a los millones de turistas que afluían a la tierra de 'la paz y el sol.' (1980: 195)[38]

But revolution from above also transfigured strategies of resistance and produced new forms of political activism. The superannuated leftist Marxist understanding of politics that focused on a notion of false consciousness and issues of falsification of history and the desecration of historical memory was being refashioned as well.[39] While it is true that there was a convergence of political and commercial rhetoric and a false conflation of (political) freedom (without free elections) with consumer lifestyle (mini-skirts, shorts, bikinis, beach holidays), there was also a new political mode to counter it. Political struggle was taking different forms: the rapid rise of political unrest (labour and student strikes, especially after the government had introduced collective bargaining in 1958), the refashioning of underground communist and leftist resistance, and the resurgence of nationalist movements (Catalonia, the Basque country).[40] It was a period of building up of civil society and civil consciousness that was not necessarily incompatible with leisure and a mass-culture industry previously thought of as contributing to political apathy. For their part, the mass media and consumer culture dwelt in much more ambivalent terrain.

As Helen Graham and Jo Labanyi point out, 'Francoism's goal of securing the permanent separation of cultural and political modernity from the modernization process was ultimately unachievable' (1995b: 10).[41] While it is erroneous to conceive of economic development as a path to democratic emancipation (since it is an assumption that coincides disturbingly with the regime's own official line about development and the much-canvassed 'miracle'), owning a car, possessing a television set and going on vacation do truly point to profoundly changed modes of transportation, communication, organization of leisure-time, gender relations and so on. No aspect of everyday life had been untouched by the availability of mass consumer goods. While keeping in mind that the modernizing project of technocrats in the mid-1950s continued to a large extent a long line of modernizing projects, all of which 'have used pseudo-universal rhetorics while in fact privileging specific dominant groups, classes, races…,' the force and importance of consumer society in contributing to social change cannot be underestimated (Graham and Labanyi 1995b: 11). The economic development and consumer lifestyle that became an integral part of Spanish culture brought complex and ambiguous changes. Thus the move towards the modern was inexorable, but never smooth. It entailed a continuous process of struggle and negotiation.

Spain experienced drastic changes from terrible political repression and the social 'immobilism' of the 1940s to the timid process of socio-economic change of the 1950s and then the impressive economic growth of the 1960s. While the 1940s were restrained by an emphasis on moderation and restriction, the celebration of *bendito atraso*, and 'an innate spiritual vocation for poverty,' the economic *apertura* of the 1960s was marked by new social and sexual mores and consumer habits of a society of leisure. The market economy and economic liberalism ceased to be anti-Spanish. The age of prosperity no longer equated economic gain and sexual pleasure with moral loss. The distinction highlighted between an ascetic Spain and an indulgent West rested on a distinction of consumer values that, if they once existed, no longer did. Thus, 'the dwindling of the sacred, this reduction of value to the secular horizon as in the function of the monetary instrument, exemplifies the "reign of quantity"…' (Goux 1990: 130,1). Not only did the nation cease to be sacred (even if sacrality was always already rhetorical), but it became profitable. As Crumbaugh has written,

> Fraga reinvented difference as an object of government activity, of planning, buying, and selling… tourism gave the regime's more atavistic cultural policies new relevance within the symbolic coordinates of liberalization, economic growth, and consumerism, since tourism magically spun notions of backwardness into highly marketable spectacles of local color. (2009: 61; 6)

The 'reign of quantity' was also anticipated in Juan Goytisolo's novel *Fiestas* (1957). Goytisolo's vivid image captures Spain's epochal passage:

> [La] fachada era de ladrillo sin revoque y se cuarteaba ligeramente hacia el terrado. Al final de la guerra habían inscrito en ella una leyenda: POR EL IMPERIO HACIA DIOS, en gruesos caracteres negros, pero el calor y las lluvias la habían desfigurado. Ahora lucía un cartel flamante: BEBA COCA-COLA, que anunciaba una hermosa mujer de pelo rubio y cara sonrosada. (1958a: 39)

The inscription of 'Through the Empire towards God' is disfigured by heat and rain, but still barely visible under the poster of blond women announcing Coca-Cola. The two worldviews (one vouched for by God and the other by Coca-Cola) affected every aspect of Spanish society and tumultuously coexisted throughout the so-called Mid-Passage of the regime and the first years of the 'Plan for Economic and Social Development, 1964–67' (or *Plan de Desarrollo*).[42] Franco showed an increasing inability to accommodate such rapid changes within his regime: 'He was presiding over a machine whose inner workings were becoming a mystery to him' (Preston 1994: 688). In his 1961 end-of-the-year speech, '[He] had described himself as the captain of the ship of Spain and the people as 'the crew and the beneficiaries' of his rectitude, virtues and skills as a navigator.' But as Preston points out, 'where the navigator was steering Spain was not clear' (1994: 698).

By 1961, the Spanish miracle and a transformation from Francoism to Fraguism, fully in motion, had triumphed. Since its inception, Franco's Spain was never a monolithic entity and the dictatorship was in constant flux. But, by the 1960s, Spain –the Mobile Nation—reached its turning point, one that prefigured the political directions of the Transition. Justin Crumbaugh has suggested that we take 'what became known in the 1960s as *fraguismo* seriously as a rationale that subtended late-Francoist public discourse, one that revolutionized the Spanish Right from within' (2009: 42). He adds: 'Significantly, this occurred not after Franco's death but during the 1960s, at the height of the dictatorship' (2009: 42).

The Mobile Nation explores the distinctive culture that emerged between two historical moments, one marked by autarky and God and the other by *desarrollo* and Coca-Cola. The book explores the social reality of mid-century Spain that was 'nothing but a fragile, symbolic cobweb' (Žižek 1991: 17).[43] Attesting to the emergence of the mobile modern subject and the transitory spaces inhabited by those subjects, the book focuses—as stated above—on a range of cultural phenomena: literature and the publishing industry, television, popular cinema, foreign tourism, and the national automobile-manufacturing industry.

In the midst of this mobile nation and its doom prophecies proclaiming the end of politics proper, its 'reign of quantity' and economic miracles, consumer frenzy, game shows, cars, washing machines and television sets, Spain was neither an apolitical post-ideological twilight or an atavistic antithesis of modern governance, nor 'a population of consumer zombies deadened by international neocapitalism' (Aub 1995: 378–80; Crumbaugh 1999: 120).[44] Goytisolo's distorted faded-brick image points to the encroaching of a global market and liberalism that would eventually contribute to the end of literature and the end of the state. Unlike López Rodó's and Fernández de la Mora's 'ends,' Brett Levinson explains that the end of a nation state does not refer to its disappearance but 'alludes to the demise of the *sovereign* state, which now must compete with other domains such as the global market and international political organizations' (2001: 1). The end of literature 'signifies that literature, which once occupied a privileged position within the state itself, must now battle for that rank and legitimacy with other forms of creation, above all, mass and popular culture' (Levinson 2001: 1, 2). No one grasped more accurately the place of mass and consumer culture then Fraga himself, who asserted prophetically that the new order functioned as a 'pedagogy of leisure' (*pedagogía del tiempo libre*) in a consumer-driven mediascape (1965: 296).[45]

Notes

1. For an excellent study of Spanish cinema that focuses on this period, see Faulkner (2006).

2. Gabriel Tortella pointed out that in the post-war period 'Spain remained virtually isolated from the international scene, both politically and economically, the promised economic recovery was not consummated, income per capita remained below the 1935 level, and the population at large suffered serious hardship' (2000: 450).

3. 'Bendito atraso' is a title of the first chapter of Carmen Martín Gaite's book *Usos amorosos de la postguerra española*. She quotes from Antonio Castro Villacañas's text published in *La Hora* on 14 May 1948. The texts reads: 'No queremos el progreso, el romántico y liberal, capitalista y burgués, judío, protestante, ateo y masón progreso yanqui. Preferimos el atraso de España, nuestro atraso, el que nos lleva a considerar que ante unos valores fundamentales deben sacrificarse los intereses materiales…Bendito nuestro atraso' (Martín Gaite 1987: 29).

4. See García Delgado (1986).

5. For statistical data on Spain's consumer patterns, see Gracia García and Ruiz Carnicer (2001) and Longhurst (2000). Their studies draw on statistics from La Fundación FOESSA (Fomento de Estudios Sociales y Sociología Aplicada) and The Instituto Nacional de Estadística. Statistic of the 1950s and 1960s are not entirely reliable and vary considerably depending on the source consulted. There are also drastic disparities in urban and rural consumer habits and spending power as well as regional differences, often dependent on degree of local development.

6. The end of peasantry was one of the most important social phenomena in the history of Europe in the twentieth century. See Hobsbawm (1994).

7. The trope of mobility was widely used in Spanish socio-political discourse, in cultural phenomena ranging from *Movimiento* to *la Movida*. See Epps (1995).

8. The period studied (1954–1964) is by no means the starting point of capitalism in Spain but rather a post civil-war re-entrance into Western consumer capitalism. For a long-term economic trends, see Tortella (2000).

9. On *franquismo sociológico* see Abella (1996: 273–286).

10. See my earlier studies. Pavlovic (2004, 2007).

11. Adorno and Horkheimer coined 'the culture industry' term in *The Dialectic of Enlightenment* (1947).

12. As Graham and Labanyi have pointed out 'question of production and consumption cannot be divorced. And consumption is never a passive or homogeneous process: not only do different sectors of the public respond differently, but the same sector can respond in ways that are simultaneously conformist and contestatory...Nor can it be assumed that the institutions that control the production of meaning identify themselves monolithically with the state, or with the establishment (not necessarily the same thing)' (1995: 5).

13. Graham and Labanyi warn us that terms such as *the popular* and *the masses* are 'a construction of the modern state; a product of modernity' (1995: 6, 7). They add: 'Postmodernist theory is mostly the product of advanced capitalist societies where, with the disappearance of a folk tradition, the terms "mass culture" and "popular

culture" have become synonymous, producing a further slippage in the meaning of the latter term' (1995: 7, 8).

14. One of the few studies that centers on audience reception of the time period, specifically cinema, is *The Mediation of Everyday Life: Remembering Cinema in 1940s and 1950s Spain* by Labanyi, J., Marsh, S., Martin-Márquez, S., Sánchez Biosca, V., Vernon, K. and E. Woods (forthcoming).

15. *La cuestión palpitante* references Emilia Pardo Bazán. For more information on the history of the expression, see Santana (2000: 160 n.1). Santana's book is an outstanding work on the Spanish reception of Latin American literature.

16. While this genre belongs mostly to popular film tradition we should keep in mind the complexity of the concept *popular cinema*. Lázaro-Reboll and Andrew Willis analyze the slippery nature of this term. They point out that films such as *¡Bienvenido Mr. Marshall!* 'are able to shift from *popular* to *middlebrow* dependent upon the taste formations of those watching. This change often reflects the broad historical shifts in the cultural status of cinema' (2004: 6). For more detailed discussion, see Lázaro-Reboll and Willis (2004).

17. Tortella has analysed in great detail the impact of emigration on economic development: 'According to the Arthur Lewis model, Spain would represent the *subsistence sector* and Western Europe the *capitalist sector*. Development within the capitalist sector caused a labor shortage which prompted a transfer of workers from Spain to Europe. This transfer, the massive out-migration of the 1960s, in turn dried up labor reserves in Spain, causing salaries to rise; this in turn stimulated mechanization in agriculture and a substantial increase of living standards, with consequent rising demand for industrial products. All these phenomena caused irreversible economic development in all its dimensions (industrialization, urbanization, and tertiarization), which even the return of emigrants and other repercussions of the 1973 crisis could not reverse, although the growth rate did in fact slow down' (2000: 444).

18. Tortella (2000) is a key work in Spanish economic history. Some other significant works on evolution of Spanish economy are Barciela, López, Melgarejo and Miranda (2001); Crespo MacLennan (2000); Fusi and Palafox (1997); Harrison (1978); Prados de la Escosura (1999, 2003); Salisbury and Theberge (1976); Salmon (1995); Townson (2007).

19. The book consists of compilation of articles originally written for *Arriba*.

20. Born in Mexico of parents who had emigrated from Santander, Waldo de Mier 'returned' to Spain in 1920s. He came of age in the tumultuous 20s in Toledo before enlisting in the Legion. Next he moved to Santander and worked as a bureaucrat in the Bureau of Mines. With the advent of rebellion in the ranks of the military, he enlisted in the Nationalist Army. He fought throughout the country and was a second lieutenant of infantry in the (in)famous Aragón offensive. While advancing with his troops toward el paso de Guadalupe, he lost his leg in battle. Almost according to script, he married the nurse that took care of him. The romance united masculine and feminine prototypes of those heady times: *la enfermera y el oficial herido*. After the war he became a journalist and wrote with same vigor with which he once fought. The battlefield became the pages of the dailies, naturally Francoist, *Alerta*, *El Alcázar*, *Baleares*, and *Arriba*.

21. As observed by both Labanyi and several other critics, the monumental, theatrical style of the Falangists (seen in García Serrano) could be traced to the very core of the foundation of the Falange in the Teatro Comedia of Madrid in 1933.

22. See Plonowska Ziarek (1998: 222).

23. Less ambiguous than Benjamin's and unlike Benjamin's 'Angelus Novus,' Waldo de Mier's 'Angelus Novus'' face never turns towards the past.

24. For a more detailed account of 1957 cabinet changes, see Preston (1994: 655-684).

25. Original quote comes from López Rodó's *Política y desarrollo* p. 44.

26. Fernández de la Mora proposes cosmopolitanism as a replacement for both socialism and liberalism since 'El cosmopolitanismo es fruto de una racionalización de la conciencia política y, consecuentemente, un factor de desideologización' (1965: 95). To illustrate the end of ideology he uses a vivid nautical metaphor: 'el socialismo vira a estribor (starboard) y el liberalismo vira a babor (port, larboard).'

27. See Fernández de la Mora (1965: 48-59).

28. For more details on the Spanish civil service, see Carr and Fusi (1981: 79-103).

29. See Ross (1996) and Boltanski (1987). Ross writes: 'As for the jeune cadre, Luc Boltanski has traced his national and international ancestry, from his beginnings in the 1930s (the word *cadre* entered French industrial vocabulary around 1936

and was used to describe men whose place in a company couldn't be precisely defined), his consolidation in the corporatist values of Vichy, through his full-fledged flowering in the late 1950s. That flowering was in fact the successful grafting or composite formation of two previously separate individuals: the engineer and the bourgeois, and it occurred under the careful midwifery of the American productivity missions conducted after the war' (1996: 167).

30. The 'statistical triumphalism' of the regime is Carr and Fusi's term (1981: 59).

31. See Tamames (1961, 1967).

32. Graham and Labanyi also point out that 'modernization is seen as having a quasiautonomic, self-sustaining quality verging on determinism' (1995: 10).

33. See *Plan de Desarrollo económico y social para el periodo 1964–1967* (Madrid 1964); Comisaría del Plan de Desarrollo Económico.

34. See Payne (1988).

35. As seen for example in Spain's Organic Democracy. Carr and Fusi write that 'Organic Democracy challenged not merely representative government based on universal suffrage but the division of powers as a safeguard for the rule of law' (1981: 45).

36. As Justin Crumbaugh has shown, Fraga's theory of state is largely supported by Carl Schmitt's model of statehood as developed in *The Concept of the Political* (1932). See Crumbaugh (2009: 41–63).

37. See Ben-Amí (1980).

38. There were nevertheless some important consequences of the press law, seen in publication of new journals such as *Cuadernos para el Diálogo* or resurrected ones such as *Revista de Occidente*.

39. Ben-Amí pinpoints the Communist Party crisis and restructuring precisely to 1965 (1980: 190). Additionally, he studies other aspects of oppositional culture of the times (1980: 165–206).

40. See Járegui and Vega (2007) and Díaz (1995).

41. Quote slightly modified. The original reads: 'Francoism set itself the (ultimately unachievable) goal of securing the permanent separation of cultural and political modernity from the modernization process' (1995b: 10).

42. This tumultuous co-existence was especially due to the fact that López Rodó's and the technocrats' entry into the new cabinet was not altogether smooth and was riddled by significant crisis, summed up in the telling name for the period, 'disorientation,' 'during which public debt, inflation and the balance of payment problems continued…being largely the legacy of autarky' (Preston 1994: 670).

43. See Žižek (1991).

44. Aub refers to Dámaso Alonso's verse from *Hijos de la ira* (Madrid, 1944): 'Madrid es una ciudad de más de un millón de cadáveres (según las últimas estadísticas).'

45. In addition to his reflection on the pedagogy of leisure, Fraga also wrote about other contemporary phenomena such as *sociedad de consumo*, mass-media, urbanism, and feminism, among other topics. On Fraga's concept of pedagogy of leisure, see Crumbaugh (2009: 41–63).

Chapter I

La hora del lector: Literature and the publishing industry

> El lector se ha convertido en protagonista activo de la creación literaria.
> Y nuestro tiempo, en el tiempo del lector.
>
> – José María Castellet, *La hora del lector*[1]

The Spanish literary scene of the 1950s was marked by a passage from social realism to a more experimental new novel that had gained readership and critical recognition by the mid-1960s. Social novelists and critics alike were questioning the premises and effectiveness of this neo-Realist model. Moreover, the disengagement from the literary paradigm of *neorrealismo* was accompanied by an unparalleled growth in the publishing industry itself. Such passage was complex and at times paradoxical: the very same intellectual figures who had advocated social realism henceforth engaged in detailed criticism of the movement, radically re-shifting the Spanish literary scene. One attempt at a taxonomy of this literary moment has been suggested by Gonzalo Sobejano. He writes:

> The social novel divides into three currents: a first wave of neorrealismo (more transcendent and of a more consciously crafted artistic density); a social realism (combining proletarian and anti-bourgeois strains); and the critical or dialectical realism that informs *Tiempo de silencio* (*Time of Silence*, 1962), a novel by Luis Martín-Santos that establishes yet a different model. (2003: 180)

Some of the major strategies and tendencies in this progression were: (1) a process of critical self-reflection and a search for new literary models that would reflect a re-articulation of the outdated political and aesthetic practices of neo-Realism; (2) a rapid growth in the publishing industry, its disengagement from neo-Realism and an accompanying search for different 'products' (linked to an increased emphasis on literary prizes as a marketing tool); (3) exploitation of the Latin American Boom, the key role of Spain's publishing houses in its 'creation' and dissemination, and the Boom's radical refashioning of Spanish literature. These cosmopolitan tendencies and global practices signalled a move beyond national and fiction-genre borders and a forsaking of provincialism and post-war 'Eternal' or immobile Spain.

The critical trends and strategies outlined above will be examined here through the literary pursuits and publishing activity of Juan Goytisolo, Spain's foremost writer in the period; José María Castellet, a renowned literary critic; and Carlos Barral, a Barcelona School poet and the country's most successful publisher.[2] Their evolving trajectories, in interplay with multiple international forces (such as literary trends, economic factors, and political censorship), re-shaped the literary field of 1950s Spain. This chapter begins with their backing of social realism as the narrative model and ends with their subsequent disengagement from the movement. For Goytisolo, this becomes clear in the realm of fiction in his shift from *Juegos de mano* (1954) to *Señas de identidad* (1966) and, in his critical endeavour, from *Problemas de la novela* (1959) to *El furgón de cola* (1966).[3] For Castellet, the shift is from *La hora del lector* (1957) to his later essays such as 'Tiempo de destrucción para la literatura española' (1968), promoting Latin American fiction and sketching new directions for the Spanish novel. For Barral, it is a move from his Colección Biblioteca Breve to the Prix Formentor, the Prix International de Littérature, and 'discovery' of Vargas Llosa and other Boom writers (Borges, Carpentier, Cortázar).[4]

Significantly, before they exhausted the possibilities of the social realist model, they had come to embody it, as an exemplar of its expression in the novel (Goytisolo), as a critic and 'creator' of the *Generación de los 50* (Castellet), and as its cultural promoter and publisher (Barral). Their original support and canonization of neo-Realism drew from the movement's four basic functions in the literary field. The first one was its informational role, vital in a country where the press was subjected to state control. Spain's writers, filmmakers and intellectuals felt an ethical burden to document another social reality behind the one promoted by government propaganda. Pointing to the novel's role as a witness, Goytisolo wrote: 'La novela cumple en España una función testimonial que en los demás países de Europa corresponde a la prensa ("Los escritores españoles frente al toro de la censura"; 1976: 60)'. Secondly, there was a question of the rupture with the immediate post-war literary generation and their anaemic, refined and outdated forms. He observed:

> En el plano puramente estético su conservadurismo se traduce, en los mejores, en el uso de esta prosa rancia y castiza que constituye para la crítica española la quintaesencia y el canon del Buen Decir: lengua refinada y anémica que convierte a quien la emplea en prisionero de un lenguaje ya creado y utilizado por otros, lenguaje incapaz de captar y expresar la novedad y complejidad del mundo moderno (solicitado por la aparición de nuevos lenguajes) y condenado, por consiguiente, a la vía muerta y al cementerio de los estilos ya hechos, ya terminados. ('Literatura y eutanasia'; 1976: 81)[5]

Goytisolo's call for a radical break with the first post-war literary generation, prompted by the 'death of the old forms', prepared the ground for thinking of the yet more definitive rupture with their contemporary generation and their linguistic limitations.

Thirdly, neo-Realism provided the Left with an artistic device by which to confront Franco's official culture and give cohesiveness to their anti-dictatorial struggle. This political dimension that marked neo-Realism was most explicit in the Communist Party's recruitment of writers from Armando López Salinas to José Antonio Ferres, Juan García Hortelano, Gabriel Celaya and Angel González. Barral was well aware of the convergence between his editorial interests and the Communist Party's cultural strategy, referring to it as a 'politico-literary project' and seeing it entrenched in Madrid. He even claimed that the party assigned literary themes to 'their' social novelists:

> La rueda de Madrid era la que soportaba los proyectos político-literarios, proyectos que podían llegar hasta el reparto de temática para futuras novelas y, por supuesto, a la distribución de presencia en los premios y las publicaciones. La rueda de Barcelona, básicamente editorial, era la que conectaba esas conspiraciones, algunos libros y la prematura gloria de algunos autores con ese mecanismo internacional que habíamos ido poco a poco construyendo. (1988: 60)[6]

Barral's discussion of Madrid and Barcelona's role in the cultural mapping of Francoist Spain brings us to the fourth and last function of neo-Realism in the literary field of the 1950s: its connection to an emerging publishing industry. Social realism provided publishers with a cultural product that could be attractive internationally. The social-realist novelist was acclaimed abroad as the voice of a new Spain on the threshold of revolutionary transformation. This model worked especially well in the French reception of Spanish novels, such as Gallimard's new collection of Spanish literature in translation that was launched in the mid-1950s. Goytisolo, their editorial adviser (*consejero de literatura española*), particularly benefitted from this trend and the favourable reception of his *Juegos de manos* in French translation was partially due to its novelty and its classification as 'a novel from Francoist Spain'.[7]

Following Ernesto Laclau's concept of hegemonic articulation, we can claim that social realism emerged only when disparate elements started to resonate together: its testimonial, literary-aesthetic, political and print-medium dimensions. Its demise, by the same token, came about when one or more of these elements became obsolete, losing their original urgency. In the forefont of disengagement and disillusionment with neo-Realism stood issues of politics and language. The two were interlinked from the start since the endorsement of neo-Realism in Spain was essentially politically motivated, yet aesthetically problematic. Goytisolo thus accurately described his generation as political non-conformists (Marxist and agnostic), yet traditionalist in terms of literary technique. He was aware of the incompatibility of a progressive Marxist ideology coupled with attachment to the Spanish literary tradition: 'Si la ideología marxista abre el horizonte del porvenir, el apego excesivo a las formas de la tradición literaria española lo cierra necesariamente' ('Literatura y eutanasia'; 1976: 93). The political engagement, it became clear, was futile without a radical aesthetic programme. In that spirit Goytisolo would later parody a reception of his *Juegos de manos* (in *Señas de identidad*), where Parisian intellectual circles claimed him—a young Spanish novelist—as an emblem of the anti-Francoist struggle. While Spain's culturo-political context in the early 1950s vindicated the practice of neo-Realism, in the view of most of its participants, it was harder to validate it by the mid-1960s. In that spirit we can understand Goytisolo's progressive distancing of himself from Spain and his prior revolutionary enthusiasm:

> Por espacio de once años vivirás física y moralmente alejado de tu país, fuera del devenir histórico, dueño del vasto olvido...En adelante formularás opiniones políticas sobre Santo Domingo, Checoslovaquia o Palestina, pero no sobre España. Su previsible evolución bajo el franquismo ha dejado de apasionarte. (1986: 82)

Juan Goytisolo

Goytisolo's parody of his own literary beginnings in *Señas de identidad* is an ironic history of his slow and, at times, painful rupture with his literary generation. The rupture is easy to trace in Goytisolo's fictional work.[8] Goytisolo's Realist phase may be said to start with his first novel *Juegos de manos* published in 1954 and end with *Fin de fiesta* published in 1962.[9] His more experimental period is initiated with the publication of *Señas de identidad* in 1966. Significantly, Goytisolo did not publish any fictional work between 1962 and 1966, a parenthesis that roughly corresponds to his re-examination of social realism.[10] Goytisolo's fictional hiatus accurately paralleled drastic change in the Spanish literary field, provoked by the internal crises of the realist literary model.

The period was nevertheless fruitful for his critical activity. During this time he published a series of essays on literature, theory of the novel, Spanish literary tradition, international literary trends, censorship and politics. These first major essays appeared in the journal *Destino* (Barcelona) between 1956 and 1957, and were later published as a collection in *Problemas de la novela* (1959). *Problemas de la novela* is a scrutiny of literary creation through the optic of what Goytisolo terms 'social motivation' (*motivación social*). It argues for the novel's social purpose and role, and proposes the emerging literary current of behaviourism as a model. Goytisolo advocates behaviourism as an authentic insight into reality, rather than the omniscient and absolute narration that characterized the nineteenth century. Promotion of behaviourism and advocacy of the social role of the novel were linked to Goytisolo's principal targets in *Problemas de la novela*: Ortega y Gasset and the earlier writer's theory of the novel. Goytisolo situates himself in opposition to Ortega's elitism of 'minorías selectas'. Goytisolo claims that during the times of Ortega and *La Revista de Occidente* 'se produce divorcio entre el novelista y la sociedad. La novela pierde sus contornos nacionales y se torna aséptica, cosmopolita, neutra. *Olvidando que sólo al nacionalizarse adquiere una literatura interés universal, los escritores se quieren universalizar, desnacionalizándose*' (1959: 84; Goytisolo's emphasis). Moreover, the socialist-realist conventions that Goytisolo adhered to and their capacity to express and expose the problems of reality were directly opposed to Ortega's assertion that 'los hechos y sucedidos mediocres de la vida corriente carecen de interés' (1959: 83). Goytisolo's reductive readings of Ortega are nevertheless effective in his agenda of 'reclaiming' Spanish reality (*los hechos y sucedidos mediocres*) for his generation. *Problemas de la novela* reads well with Goytisolo's article 'Para una literatura nacional popular' published in 1959, where Goytisolo calls for the novel to concern itself with reality and, above all, the reality of the country in which it is produced. Literature, according to his manifesto, should become once again a 'national' literature. Paradoxically, Goytisolo's call for reclaiming of national literature is embued with a Catholic-Nationalist rhetoric. Nevertheless, the strategy is effective as an attempt at the reappropriation of the concept of the 'national', which had become such a heavily charged political term in post-war Spain. It is significant to add that, throughout his career, Goytisolo would continue to reassert the importance of the Spanish national literary tradition to his writing, while not adhering to any national nostalgia.

But above and beyond, *Problemas de la novela* illustrates Goytisolo's struggle to reconcile and resolve the conflict between textual pleasure and socio-political critique, essentially a dilemma between form and content. Goytisolo's rejection of pure formalism 'la novela no puede perder su contacto con la realidad en nombre de una abstracción superior, so pena de convertirse a largo plazo en algo formal y muerto' reflects his ongoing inability to resolve this false dichotomy (1959: 37, 38). Very telling is Goytisolo's choice of appendix to *Problemas de la novela*—extracts from Lukács, Malraux, Brecht and Vittorini which reflected the critical-Marxist spirit of the times, one where political commitment was seen as incompatible with stylistic experimentation. But soon, Goytisolo would begin to see political oppression as an essentially discursive phenomenon and would postulate the need for a decodification of repressive codes of an 'official' language or any language that normalizes and naturalizes them. In *El furgón de cola*, a subsequent collection of essays, Goytisolo insisted that 'la negación de un sistema intelectualmente opresor comienza necesariamente con la negación de su estructura semántica' ('La actualidad de Larra'; 1976: 32 n.2).

Rejecting his 'Marxist' beginnings, Goytisolo later characterized these early texts as 'producto de una bulímica lectura de Gramsci' (1986: 21). Moreover, he felt relieved that the volume was 'felizmente agotado hoy' prohibiting re-publication of these 'poco meditados articulillos recogidos en el volumen *Problemas de la novela*' ('Cernuda y la crítica literaria española'; 1976: 141 n.4). Much more recently, Goytisolo revised his stance with some maturer reflections:

> Me entrego a generalizaciones a vuelapluma...Para concluir, con juvenil apresuramiento y escaso caletre, que 'la novela objetiva (?), basada en una apreciación sintética (?) y real (?) de la conducta humana, se ha convertido, gústele o no a escritores y críticos, en el único medio eficaz de novelar a nuestro tiempo.' (Y con ello condeno a la ineficacia la totalidad de mi labor literaria a partir de *Don Julián*). (2005: 16)

In the same spirit, Goytisolo came to lament Lukács's mentorship in those early years: 'Luego en París, empecé a leer al propio Marx, Engels y, sobre todo, Lukács que fue desdichadamente por espacio de cuatro o cinco años, mi inseparable mentor' (1985: 220). Nonetheless, rather than a 'bulimic reading of Gramsci', one can see Goytisolo's *Problemas de la novela* (as well as Castellet's *La hora del lector* [1957] discussed hereafter) as literary manifestos of their generation that outlined the political and cultural underpinnings of social realism, disavowing 'sacred' texts of the Francoist regime and previously entrenched theoretical currents.

El furgón de cola (1966), Goytisolo's second major collection of essays, was written between 1960 and 1966 for various European and Latin American literary journals. *El furgón de cola* marks a break with Goytisolo's realist mode due to its twofold 'failure'. The aesthetic shortcomings of the social novel were coupled with an awakening to the political futility of literary works and their failure to transform reality as was believed: 'políticamente ineficaces, nuestras obras eran, para colmo, literariamente mediocres' ('Literatura y eutanasia'; 1976: 87). *El furgón de cola* consists of fourteen essays ranging from the analyses of the Golden Age, Romanticism and the Generation of 1898 to essays on writing, censorship, tourism, economics and language. Of importance in the context of this chapter are the Introduction entitled 'El furgón de cola', 'La actualidad de Larra' and 'Literatura y eutanasia'. The first two are clearly written in the spirit of post-war debate on

Spain's essence and concerns for Spain's 'backwardness'. These had become familiar from the dispute between Laín Entralgo (*España como problema*) and Calvo Serrer (*España sin problema*).[11] The contemplations of Spain's belated modernity, so ubiquitous in Spanish thought from the 1898 Generation on, are reflected in the very title 'El furgón de cola'. Inspired by Machado, the essay revives question of Spain's relationship to 'Europe', Spain historically being its 'furgón de cola'.[12] The sardonic reference is to a railroad train with its caboose (US) or guard's van (UK) (*furgón de cola*) trailing in the rear. Rejecting easy and comfortable rhetorical tropes inherited from those disputes, such as 'me duele España', 'queremos a España porque no nos gusta', 'Españohogándose' ('El furgón de cola'; 1976: 11), Goytisolo calls for a new type of commitment 'más razonado y menos espontáneo, más científico y menos moral' ('El furgón de cola'; 1976: 14). Spain is still a problem for Goytisolo, but its solution clearly no longer lies in that meditation and reflection proposed by the Generation of 1898.

El furgón de cola targets intellectuals who, incapable of imagining new tools, continue believing in the same old revolutionary ideals they had in the autocratic, isolationist Spain of the 1950s while living in the neo-Capitalist, consumerist Spain of the 1960s. The lack of historical progress lies in a lack of sense of historicity, expressed in a continual attachment to an anachronistic figure Goytisolo terms 'español eterno' ('Examen de conciencia'; 1976: 249). This inert mode of Spanishness of an Eternal Spain leads to dire consequences in cultural and economic realms:

> Durante muchos años los benificiarios de nuestro inmovilismo divulgaron una teoría según cual, los españoles, por el mero hecho de ser españoles, poseíamos un destino particular en el planeta, ajeno a las leyes sociales y económicas del mundo moderno (una concepción metafísica del hombre). ('La actualidad de Larra'; 1976: 35 n.4)

In sum, 'Para España no pasan días, decía Larra; para la intelectualidad progresista española, añadiría yo, tampoco' ('El furgón de cola'; 1976: 11). It is within this context that Goytisolo would accuse Spain of 'growing fat, but remaining silent' (*España engorda, pero sigue muda*) ('Examen de conciencia'; 1976: 253 n.3).

It is, however, in 'Literatura y eutanasia' (1966) that Goytisolo fully centres on the problematic of language essential to his rupture with social realism.[13] While still reiterating the strategic merits of the movement (such as its testimonial value and break with the religious and epic style of the post-war writers), this essay is mostly an analysis of its shortcomings.[14] It is here that Goytisolo proposes a radically new literary direction, stemming from his redefinition of the relationship between the world and literary text. Goytisolo questions a misguided identification of literary and political commitment reinforced by a paralysing respect for the Spanish language and literary tradition: 'un respeto excesivo a la tradición literaria española y a su agarrotado lenguaje' and 'una generalizada confusión entre política y literatura, entre compromiso político y compromiso literario' ('Literatura y eutanasia'; 1976: 84). Political oppression is seen as a form of discourse which bespeaks a need for decodification of its repressive formulae of 'official' language.

Goytisolo's theoretical preoccupations with language date back to his arrival to Paris in 1956. His contact with French intellectuals corresponds to a lingusitic turn in literary studies in the late 1950s, and the progression from *Problemas de la novela* to *El furgón de cola* can be read as the transition from Sartre and Lukács to Barthes. As we have already seen, Goytisolo disavowed Lukács' mentorship as much as he departed from Sartre's Existentialist account of literature and concept of comittment crucial to the Spaniard's early criticism. Goytisolo's move away from Sartre to Barthes corresponds to Barthes own (dis)engagement with the dominant intellectual trends of the day, notably Marxism and the Existentialist movement in literature, criticism and philosophy. Barthes' *Le Degré zéro de l'écriture* (*Writing Degree Zero*) was published in 1953, the year that Goytisolo travelled to Paris for the first time. *Le Degré zéro de l'écriture* engages with Sartre's 'What is Literature?' ('Qu'est-ce que la littérature?') giving both a reassessment of Sartre and a rehabilitation of supposedly uncommitted authors such as Flaubert, Mallarmé and the Surrealists.

It is Barthes' reframing of Sartre's idea of commitment that would become key to Goytisolo's later writings. Now to the forefront comes the artist's commitment to the nature of *the work of art itself*, that is, a commitment to literature itself. In this spirit, Goytisolo sees the failure of the social realist novel not in its political dimension, but rather in its neglect of the duty to literature itself: 'La literatura de la generación del medio siglo es como suele decirse, una literatura 'comprometida,' pero el compromiso aparece en ella externo y ajeno a la especificidad de la obra literaria' ('Literatura y eutanasia'; 1976: 84). Above all, this realization is a reflection on his own early novels in which radical content (incest, murder and other transgressive topics) was undermined by their traditional literary form:

> Encastillados en el imperfecto de indicativo y en la primera o tercera persona del singular, no hemos explorado hasta ahora las inmensas posibilidades de la sintaxis: aferrados a una terminología de valores congelada y estática nos hemos mostrado incapaces de llevar el empleo del lenguaje moderno hasta sus últimas consecuencias. ('Literatura y eutanasia'; 1976: 93)

Goytisolo's early mode of writing or mirroring of reality that he would refer to as 'photographic reality' is replaced by the call for attention to the forms of the intelligibility in which the real is produced. The outside world is always mediated by language and narrative, however naturalized by any supposed transparency of realist language. It is in language, according to Barthes, that the author engaged with reality most profoundly and at its most relevant level: 'como dice Roland Barthes, la obra más "realista" no será la que "pinta" la realidad, sino la que sirviéndose del mundo como contenido…explora lo más profundamente posible la *realidad irreal* del lenguaje' ('Los escritores españoles frente al toro de la censura'; 1976: 60 n.4).

Together with the turn to language, Goytisolo pinpoints a failure of social realism to its lack of complexity, especially its neglect of what he terms 'double' vision, that is, an ironic dimension that always accompanies the dramatic one:

> Si nos limitamos al punto de vista dramático mutilamos la realidad y la empobrecemos…fenómeno curioso entre nosotros: en una literatura que cuenta antecendentes cómicos tan ilustres como los de Cervantes y Larra…Quevedo y la novela picaresca…desde el 98 acá parece que hemos perdido la antigua afición a la sátira y hasta la facultad de sonrisa. ('Literatura y eutanasia'; 1976: 88, 89)

For Goytisolo, irony is precisely the element of language that opens up the possibility for a break from convention of 'photographic' realism. Aware of the perils of political commitment that envision art primarily as *engagement* and obligation in the line of Sartre and Lukács, the Goytisolo of *El furgón de cola* searches for a transformative relation between language and the socio-political order.

Goytisolo ends the essay with a call for a literature that postulates destruction and transgression as a textual, political and moral act. Goytisolo becomes positively hostile (creates by destroying): 'el mundo en que vivimos reclama un lenguaje nuevo, virulento y anárquico. En el asto y sobrecargado almacén de antigüedades de nuestra lengua sólo podemos crear destruyendo' ('Literatura y eutanasia'; 1976: 93). Or to put it in his more colourful terms, one that uses dynamite and laxative to obliterate Castilian prose: 'nuestro anquilosado lenguaje castellanista exige, en efecto, con urgencia, el uso de la dinamita o el purgante' ('Literatura y eutanasia'; 1976: 94). The need for destruction of the fossilized Castilian language will lead Goytisolo to propose the Latin American model (the novels of the Boom) as one capable of refurbishing literary language (as it will Castellet and Barral). The Boom illustrated the possibility and the power of literature to resignify and supplant reality. The model fits well Goytisolo's increasing refusal to respect national boundaries (its sacred texts, borders and linguistic norms), as well as his progressive move toward formalism(s): from the avant-garde to the French *nouveau roman* and finally the Latin American Boom.

As we can see, Goytisolo's central preoccupation in this period is how to negotiate his social concern and translate it into aesthetic practice. A critique of society through the critique of language reconciles social and artistic commitment, especially crucial in the context of Spain's growing materialism and neo-Liberalism. A 'linguistic turn' corresponds to the questions of the social responsibility of the writer in this new historical context. Reflections and changes of directions in *El furgón de cola*, also visible in *Señas de identidad*, form a foundation of Goytisolo's later more experimental writing. From that moment on there will also be a greater correspondence between his theoretical writing and his fiction. Thus later Goytisolo's work is marked by a metafictional turn, where a critical work will be located at the core of his fictional one. Creation, literature, destruction and literary theory all overlap in his fiction. But even then, Goytisolo, a restless thinker, would continue to constantly re-evaluate the role of the writer and the nature of 'commited' art. The contradiction that surfaces between the search for linguistic limits and desire for social commitment becomes a base of Goytisolo's novelistic and theoretical enterprise, and its paradoxical traits are integral to his structural base.

Fundamentally, Goytisolo's criticism of his generation is also an assessment of his own work. He is conscious that his writing is *not yet* so different from the Spanish tradition he impugns. His generation's conceptual confines are his own. Describing their literary pursuits through bull-fighting imagery, he will grant them their place in Spanish literary history—that of the break with previous arm-chair bullfighters of literary salons—yet hold them accountable for their lack of skills of trade (language) or incapacity to engage more profoundly with the form: 'un grupo de floridos toreros de salón (incapaces de afrontar el toro de nuestra siniestra realidad española) ha sucedido otro de toreros (y maletas) valientes y bravos, pero desconocedores (por lo común) del mecanismo sutil del arte de la lidia' ('Literatura y eutanasia'; 1976: 83). In that critical spirit, and leaving behind adherence to social-realist conventions that conceives of language as a transparent medium, Goytisolo initiated a project of stylistic experimentation, embraced in this period and fully deployed by the time of the publication of his *Reivindicación del Conde don Julián* (1970). As Goytisolo himself concluded:

> Un conjunto irrepetible de circunstancias políticas, literarias y personales me impulsó a un proceso de ruptura y desposesión en virtud del cual el primitivo exilio político se transformó en un exilio social, literario, moral y sexual. Me desprendí de la fratria generacional y emprendí un rumbo solitario por aguas para mí desconocidas. (2005: 15)

José María Castellet

The literary and theoretical concerns that permeate Goytisolo's writing are strikingly similar to those of José María Castellet due to their common background: the cultural milieu of post-war Barcelona, shared literary influences, the proximity of French thought and an anti-Francoist political stance. While Goytisolo was a pre-eminent writer of the 1950s, Castellet was its critical voice. He is the theorist of Goytisolo's generation, those 'courageous and brave bullfighters unaware of the mechanism of the subtle art of bullfight'. Castellet was a voice of cohesion that gave expression to a fractured community of writers of the 1950s. Through Castellet's critical endeavour this alienated community became the Generation of the Mid-Century or the 1950s Generation.

The literary and theoretical evolution seen in Goytisolo can be traced through Castellet as well: the fervent promotion of a social novel evolving into a more complex interrogation of realism—and of reality itself—and finally reaching disillusionment over its own effectiveness as either literary or political tool. The dissonance between Castellet's early adherence to Marxism and subsequent (post)-structuralist tendencies reinforces the tension between pragmatism and utopia that runs through his work.

Castellet's literary and critical beginnings were tied to the student circles of Barcelona University, tertulias such as the one in Café El Turia or the Bar Club, and literary journals: *Estilo*, *Qvadrante*, *Laye* and *Revista*.[15] Several of these journals were part of the cultural production of SEU (Sindicato Español Universitario), an official and mandatory student union. *Laye*, SEU's most significant literary and cultural journal—envisioned as an instrument of official culture and created within the limits of official culture—became a voice of opposition within those limits.[16] Castellet's first writings for *Estilo*, *Qvadrante* and *Laye*, mostly articles on contemporary European and American narrative or cinema, date back to 1945. But it was those essays written for *Laye* that contained key elements of what would become his most influential theories. Not surprisingly, Castellet and Jaime Gil de Biedma always refered to *Laye* as 'unforgettable' (*la inolvidable*) (Marsal 1979: 93). Collaboration for *Laye* was an essential experience for Castellet and his generation because of the shared cultural capital aquired there. Some of the most significant texts that were read and circulated were those by Ortega y Gasset, Heidegger, Proust, T.S. Eliot, Joyce, Kafka, Sartre, Camus, Gide, Moravia, Faulkner, Dos Pasos and Hemingway. These influential texts later became the building-stones of their own theoretico-literary edifice. Castellet sums up this formative experience in these words:

> En todo caso, la experiencia de 'Laye' fue determinante para mí en muchos aspectos. Allí encontré la satisfacción de un trabajo en común, con viejos amigos de la universidad (los Ferraté, Barral, Gil de Biedma, Ferrán, Costafreda, los Goytisolo, etc.). Allí encontré nuevos y valiosos amigos como Esteban Pinilla de la Heras, Ramón Carnicer, etc. Allí se publicaron algunos de mis primeros trabajos válidos, algunos de los cuales -- aparte de los recogidos en *Notas sobre literatura*...—formaron el germen de mi primer libro 'serio,' *La hora del lector*. Allí conviví crisis políticas y espirituales que tanto ayudan a la formación. Allí discutí sobre temas variados con personas de procedencia e ideologías distintas—y también eso ayuda a formarse. (Marsal 1979: 92)[17]

Besides his critical activity, Castellet was also active in organizing cultural events housed in the Instituto de Estudios Hispánicos, such as the Juan Boscán Poetry Seminar where he forged closer ties with several writers and intellectuals who would figure prominently in his future cultural undertakings such as José Agustín Goytisolo, Jaime Gil de Biedma and Carlos Barral. As Castellet emphasized, the Institute provided scope for the group's increased politicization:

> Por aquel entonces renové la amistad con alguna gente de la universidad y de la oposición y a través del Instituto de Estudios Hispánicos hicimos una determinada evolución ideológica hacia el 'marxismo' (entre comillas) porque era un marxismo sin textos, casi puramente intuitivo. (Marsal 1979: 89)

Gabriel Celaya has mockingly called this intuitive marxism, 'a marxism by word of mouth' (*un marxismo de tradición oral*).[18] *Laye* and the Instituto de Estudios Hispánicos provided space for the initial formation and political apprenticeship of Castellet's generation within the limits of a dictatorial structure and in place of a more coherent intellectual formation.

Notas sobre literatura española contemporánea (1955)

This increased politicization and sense of generational belonging is the backdrop for Castellet's first important collection of articles, *Notas sobre literatura española contemporánea* published in 1955 in Ediciones Laye of Barcelona. The political intention of the text becomes evident from the section called *Justificación* that preceeds the volume:

> En otras circunstancias no estaría justificado, creo yo, reunir en un volumen unas notas como las presentes, escritas a filo y con las prisas de la actualidad y ya publicadas en diversas revistas del país, durante los tres últimos años; pero se me ha pedido que lo haga, no por el interés de la crítica literaria que pueden tener—si lo tienen—, sino por lo que su postura, abierta y honradamente inconformista, representa frente a una situación cultural anómala y confusa como la actual. Por ello he recogido, especialmente, aquellas notas que de un modo u otro hacen referencia a esta situación. (1955b: 7)

The political dimension is placed before the literary one, and the very value of Castellet's writing resides in his non-conformist stance within what he himself terms 'the confused and anomalous cultural situation of Spain' which the reader should implicitly understand as having been produced by dictatorship.

Second, his *Justification* highlighting the issues of writer's non-conformism is strategically tied to generational questions in a Prologue entitled 'Una generación sin inconformistas'. The title refers to Castellet's being dubbed 'el crítico más caracterizado por su inconformismo dentro de los de [su] generación' (1955b: 11).[19] This individualist stance of the author is strategically used to express the collective dimension and works as a springboard for Castellet's reflection on the role of writers of his generation, conditioned by the 'anomaly' of the political structure of dictatorship that they inherited. For Castellet, the question of writing becomes inseparable from what he terms 'a realization of awareness' (*toma de conciencia*), an axiom reiterated throughout his text, and clearly indebted to Marxist and Sartrian language and thought (*falsches Bewußtsein*; *prise de conscience*). Castellet's text functions as both an interpolation and a 'call' to consciousness and a warning:

> Temo por el porvenir de una generación sin inconformistas, eso es, sin conciencia crítica, sin 'daimon.' Y por ello, estas líneas, que son antes una confesión que una acusación, buscan despertar una conciencia, revelar un problema que es, quizás, el problema de nuestra generacíón. (1955b: 13)

This intersection of the literary and political along with the individual and the collective, reiterated throughout *Notas sobre literatura española contemporánea*, forms the groundwork for theme of generational question which preocupied Castellet throughout his career. Articulated in *Notas*, it will be investigated deeper in his first major work *La hora del lector*, that is dedicated 'A los escritores españoles de mi generación'.

Besides its political urgency for Castellet, the question of generation is also the bases for a methodology in literary studies. Castellet appropriates various generational theories for his own historical context of the 1950s in Spain: from *la generación perdida* and Hemmingway's generational concept in American literature to Spanish generational theorists such as Ortega y Gasset and his disciple Julián Marías.[20] It is significant that Castellet delimited his 'Generation of the Mid-Century' to authors born between 1922 and 1936. His timeframe draws from Ortega's concept of *vigencia*, the fifteen years that Ortega assigned to a generation:

> El sistema de vigencias en que la forma de la vida humana consiste, dura un período que casi coincide con los quince años. Una generación es una zona de quince años durante la cual una cierta forma de vida fue vigente... La afinidad no procede tanto de ellos como de verse obligados a vivir en un mundo que tiene una forma determinada y única. (Ortega y Gasset 1971: 104, 105)[21]

Orteguian time span (*vigencia*) together with the pro-Nazi scholar Julius Petersen's eight postulates of generational formation—herencia común; fechas de nacimiento; elementos educativos; comunidad personal; experiencias de la generación; guía o caudillo; lenguaje común and anquilosamiento de la vieja generación—enabled Castellet to place his generation in contrast to the Civil War generation (Generation of 1936) or authors born between 1906 and 1921.[22] The strategy is again political and it revolves around the question of inheritance, accountability and the necessity for rupture with the previous generation. The War generation—mutilated, stunned by civil conflict, infatuated with fascism—was perceived as unwilling or incapable of political and aesthetic renewal. To the 1950s generation, in contrast,

> ...le está encomendada una labor [manifestarse acerca de la patria, la sociedad y su concepción de la literatura] ingrata, de gran esfuerzo y, seguramente, de provecho tardío. En todo caso, si logra cumplir con su misión, le habrá cabido el honor de ser la primera generación que, después de la guerra, se haya asomado al interior de España con un decidido afán de renovación y al exterior de ella con la tenaz humildad de querer estar de nuevo presente en el mundo, representando a su patria, mostrándose tal cual es: una generación en la que sus hombres buscan la reconciliación y la reconstrucción nacional, luchando día tras día por una libertad que les abra el camino hacia ellas. (Castellet 1958a: 52)

Castellet's 'zealous' generation are the poets José Hierro, Eugenio de Nora, Carlos Bousoño, Lorenzo Gomis, Alfonso Costafreda, José Manuel Caballero Bonald, José María Valverde and Jaime Ferrán; playwrights represented by Alfonso Sastre, and the novelists Juan Goytisolo, Jesús Fernández Santos, Ignacio Aldecoa, Rafael Sánchez Ferlosio, Mario Lacruz and Ana María Matute. According to Castellet, their eagerness for renewal required search, sense of mission and intensity of labour, yet the effort was rewarded by freedom and a recovery of their place on the political and world map. Castellet's heavy Marxist/Sartrian tone is at time punctuated by National-Catholic, not to say Fascist strains. Castellet, moving through precarious political terrain, still contaminated by the ubiquitous messianic language of the post-war Falange, summons this emerging community of the mid-century to labour and commitment.[23] This gesture shows that for Castellet 'history does not belong primarily to time, nor to succession, nor to causality, but to community, or to being-in-common' (Nancy 1993: 143).

Castellet's use of the generational concept has been criticized from several angles. Most importantly, as Laureano Bonet warns, Castellet failed to consider important writers of the immediate post-war period, several of whom were completely absent from Castellet's account of Spanish literature:

> Sin duda aquí un Castellet comprometido con la generación de los 50—la suya, no lo olvidemos—es un tanto injusto en su tratamiento de la literatura de la primera postguerra y, en el anhelo por destacar lo que él llama la 'reconstruction of the Spanish novel structure', destruida por el conflicto civil, desdeña interesantes aportaciones—por discutible que fuese alguna de ella en lo ideológico—de escritores como G. Torrente Ballester, M. Delibes, R. Sánchez Mazas, J.A. Zunzunegui o J. Suárez Carreño. (1994: 112, 113)[24]

But, instead of the attempt to do better justice to the post-war generation discernable in Bonet's comment, we can construe this oversight as Castellet's strategy. His gaps were intentional and his neglect of the select post-war literature a necessary tactic in his re-formulation of the Spanish literary canon, contours of which we may still follow today. Castellet's classification 'errors' gathered a somewhat dispersed group into a generation, serving Castellet's own culturo-political project.

As is well known and as Manuel Vázquez Montalbán also pointed out, 'la literatura española padece un abuso de generacionismo' (1988: 127). But as we have seen, Castellet's abuse of *generacionismo* enabled him to systematize and politicize the generational concept, despite his barely original generational postulates. Castellet's strategy is also an invention of genealogy. Besides issues of accountability, it is obvious that the earlier avant-garde legacy was much more appealing than the aesthetics that marked the War generation, in its love affair with Fascism. Castellet's orphaned generation, living in the stagnant Spanish cultural panorama of the 1950s and cut off from their philosophical and literary heritage due to the repressive political post-war climate, saw the question of writing as a question of patrimony as well. This traumatized 'fatherless generation' erased their immediate ancestors, reclaiming the Modernist or avant-garde lineage of their litarary grandfathers.[25]

The principal question of generation addressed in the Prologue is followed by four other sections of *Notas*: 'Notas de sociología literaria', 'Tres notas inconformistas', 'Dos notas afirmativas' and 'Tres notas sobre los jóvenes'. The first one, 'Notas de sociología literaria' is theoretical, while the following three sections provide concrete examples to illustrate the arguments expounded there. The heart of the book comes in an essay 'Notas sobre la situación actual del escritor en España' sandwiched into the 'Notes on literary sociology'. It contains the core of Castellet's 1950s thought. Since the main themes addressed in *Notas sobre la literatura española contemporánea* are recast in Castellet's following book *La hora del lector*, the following section expands upon them.

Before moving on to *La hora del lector*, however, it is important to point out that the highly political nature of topics addressed in *Notas sobre literatura española contemporánea* and Castellet's critical tone caused the book to be pulled from the market after three months. As Castellet vividly describes it: '...they burned it or put it to the guillotine' (*lo quemaron, o guillotinaron*) (Marsal 1979: 88). With this early work, Castellet showed that he indeed had the pulse of Spanish reality or its *actualidad*. Prohibition of *Notas* together with the imminent closure of *Laye* validates Castellet's assessment that 'alrededor de 1956 todos [los colaboradores de *Laye*] sin excepción éramos ya intelectuales democráticos en oposición al Régimen' (Marsal 1979: 92).

La hora del lector (1957)

Castellet's assertion that literature performs an important fundamentally cathartic role and it can and must come to be the reflective consciousness of a community (1955b: 24) is the driving idea behind his second collection of articles entitled *La hora del lector*. This linking of literature to social consciousness is not surprising given that 1956, the year between the publication of the two collections, was a year of a student unrest and of a cancelled University Congress of Young Writers (el Congreso Universitario de Escritores Jóvenes), two events that profoundly affected the Spanish political and cultural milieu. The book returns to queries already engaged in *Notas sobre literatura española contemporánea* such as questions of generational methodology, literary techniques, Spain's lack of cultural modernity, the country's anachronism vis-à-vis Europe, the ambivalent role of literary prizes and the intersection of political and literary commitment. Above all, *La hora del lector* was an attempt to systematize the role of reader and readership in contemporary Spanish literature.[26] The aesthetics of reception is proposed by Castellet as an alternative methodology, with potential for renovation of the stagnant Spanish literary scene. As the title indicates and the new 'Justificación' that precedes the text also clarifies, *La hora del lector* postulates a literature that now belongs to the reader:

> esta obra quiere, ante todo, subrayar la importancia que el lector adquiere, en nuestros días, como activo creador de la obra de arte literaria. El lector es, pues, hoy, nuestro tema y, para intentar ayudarle a tomar conciencia de su importancia en la literatura de nuestro tiempo, se han escrito estas páginas. (1957a: 11)

Participation of the reader or spectator of the work of art in the production of its meaning had been postulated by several thinkers before Castellet, but Castellet systematized the concept and diffused it for a generation that was cut off both from the pre-war philosophical and literary tradition and from the then-contemporary European literary currents.[27] Like *Notas sobre literatura española contemporánea, La hora del lector* is clearly influenced by Ortega y Gasset, particularly Ortega's contemplations of objects of art and his theory of the novel. In his *Ideas sobre la novela* published in 1925, Ortega's stated that 'sólo a través de un mínimo de acción es posible contemplación' (1982: 40,

41). This idea, further developed in the philosopher's famous discussion of the atrabilious nature of a hypothetical character called Pedro, forms the core of Castellet's argument in *La hora del lector*. Castellet cites Ortega:

> Si en una novela leo: 'Pedro era atrabiliario,' es como si el autor me invitase a que yo realice en mi fantasía la atrabilis de Pedro, partiendo de su definición. Es decir, que me obliga a ser yo el novelista. Pienso que lo eficaz es, precisamente, lo contrario: que él me dé los hechos visibles para que yo me esfuerce, complacido, en descubrir y definir a Pedro como ser atrabiliario. (1957a: 47 [Ortega 1982: 22])[28]

Hermeneutics in general and Ortega's interpretation of aesthetics of reception in particular, especially the philosopher's insistence on an *arte de novelar* or narrative skill that entices responses in the reader, influenced Castellet's own conception of the dynamic reader. The reader's active engagement and willingness to participate with the text became the groundwork for Castellet's own theory of readership. The spirit of the times together with the texts themselves required 'la progresiva desaparición del autor' (1957a: 15) or a writer who was willing to let go of his privileged place as author of the literary work. The new reader became burdened by the task of deciphering a novelistic world, yet rewarded by the freedom of re-creating it: 'El lector se ha convertido en protagonista activo de la creación literaria. Y nuestro tiempo, en el tiempo del lector' (1957a: 62).

Besides Ortega's influence, Castellet's scrutiny of the readers of those times is supported by the theoretical work of Jean-Paul Sartre (*¿Qué es la literatura?*), Claude-Edmonde Magny (*La era de la novela americana*) and Alain Robbe-Grillet (*Un camino para la novela futura*). The excerpts from these works are included in the book's appendices and each one forms an important part of Castellet's argument in *La hora del lector*. Castellet's critical bibliography of the readership problem is therefore sustained by theoretical postulates from existentialism (Sartre), the *nouveau roman* (Robbe-Grillet) and the American realist novel (Magny). Existentialism provided a moral backdrop to *La hora del lector*, while American realism and the *nouveau roman* provided new techniques that would replace the ossified nineteenth-century narrative models. At times these influences overlap, dialogue with each other or even come in conflict. Before entering any discussion of *La hora* itself, therefore, I will briefly indicate each theorist's particular impact on Castellet.

Castellet first read Sartre's *Situations, II: Qu'est-ce que la littérature*? in the original French edition just before his trip to Paris sponsored by a scholarship from the Delegación Nacional de Educación in 1953.[29] Castellet elaborates:

> Cuando llegué a Paris…yo era ya un sartriano convencido, a pesar de que mis lecturas de Sartre habían sido escasas a causa de la dificultad de encontrar en España sus libros y, aun, en las reboticas de unas

> pocas librerías progres. Uno se convierte a lo que está predispuesto. Yo había leído ya 'Situations II' y, ¿qué mejor regalo para un joven literato antifranquista e izquierdoso que aquél volumen que ofrecía nada menos que la 'Presentación de Temps modernes' y '¿Qué es la literatura?'. Maná caído del cielo o cosquilleo intelectual venido de las llamas del averno: lo que ustedes quieran...Había, pues, que escoger, primero y comprometerse, luego, con la opción adoptada. Así fue de simple mi adscripción a un cierto sartrianismo al que fui fiel durante muchos años—una quincena, quizás—y del cual se encuentran algunas referencias en mis libros, especialmente, claro está, en *La hora del lector*. (1990: 2)

What is Literature?, liberally quoted and paraphrased throughout *La hora del lector*, makes clear Sartre's influence on Castellet. The most important Sartrian concepts Castellet draws on are: the notion of committed literature (*littérature engagée*), praxis (human activity in its material context) and the ethics of authenticity. Following Sartre, Castellet addressed the problem of 'writing for our time' through existentialist ethics and existentialist humanism. In his writing Castellet also simulated Sartre's joining of Existentialist vocabulary of the 1940s and early 1950s with the Marxist lexicon of the late 1950s and 1960s. Departing from Sartrian foundation, Castellet's life-long critical project centres on questions of writing and historical responsibility, the historicity of texts (historical materialism), attention to contemporariness or *la actualidad*, the artist's responsibility to society, and the social and political function of literature at large.

While Sartre provided an Existentialist grid for Castellet, Claude-Edmonde Magny introduced him to American realism.[30] Castellet's general interest in American literature goes back to the late 1940s but by the mid-1950s and under French influence, he refocused his interest towards the American realist novel and *roman noir* in particular.[31] The American realist novel, filtered through Magny's interpretation, was instrumental in introducing Castellet to behaviourism and use of cinematic techniques in contemporary literary production:

> En América ha florecido una escuela filosófica llamada 'behaviorismo;' esta escuela se define por considerar solamente real, en la vida psicológica de un hombre o de un animal, lo que podría percibir un observador puramente exterior, representando en el límite, por el objetivo de una cámara fotográfica; por eliminar cuanto no pueda ser conocido más que por el mismo sujeto, por medio de un análisis interior...(Magny cited in *La hora*, 1957a: 156)

While the American realist novel introduced Castellet to 'objective' narrative tools, its subgeneric variant *roman noir* or hardboiled fiction provided Castellet with an insight into the literary innovations that this low-brow genre offered.[32] It showed him the possibility of articulating a social critique through a form that fitted parameters of social realism yet departed from its ideological rigidity.

The third key voice of *La hora*, Alain Robbe-Grillet, was instrumental in introducing Castellet to the theory of the *nouveau roman*, with its innovative forms and radical narrative experimentation.[33] Robbe-Grillet's 'Un camino para la novela futura', included in the appendix, highlights the preeminence of objects and gestures in the novelists's thought: 'En este universo novelesco futuro, gesto y objetos estarán *ahí* antes de ser *cualquier cosa*' (Robbe-Grillet cited in *La hora*, 1957a: 159).[34] The New Novel, often unreadable, lacked humanity and insisted on erasing the interiority and psychological dimensions of the literary work that characterized the previous century:

> Que los objetos y los gestos se impongan, ante todo, por su *presencia*, y que esa presencia prosiga continuamente hasta dominar, por encima de cualquier teoría explicativa que tendiera a encerrarlos en un sistema cualquiera de referencias: sentimental, sociológico, freudiano, metafísico, etc. (Robbe-Grillet cited in *La hora*, 1957a: 159)

Similar in spirit to (Magny's) behaviourism, Robbe-Grillet's theory of objects is clearly a precursor of postmodern celebration of surface or 'la destitución de los viejos mitos de la "profundidad"' (Robbe-Grillet cited in *La hora*, 1957a: 160). Rejecting interiority, Robbe-Grillet stated that 'Los objetos...perderán poco a poco su inconstancia y sus secretos y renunciarán a su falso misterio, a esa sospechosa interioridad que Roland Barthes ha llamado el "romántico corazón de las cosas"' (Robbe-Grillet cited in *La hora*, 1957a: 159). An exaggerated concern with visual perception and focus on inanimate and seemingly trivial objects is an attempt to show how 'reality' was constructed or invented by our perception and conception in the first place. The focus on objects reflects the excessively formalist tendencies of the *nouveau roman* and stresses the realities of representation over any representation of 'reality'. But Robbe-Grillet and the New Novelists transformed the possibilities of fictional practice, redefined the novelistic domain and encouraged readers to read afresh—all aims of Castellet's own pedagogical enterprise.

The main body of *La hora* is divided into four sections: 'Las técnicas de la literatura sin autor', 'La hora del lector', 'Una literatura sin lectores' and 'Hacía la literatura del futuro'. While the first two sections centre on the question of authorship, literary point of view and new novelistic techniques, the last two belong to the sociology of literature, relating the question of reading to the question of justice.[35] 'Las técnicas de la literatura sin autor' advocates a progressive disappearence of the author, only possible as a result of the crisis of bourgeois thought that calls for alternative political and literary models. This agony of the bourgeois world, condensed in the 'grito nietzscheano que proclamaba *la muerte de Dios*', is accompanied by the death of old forms, that is, the death of the moral, social and spiritual values of the bourgeoisie (Castellet 1957a: 24). The death of God bolstered the death of the 'novelist God' 'que quedaba automáticamente incluído entre los valores que iban a desaparecer, arrastrados por el derrumbamiento de toda la concepción burguesa de la vida' (1957a: 25). A break with the divine, authoritarian and absolute point of view that characterized nineteenth-century literature is accompanied by more modern mediums of expression influenced by existential philosophy and behaviourist psychology. The fiction that belonged to the time of the new reader rejected essentialist psychology, linear chronology, the notion of a coherent whole, a meaningful literary universe and notions of psychological interiority. Nevertheless, social realism, like mid-twentieth-century Marxism, still had scientific pretentions to objectivity. Despite that element, the accent was on liberating the novel from the imperatives of traditional fiction, the metaphysical assumptions these novels implied and the aesthetic formulas they encouraged. The omniscient narrator, a holder of monolithic values of bourgeois society, is now replaced by objective narration and its corresponding cinematic techniques. Besides, as Brad Epps has noted, '...the role of the engaged intellectual translates into an apparently disengaged author—disengaged, that is, from an intrusive, even dictatorial, telling of the tale' (2003: 195, 196).

The disappearance of the 'novelist God' and his omniscient narrator calls for a reinvention of literary language which would signal the possibility of participation by the reader in the production of meaning. In *La hora del lector* Castellet outlined three fundamental techniques of literature without the author: first-person narrative, interior monologue and the objective technique of narration ('la técnica objetiva'). He recapitulates:

> El autor ha ido autoeliminándose, progresivamente, de sus narraciones. En primer lugar (*relatos en la primera persona*), ha pasado de creador de personajes, a ser él mismo personaje, con la única diferencia o superioridad sobre los demás de conservar su situación de narrador. Más tarde (*monólogo interior*), deja de intervenir absolutamente en la narración, para ofrecer al lector el mundo íntimo, los pensamientos, los deseos ocultos e, incluso, la estructura psíquica inconciente de sus personajes, con lo que su papel se limita al de simple transmitor—casi diríamos de estenógrafo—del libre curso mental de éstos. Por último (*narraciones objetivas*), el novelista se borra totalmente de sus obras y su misión queda reducida a registrar, con total y fría objetividad, los acontecimientos externos de los que son protagonistas los personajes. (1957a: 18)

While the first two techniques were used in previous literary epochs and have slowly evolved to fit contemporary expression, the objective technique is a radical departure as narrative mode that belongs solely to the literature of the future. 'La técnica objetiva' is not plagued by 'privilegios residuales' of first-person narrative and interior monologue (1957a: 29). It is a culmination of literature without author that revolutionized literature, he states, and its pinnacle is the author's absence from the pages of the book. Key to the objective technique is the writer's resemblance to a film camera. This new hybrid is even denominated *el novelista-cámara* since he 'enfoca y reproduce—concreta, directa y obligatoriamente—conductas humanas *en situación*' (Castellet 1957a: 37). The goal of *el novelista-cámara* is

> narrar historias con la misma objetividad con que lo haría una cámara cinematográfica, esto es *reproduciendo fielmente*—sin añadir el menor comentario, ni intentar el menor análisis que representa la presencia de una subjetividad aparte del mundo en que se desenvuelve la anécdota—*lo que es pura exteriorización de una conducta en una situación dada.* (Castellet 1957a: 36)[36]

All three literary modes are deeply embedded in social structures, and Castellet, in keeping with a progressive vision, attempts to show an evolution from nineteenth-century bourgeois models of realism to the committed and objective writings of his own times. Castellet illustrates this notion of 'literary progress' through the 'model' texts that he includes in the appendix of the book. Cervantes's *Don Quijote de la Mancha*, Tolstoy's *War And Peace* and Proust's *Swann's Way* are models for traditional narrative modes (*los modos narrativos tradicionales*). *La vida de Lazarillo de Tormes* and Hemingway's *To Have and Have Not* are models for first-person narration (*los relatos en primera persona*); Joyce's *Ulysses* and John Dos Passos's *The Big Money* are models for interior monologue (*el monólogo interior*); and Dashiell Hammet's *The Glass Key* and Rafael Sánchez Ferlosio's *El Jarama* are models for objective technique of narration. Literary progress parallels, perhaps too neatly, the historical one, and this progression of narrative styles culminates in the most—politically—progressive one: *la técnica objetiva*. However, Castellet is neither able to explain convincingly the evolution of these literary techniques nor to distinguish what he calls earlier, inauthentic models of these techniques from the ones that evolved into the authentic, contemporary counterpart of which he approves. Neither this evolutionary model nor Castellet's claim for the objective mode's intrinsic relation to progressive social agendas persuades us. Castellet's taxonomy or classification of literary models is interesting politically, yet theoretically ineffective.

While the first chapter outlines literary techniques, the second one that gives the collection its name—'La hora del lector'—centres on the factors which distinguish contemporary narrative from that of the previous century. According to Castellet, these are: (1) a change of narrative focus that brought to an end the nineteenth-century novelist's habit of interfering in the action and commenting on characters ('en las novelas de nuestros días, al autor no le están permitidas ingerencias en la acción', 1957a: 46), (2) intricate narrative constructions with simultaneous use of different literary techniques. This mode complicates the chronological progression of the novel, which may no longer be reduced to the linearity which characterized nineteenth-century novels ('una complejidad que no respeta la normal sucesión del tiempo', 1957a: 46), and (3) the use of a different kind of language characterized by Castellet as *lenguaje oscuro* that replaces the analytic expression of the nineteenth century ('progresivo oscurecimiento de la expresión y de complejidad narrativa', 1957a: 45). The most striking trait in this chapter is Castellet's theorizing of *lenguaje oscuro*. Castellet advocates a narrative complexity appropriate for the new era, while warning against its possible false masquerades:

> Señalar la inautenticidad formal de las obras que, bajo pretexto de modernismo y de 'estar al día', han sido escritas con una falsa intención 'oscurecedora', para mostrar preocupaciones técnicas que, en realidad, no han sido nunca comprendidas ni vividas auténticamente como tales (1957a: 78, 79)

Castellet's irresoluteness on this issue points to an inability to reconcile formal experimentation with political commitment. It is the problem that troubled Goytisolo in his theorizing of language and commitment which we observed in *Problemas de la novela* and *El furgón de cola*. Like the Goytisolo of those early texts, the Castellet of *La hora* was also unable to negotiate what he perceived as the incompatibilities between Modernism with its emphasis on technique and social realism with its emphasis on common justice. Furthermore, deliberate obscurantism and the stratification of cultures discernible in Modernism was what Castellet objected to politically, but could not resist aesthetically.

As the book progresses, political issues take primacy over formal procedures and literary experimentation. Thus the last two essays in the book 'Una literatura sin lectores' and 'Hacía la literatura del futuro' have more of a sociological than a literary focus. One of the main issues is the question of praxis and readership. The active reader envisioned by Castellet in 'La hora del lector' does not exist or, as Castellet phrased it, 'la realidad no responde aún a los buenos deseos de la teoría' (1957a: 68). Only an ideal reader of utopian proportions would have been able to rise to the demands of Castellet's theoretical postulates. We are therefore confronted with the central paradox of contemporary literature:

> en el momento en que la evolución de determinadas técnicas expresivas ha llegado a hacer imprescindible la colaboración del lector para el acto creador literario; en el momento en que, por lo mismo, el lector accede al

> proceso de creación de la literatura; en este momento, la literatura se va quedando progresivamente sin lectores. (1957a: 85)[37]

This paradox of a literature without a readership is the result of a disconnect between the unskillful or uninterested reader and the paternalistic or elitist writer. On the one hand, the writer can not relinquish his divine arrogance inherited from the Novelist-God of the previous epoch: 'El error consiste en seguir considerando al lector como un ser absolutamente menesteroso y desvalido, a pesar que haya conseguido su independencia y libertad con respeto al autor' (1957a: 76). On the other hand, the reader continues to be passive, a trait also inherited from the previous era:

> la inercia intelectual de los hombres, a su inevitable pereza mental frente a las novedades, a sus dificultades de adaptación ante acontecimientos o situaciones inéditas y, en el caso que nos ocupa, a la resistencia de los lectores ante las nuevas técnicas, los nuevos modos de decir que traducen—y en ella se justifican—una nueva concepción del mundo. (1957a: 70)

According to Castellet, the solution to this paradoxical twist lies in the effort required of both writer and reader of contemporary literature. Using the metaphor of a worker-writer, he describes the literary endeavour of the future as a conundrum of self-exertion:

> Escribir una novela consiste...en construir un edificio, fragmentarlo como un *puzzle*, y volver a montar en un orden distinto, el que exige la estructura interna de la novela...y, en fin, en trabajar humilde y pacientemente, como un obrero cualquiera, con su misma forzada resignación y con la única esperanza de encontrar un lector de buena voluntad que quiera completar su labor. (1957a: 57, 58)

This quixotic notion, grounded in Castellet's Marxist belief and clearly reminiscent of the Second Republic's educational mission, is not just a utopian project but also one of social equality and justice. Castellet's avant-garde mind wants experiment, while his heart longs for justice, which is what creates the impasse between social literature and Modernist fiction. His writing at this time therefore continues to be nourished by the tension between art and society, language and reality.

Given the most strident direction of Castellet's writing, it is not surprising that his last essay 'Hacía la literatura del futuro' holds Spain's socio-political configuration accountable for the split between elitist writer and uneducated reader. Castellet states: 'La literatura es, ante todo, un hecho social y su porvenir, como el nuestro, depende de la sociedad—o sociedades—en que se encuentra inserta' (1957a: 85). Castellet implies that the shortcomings of the readers do not stem simply from their inner limitations but are a consequence of fundamental impediments and the backward educational politics of dictatorial Spain. Insisting on 'elevación cultural del lector medio' (1957a: 89), his last chapter raises the issue of the interrelations among social condition, art and inequalities of justice. Castellet calls for a radical transformation of the world, linking his own and Spain's immediate cultural-political circumstances to a broader universal dimension.[38]

La hora del lector is a radical work in the context of 1950s Spain. Where Castellet has most success is in his appropriations and amalgamation of Sartre, Robbe-Grillet and Magny and connecting their thought to the question of freedom. On the one hand, the question of freedom is deeply implicated in Castellet's own precarious historical moment, the dictatorship under which he lives and writes. Castellet's antidictatorial struggle and his proletarian literary utopia go hand in hand. It is, in sum, a belief in praxis or *la práctica de la literatura* and the impact of this on the antifrancoist struggle. On the other hand, the very freedom and essence of writing are at stake:

> el escritor no puede olvidar que la creación no podrá surgir nunca fresca, esto es, original y eficaz, si no mana de su más íntima y auténtica libertad personal...La suerte de la literatura está íntimamente ligada, pues, a la libertad del escritor, como lo está a la del lector. (1957a: 101, 102)

The possibility of freedom, linked to the notion of authenticity, is multiform: existentialist freedom, freedom from old forms and freedom from the authorial presence. In view of the above, it is hardly surprising that Castellet's book closes with a long quote from Camus:

> Creo que los hombres no han dejado nunca de avanzar en la toma de consciencia de su destino...Sabemos que vivimos en contradicción, pero debemos rechazarla y hacer lo que sea posible para reducirla. Nuestra tarea de hombres consiste en encontrar algunas fórmulas que rebajen la angustia infinita de las almas libres. Tenemos que coser lo que está desgarrado, hacer imaginable la justicia en un mundo tan evidentemente injusto y significativa la felicidad para los pueblos envenenados por el mal del siglo. Naturalmente, ésta es una tarea sobrehumana. Pero llamamos sobrehumanas a las tareas que los hombres tardan largo tiempo en cumplir: eso es todo. (Camus cited in *La hora*, 1957a: 103, 104)

This final quotation also brings us back to the central inconsistency of *La hora del lector*, its conflation of critics with widely dissimilar traits. Castellet demanded that the writer should 'vibrar con la sensibilidad de la época', yet there is a noteworthy anachronism in his own attempt to draft Sartre, Camus, Robbe-Grillet and Magny for his own critical project. Castellet's mission in *La hora del lector* is pedagogical, yet he does not provide his readers with the historical and literary background of his core theorists. For example, Magny's 'The Age of the American Novel' gained prominence back in the 1930s and 1940s, signalling—in Sartre's expression—'a veritable revolution in the art of telling a story' (1946: 116). Its success in the European milieu was due to a perceived raw and barbaric energy that stale European society lacked. Similarly, Existentialism belonged to that dispirited and introspective moment following French liberation and the general destruction of the Second World War. Yet again, the New Novel was to become the most important French literary phenomenon of the late 1950s and early 1960s closer to Castellet's prime, when rapidly developing Western European consumer capitalism may have encouraged the primacy of pure objects over earlier humanistic beliefs. On top of this, by the time Castellet wrote *La hora*, it was clear that the *nouveau roman* constituted a very different kind of fiction; one that did away with both the methods of the nineteenth-century novel and the premises of Existentialism that had dominated Parisian circles in the immediate post-war era. The fictions of the New Novelists stood as distant from nineteenth-century versions of Realism as they did from the post-war Existentialist concerns of Camus, Sartre or Simone de Beauvoir. Despite this, Castellet insisted on marrying Sartre's ideas on commitement (*engagement*) to *nouveau roman* postulates that remained utterly insensitive to sociopolitical issues and were more concerned with their own formal procedures and experimentation. Existentialism, so deeply invested in human beings both in their potential and in their ethical duty (*posibilidades y deberes*), was hard to reconcile with the New Novelists' focus on objects and breaking the mold.

Although Castellet recognized the importance of Sartre, Marxism and revolutionary politics, he profoundly misunderstood all of them. The same could be said for his misinterpretations of Magny and Robbe-Grillet. In this sense, we could also tie Castellet's puzzling accumulation of French thought and alien authorities to Harold Bloom's notion of 'anxiety of influence' in the tyro writer. Finally, one can try to read Castellet's gesture as strategic, maintaining that the Spanish cultural landscape was ripe for his amalgamation due to the strange time-warp in which Spain found itself stranded during the 1950s. Castellet's ad hoc theorizing might have been a consummate fit for a country with one foot in a burgeoning market capitalism and the other in Marxist anti-dictatorial struggle. While the importation of hard-boiled American Realism and the French New Novel did indeed give Spanish fiction an air of experimentalism, humanistic Existentialism also nurtured the idea that writing should engage and transform reality and provide a moral backdrop in the call for a new society.

French Collioure and the *Colección Collioure* (1959)

The publication of *La hora del lector* established Castellet as a contentious voice on the Spanish literary scene. The political dimension of Castellet's writing gained even greater impact through his publishing activity where he closely followed his own postulates of a literature of the future. One of the most important projects after *La hora del lector* was the series of poetry volumes entitled *Colección Collioure* directed by Castellet and edited by Jaime Salinas.[39] *Colección Collioure* was inspired by a homage to Antonio Machado that took place in Collioure, France (where the poet died fleeing the Nationalist victory), between 21 and 23 February of 1959. The gathering on the twentieth anniversary of Machado's death brought together numerous poets of the 1950s—Carlos Barral, Jaime Gil de Biedma, José Agustín Goytisolo, Ángel González, Alfonso Costafreda, and Juan Ferrater—and so provided a binding element for this whole generation: '...una generación que se ha sentido unida y en movimiento, precisamente conmemorando el XX aniversario de la muerte de Antonio Machado' (Castellet 1960b: 55).

Among the volumes of the *Colección Collioure*, Castellet and Salinas published Gabriel Celaya's *Poemas de Juan de Leceta* (1961); Angel González's *Sin esperanza, con convencimiento* (1961); José Agustín Goytisolo's *Años decisivos* (1961); Jesús López Pacheco's *Canciones del amor prohibido* (1961); Carlos Barral's *Diecinueve figuras de mi historia civil* (1961); Angel Crespo's *Sume y sigue* (1962); Gloria Fuertes's *Que estás en la tierra* (1962); José Manuel Caballero Bonald's *Pliegos de cordel* (1963); José Angel Valente's *Sobre el lugar del canto* (1963); Jaime Gil de Biedma's *El favor de Venus* (1965) and Alfredo Costafreda's *Compañera de hoy* (1966). This collection clearly had an antifrancoist literary-political agenda emphasizing the editors' promotion of *littérature engagée* and their penchant for historical realism and *poesía social*. While the *Colección Collioure* was not exclusively or unanimously a collection of activist literature (as was obvious in the case of Barral and Caballero Bonald), it gathered together politically engaged writers who resisted Francoist culture and the reactionary moral tradition that upheld it. But the discrepancy between political support for social literature and the aesthetic resistance to it became especially noticeable in those poets of the Barcelona School who were featured in the *Colección Collioure*. Carme Riera observes:

> En un caso como el de Jaime Gil, la fecha de publicación ya tardía, 1965 y el tema del poemario, erótico, le apartan del 'compromiso.' En otro, como en el de Barral, el primero en publicar en la colección, su texto *Diecinueve figuras de mi historia civil* (1961) es una contribución muy personal a los postulados de Castellet, pese al considerable esfuerzo realizado por el poeta para emplear un lenguaje coloquial y renunciar al hermetismo de su producción anterior. Es José Agustín Goytisolo, entre

> el 'grupo de los tres,' el que más cerca está del 'realismo crítico' en *Años decisivos*. (1988: 220, 221)

Barral's decision to include his own *Diecinueve figuras de mi historia civil* is a telling gesture. Even within the text itself, there is a tension between his predilection for art for art's sake and his desire for political commitment. Barral's poetic language underscores the gap between the word and the world; between art and politics. At the heart of this tension is the function or task of the writer and the commensurability of art and political commitment. Barral's palpable ambivalence towards this line of social poetry was the same old stickler articulated by Goytisolo and Castellet and a principle reason for the trio's abandonment of social realism.

Despite this frank hesitation towards social realism, Barral's political commitment was fully realized in his strategic and successful publishing enterprise. The *Colección Collioure* was symbolic of anti-Francoist opposition, even if some of the works published resisted or even resented any notion of committed literature. The *Collioure* endeavour was really a unique fusion of Castellet's critical voice, Salinas's conceptual ability and Barral's pragmatism. Barral's inspiration to build a bridge between Castellet's criticism and his publishing activities was vital to the sucessful diffusion of the socialist-realist novel. Castellet became a pivotal figure in the imprint Seix Barral both as literary editor and as director of Seix Barral's new prose fiction collection *Biblioteca Breve*. Barral saw Castellet's sense of his own generation as a way of shaping of literary history:

> Algunos centenares de cartas enviadas a la prensa con la firma de José María Castellet...explicando nuestro propósito, habían predispuesto a favor de la idea a unos cuantos críticos principales que hablaban de nuestros libros subrayando el esfuerzo de su publicación a contracorriente y a contrapelo de los cálculos comerciales...Pero es evidente que la complicidad de unos y otros ayudaba a mantener el orden de batalla. (1978: 141, 142)

This marriage of politics, commerce and idealism discernible in the *Colección Collioure* would become the cornerstone for Castellet, Salinas and Barral's other publishing adventures. In that spirit, Barral concluded: 'Desde lo de Collioure todo se va en 'política de generación.' Entrevistas, frente común, política de publicaciones, antología... Etcétera...Lo del frente generacional es, sin embargo, divertidísimo y no inútil, según parece' (1978: 191). The politics of the 1950s generation was clearly carried forward by the aggregate of Castellet and Barral's literary and publishing interests. The theoretical ambivalence already seen in *La hora del lector* was mirrored in this very publishing venture, in its embrace of the literary and commercial.

The meetings at Formentor (1959; 1960)

The political and publishing strategies of the *Colección Collioure* were further strengthened by an international literary gathering held in Formentor in Majorca between 26 and 28 May of 1959, only a few months after the homage to Machado in France. The generational front created in Collioure and so involved in national literary debates and social preoccupations was now put on international display. On the home front, the gathering served to promote the prestigious literary prize *Premio de Novela Biblioteca Breve*, established only a year earlier in 1958 and won on that occasion by Luis Goytisolo for his novel *Las afueras*. In Formentor, Castellet, as literary editor for Seix Barral's *Biblioteca Breve* collection, was together with the scion of the house Carlos Barral and Jaime Salinas a key member of the jury. They awarded the 1959 *Biblioteca Breve* Prize to Juan García Hortelano's *Nuevas amistades* (1959). The politics of social realism as litmus test for winning novels was by now clearly institutionalized through the mechanism of literary prizes.[40]

On the international front, the Formentor's symposium—organized around different literary themes and with participants from various European and Latin American countries—now placed Spanish literature in a global context. The Spanish delegation took advantage of the occasion to organize its First International Colloquium on the Novel (Primer Coloquio Internacional sobre novela) and used it as a platform for awarding the second *Biblioteca Breve* Prize for the novel. Each session of the Colloquium addressed different themes such as 'El novelista y la sociedad', 'El novelista y su arte' and 'El porvenir de la novela'. In essence, the Colloquium voiced opposition between socialist-realist models (Sartre's Existentialy committed art or Italian neo-Realism) and *nouveau roman* trends. In 'El novelista y la sociedad' session, for example, Elio Vittorini defended the novel's historical purpose and its role in the transformation of society against Angus Wilson and the latter's claims that any question of the real is really a question of imagination. Castellet clearly favoured the practice of neo-Realism and Vittorini, its Italian representative. Believing in the necessity of realism, he concluded: 'Mientras que Robbe-Grillet, Calvino y Coindreau creen que la necesidad absoluta de realismo es circunstancial o innecesaria, a los novelistas españoles les parece esencial, para que la novela alcance un fin social que no puede eludir' (Castellet 1959: 19). This division between the French and the Spanish politico-cultural milieux that leads to incommensurable aesthetic necessities is also highlighted by Goytisolo in *El furgón de cola* where he juxtaposes French and Spanish writers, noting that: 'Para los escritores españoles la realidad es nuestra única evasión' ('Los escritores españoles frente al toro de la censura'; 1976: 60).[41]

The debates at Formentor, highly symbolic of Spain's growing *apertura* and international acceptance, harked back to Castellet's earlier meditations in *La hora del lector*, but were now given much wider exposure. Moreover, this international involvement lent the cultural-political enterprise of the 1950s Generation a more universal and cosmopolitan flair as Formentor turned overnight into the meeting place of power, criticism, creativity, art and commerce. The second Formentor Colloquium in May of 1960 turned its eye more towards the politics of publishing. Its central sessions 'El editor y el novelista' and 'El editor y el público'—highly pertinent to Seix Barral and their editorial operations—are discussed in greater detail in the section of this chapter devoted to Barral himself.

Veinte años de poesía española (1939–1959) (1960)

Castellet's controversial anthology of poetry *Veinte años de poesía española (1939–1959)* was published in 1960 in Barral's *Biblioteca Breve*. The date of publication is significant: right after Machado's homage in Collioure and between the two Formentor literary gatherings. The anthology, published at the height of Castellet's commitment to social realism, was a collective project.[42] Castellet articulated the project together with Carlos Barral, José Agustín Goytisolo and Jaime Gil de Biedma, all of them also featured in the anthology.[43] The generational ethos forged at Collioure was now clearly put into practice.

As with his other works, Castellet prefaces the text with a *Justification*. Here he directly quotes Christopher Caudwell (1907–37) on modern poetry, saying:

> Es imposible comprender la poesía moderna, a menos que no la entendamos históricamente, es decir, en movimiento. De un estudio de la poesía como 'estática obra de arte', no podremos sacar más que fórmulas muertas—congeladas y osificadas. Eso es particularmente cierto, cuando la poesía es el producto orgánico de toda una sociedad violentamente en movimiento. (1960b: 11)

Castellet keeps company with Caudwell on his Marxist-historical reading of poetic context, but places more stress on the issue of the writer's historical responsibility and on what kind of role literature can play in addressing the matter of social justice, themes already familiar to his readers from *La hora del lector*. But, above all, *Veinte años de poesía española* remains a manifesto of historical realism and social poetry. Identifying with the British poet Caudwell and troubled by his own society (now in the throes of intense change), Castellet continued to believe in the political effectivness of literature.[44]

Castellet situates his theoretical concerns in the context of both the European and the Spanish poetic traditions. The movement from Modernist symbolism to neo-Realism in European and national contexts is presented as a literary evolution in which realism and principle of mimesis are clearly privileged. In a strategic move, Castellet traces literary history itself to support his claim of the superiority of historical realism. The inadequacies of symbolism are summarized by him under four key heads. The first argument addresses readership and the accessibility of a literary text. The inaccessibility of symbolist poetry lies in its inability or unwillingness to connect to the social sphere, which results in the poet's 'self-absorption' (*ensimismamiento*):

> El poeta intentó resolver en el plano ideal de la creación literaria la contradicción que le atormentaba: la de escribir para nadie. Por eso se creó un mundo propio, tan inaccesible para la burguesía como para el pueblo. Y por eso, también, resucitó y perfeccionó la teoría del arte por el arte, lo que le permitía justificarse ante sí mismo por su carencia de público. (1960b: 33, 34)

The second argument affirms the importance of historical perspective and highlights the social mission of the poet: '...el poeta no es un ser privilegiado, un solitario, un iluminado, un encantador de palabras' [...] 'no es más que un hombre entre los demás, que participa con ellos en una misma empresa social, cantando en sus versos la vida del hombre desde una perspectiva histórica' (1960b: 34). The third argument revolves around questions of realism. Symbolist poetry is self-referential and unwilling to be accountable to 'reality' or to any force outside poetry itself. It is a direct outcome of the previously outlined shortcomings: the creation of the poet's exclusive and esoteric world and his indulgence in his art. He states:

> En la poesía de tradición simbolista, la validez de la experiencia poética se considera absoluta y más allá de sí misma, en la de actitud realista se considera válida únicamente en tanto que síntoma y expresión de otra experiencia, la real y personal que el poeta comparte con otros hombres y que el poema tipifica. (1960b: 35)

The fourth and last argument quizzes the question of language and Castellet advocates its transparency:

> El lenguaje de la poesía de tradición simbolista...busca alcanzar al lector a través de la musicalidad y la sugestión sensual de las palabras, el lenguaje del poeta de actitud realista tiende, inexcusablemente, a restituir a la palabra la función comunicativa de un significado inmediato y real: se pasa así de una poesía esotérica y enigmática, a una poesía de clara significación humana, escrita en un lenguaje coloquial y llano. (1960b: 35)

By this time, Castellet's thought grew more coherent theoretically, yet more forceful ideologically. Castellet's theorizing of a progression from symbolism to historical realism invokes two seminal poetic voices: Antonio Machado and Juan Ramón Jiménez.

Machado, as we have seen from his homage in Collioure, is a poet who both inspired the anthology and was its central figure. Juan Ramón is not represented in the selection, but only discussed in the Prologue. In an anthology featuring 40 poets, some represented with several poems, Juan Ramón Jiménez becomes strikingly present through his absence. Castellet's ideological reading of these two poets stems from his need to distinguish realist from symbolist tradition, resulting in a forceful distortion of their thought. For example, Castellet argues that besides being elitist and ahistorical, Juan Ramón Jiménez's poetry is also removed from contemporary times and sensibility ('su poesía está, en tantos aspectos, lejos de nosotros' (1960b: 41); 'su visión exclusivista y a-histórica del mundo'... 'su tiempo no es el tiempo histórico, sino el tiempo interior' (1960b: 41, 42).[45] Castellet is equally unjust to Machado. He repudiated several crucial elements in Machado's poetic opus in order to present him as a precursor of critical realism or as a realist poet *tout court*: from a disavowal of Machado's semi-secular Krause-inspired faith to a distortion of his theories of poetic language in the guise of Juan de Mairena (1936). This 'other' Machado is overlooked and sacrificed to Castellet's political programme.[46]

It is beyond the scope of this chapter to dwell in greater detail on Castellet's misappropriation of Juan Ramón Jiménez and Antonio Machado. However, it is useful to understand how Machado became an exemplar for the social realist movement. As seen in the Collioure homage, the lionization of Machado was a decisive factor in the formation of generational identity. Machado's tragically timed death coupled with his anti-Fascist stance during the war were political elements that enabled his canonization. But that would not have been sufficient, were there no aesthetic elements that made Machado fit the 1950s Generation's own poetic needs. Gabriel Celaya has perceptively articulated ways in which the slippery differences between Machado's and his own generation's conception of art enabled Machado to be reclaimed as the standard-bearer of social poetry:

> Lo que nuestro poeta estaba anunciando en este texto y en otros similares era algo cuyo alcance y cuya importancia no ha solido advertirse: Era el fin de la Modernidad, entendiendo por Modernidad la poesía que arranca de Baudelaire y viene a extinguirse en los vanguardismos. Por eso justamente la Poesía social hizo de Antonio Machado una bandera. Porque también nosotros luchábamos contra 'la pérdida de la familiaridad comunicativa' (H. Friedrich), contra el egocentrismo y el hermetismo, contra la poesía como magia más que como expresión o 'modo de hablar,' contra el neutralismo y la frialdad de la Poesía Pura, contra la falta de contacto con el hombre de la calle, etc. A estas razones de orden estético hay que añadir otras politicosociales que convirtieron a Machado en un símbolo de la poesía antifranquista. (1979: 119, 120)

Other than contemporary poetry in his *Veinte años* anthology, Castellet also dedicates a few segments to novelists of his generation who shared the premises of social realist poetry. He includes Juan Goytisolo, Rafael Sánchez Ferlosio, Jesús Fernández Santos, Luis Goytisolo Gay, Jesús López Pacheco, Juan García Hortelano, Antonio Ferres and Armando López Salinas (Castellet 1960b: 103).[47] Most poets and novelists promoted by Castellet became more visible and influential shortly after the publication of the anthology. Seeing the anthology as a tool of generational politics, Jaime Gil de Biedma confirmed Castellet's decisive role in Spain's literary scene in these terms:

> Las antologías sirven como las guías de ferrocarriles. Tienen una finalidad utilitaria. En ese caso, detrás de la primera antología de Castellet estamos Carlos Barral, José A. Goytisolo y yo mismo, que fuimos el grupo que la movió. Volviendo a la comparación con las guías de ferrocarriles: os habréis dado cuenta de que en las guías de vez en cuando hay anuncios. Bien, pues en las antologías también hay anuncios intercalados entre los expresos que llegan y los rápidos que parten. Es decir, que fue una operación de política generacional, como lo fue en 1932 la antología de Gerardo Diego…(Gil de Biedma cited in B. Mesquida y L.M. Panero, 1977: 42)

The Castellet of *Veinte años de poesía española* is a strategist and a forceful advocate of social realism. His anthology together with his critical effort is vital for understanding the problematic of canon formation in post-war Spain, and the politics of canonization in Spanish post-war literature can be traced through the changing function of aesthetics, ethics and politics in Castellet's own writing.

Paradoxically, the height of Castellet's promotion of the social realist movement is also the beginning of its twilight. His progressive saturation with social realist postulates is best seen in a corrected and broadened version of *Veinte años* entitled *Un cuarto de siglo de poesía española* (1965). Castellet's words in the anthology evidence signs of the exhaustion of critical thought and political motivation that sustained faith in social realism:

> En la primera edición (que luego se convirtió en *Un cuarto de siglo de poesía española…*) había una parte excesivamente cálida en favor de este tipo de poesía ['poesía social']; rebajé luego la adjetivación y sólo mantuve las líneas generales del prólogo. Ya habían transcurrido cinco años y muchas cosas me resultaban un tanto exageradas a mí mismo. (Campbell 1994: 298)[48]

Castellet's reevaluation of the movement can be seen in the critic's exclusion of the novelists until then seen as exemplary of the movement. In *Un cuarto de siglo de poesía española* Alfonso Sastre, Carlos Muñiz and most importantly Luis Martín-Santos replace the now outdated Jesús López Pacheco and Armando López Salinas.

The mid-1960s marked the closure of an epoque informed by social realism.[49] The most symbolic and poignant sign of the break with the social realist mode is the second Machado commemoration that took place in February 1964 in Collioure (marking 25 years of the poet's death). The two commemorations were barely separated by 5 years yet the celebratory mood that marked the first drastically changed. Long gone was the critical and ethical enthusiasm aroused by the figure of Machado who had pushed social realism into the spotlight and given coherence to the Generation of Mid-Century. The visit to his grave was marked by the same solemn ritual, yet faith in the power of literature to affect political change or 'reality' seemed exhausted. Jaime Gil de Biedma perceptively saw it as nothing more then a *revival* of the first accolade. Carme Riera adds:

> El grupo que se sintió unido y en marcha conmemorando el veinte aniversario de la muerte de Machado, como le gustaba asegurar a Castellet, se sentía, celebrando el veinticinco, disperso y casi inmóvil, o, al menos, caminando lentamente hacia metas distintas. (1988: 239)

'Tiempo de destrucción para la literatura española' (1968)

Castellet's radical change of direction is reflected in the title of his essay 'Destruction Time for Spanish Literature' ('Tiempo de destrucción para la literatura española') (composed 1967, published 1968), which appeared in the French journal *Les Lettres Nouvelles* and the Mexican journal *Siempre*.[50] Significantly, Castellet's title echoes Martín-Santos's *Tiempo de destrucción* ('Destruction Time'), the latter's incomplete sequel to *Tiempo de silencio*, the novel that signalled an effective end to social-realist literary practice. In 'Tiempo de destrucción para la literatura española', Castellet distanced himself from social realism, reflecting on its shortcomings (just as Goytisolo had done in 'Literatura y eutanasia').

It was not only internal exhaustion in the literary model that prompted this, but also a *Zeitgeist* shift that forced Castellet to restructure his theoretical system. An avid advocate of historically situated thought, Castellet was now challenged by history itself. He was faced with revolts within the Soviet sphere, from the 1956 invasion of Hungary to the Prague Spring of 1968. His early trust in a socialist alternative now turned into questioning of its effectivness. Elsewhere, the Western Left's intellectual infatuation with the Soviet Union was rapidly dissipating. This was particularly poignant for Castellet in his 1968 trip to the Soviet Union. He recalled in his memoirs: '...a las cuarenta y ocho horas de estar en la Unión Soviética había topado con un régimen que ya sabía de antemano cómo era, pero me resistía a creer que se manifestara de una forma tan grosera' (1988: 41). Castellet's change of direction was, once again, motivated by the political context and a need for rearticulation of his own stance towards it. The tumultuous year 1968 was also the year of Castellet's trip to Cuba. There he articulated theoretically what he had grasped intuitively on his trip to the Soviet Union. In Cuba, Castellet participated in the 'Ciclo sobre literatura Latinoamericana actual', where he presented a talk entitled 'La actual literatura latinoamericana vista desde España'.[51] The talk juxtaposed 'un realismo socialista de tipo vulgar' with 'una auténtica literatura de creación'. Leftist thought, he claimed, was in need of another anchor, hence the gaze of leftist intellectuals shifted to Latin America, while the revolutionary model likewise moved from Eastern Europe to Latin America. According to Mario Santana, the international reception of social realism was so deeply mired by that time because of a need 'to find a new historical hero in every Third-World country in turmoil, a role for which Franco's 'exotic' Spain easily qualified' (2000: 54). Nonetheless, in an odd twist, Castellet's *realismo histórico* ('historical realism') was now replaced by *realismo mágico* ('magical realism'). The Boom worked well as a new literary model because it was motivated by political change (Latin American revolutions), yet it managed to integrate its political disposition within a striking narratological renovation. Moreover, it responded far better to the global political turmoil of the 1960s than did the *nouveau roman*. This was obviously an appealing paradigm for Castellet who had struggled from the beginning of his career with what he perceived as the incompatibility between political and formal dimensions or a struggle between social commitment and aesthetic autonomy.

In 'Tiempo de destrucción para la literatura española', Castellet traced the intellectual evolution of the Generation of Mid-Century from their radical rupture with immediate post-war literature to the decrepitude of their own literary model. As the title of the essay suggests, this text was Castellet's attempt to synthesize the causes of his generation's demise, its passage from: '...la dinámica renovadora del mundo literario español en lengua castellana' to 'un cierto fracaso y desánimo y la desorientación consiguientes' (1976: 136, 138). The political enthusiasm that surfaced around the university turmoil of 1956 baptized the 1950s Generation as a group, while the economic boom of 1962 dispersed them:

> Con amplia conciencia generacional, entre 1956—año del estallido de la Universidad a raíz del prohibido Congreso de escritores universitarios—y 1962—momento en que el crecimiento económico español entra de lleno en una dinámica propia—estos escritores no sólo se sienten unidos por una misma actividad de resistencia política, sino que también se inscriben a un cierto credo estético, el del realismo. (1976: 137)[52]

This ending was also attached to the loss of *vigencia histórica* or historical validity of the Mid-Century Generation, a concept important in Castellet's theory of generational limits.[53]

The tone of Castellet's essay, one of sober reflection, distinguishes it from his previous essays typically immersed in the moment itself (*actualidad*). The sense of critical distance gives the essay its depth and enables Castellet to put in perspective both literary accomplishments and the setbacks of his generation. The generational demise, he maintains, is attributable to three fundamental causes: (1) Lack of mentors, (2) social-realist testimonial rather than literary function, and (3) political naivete and inadequacy in leftist thought and political practice.

Lack of mentorship, due to an intellectually impoverished post-war Spain, resulted in the autodidacticism of Castellet's generation. Goytisolo would term this autodidacticism 'la discontinuidad cultural española' and 'la indigestión doctrinal' (2005: 14, 17). The cause of Spain's cultural void in the 1950s, permeated by what Castellet has called 'inoperancia formativa' or the ineffectivenes of their intellectual formation, was itself twofold:

> Buena parte del pensamiento de los noventayochistas o del mismo Ortega—la tradición inmediata—ya no era válido y operante en el mundo de la posguerra mundial. Era curioso comprobar que libros que, por una parte, casi eran considerados como clandestinos, no ofrecían, por otra, el alimento intelectual que exigía el momento. Y los libros que aportaban el nuevo pensamiento europeo y de los que llegaban velados ecos desde el extranjero, no se podían encontrar en España. (1976: 139)

The second reason given by Castellet for this generational demise is the one that Goytisolo had already highlighted in *El furgón de cola*, where he warned of the perils of allowing social realism's testimonial function to overshadow its literary aspect. The ethical burden to document some other social reality than the one posited by the dictatorship transformed novelists into journalists. Besides, the repressive climate also eradicated many forms of critical expression: 'Faltaban los fundamentos básicos para la existencia de cualquier clase de crítica: la libertad, la independencia, la información, la responsabilidad' (Castellet 1976: 140). Moreover, documentation of existing social reality proved entirely unsuccessful:

> En vez de 'realismo,' se había practicado una especie de naturalismo muy del siglo XIX y, por si fuera poco, el crecimiento económico había transformado notablemente las estructuras de la sociedad española, hasta el punto de obligar a nuevos planteamientos tácticos de la izquierda. (Castellet 1976: 142)

In sum, Castellet emphasized a weakness of leftist thought that was neither able to reflect the complexity of post-war Spanish reality nor capable of proposing new political directions. Besides, literary texts were plagued by 'maniqueísmo elemental' and politicization of literature in that period stripped it 'de uno de los requisitos elementales de la *buena* literatura: la presentación del mundo como un complejo de contradicciones que reflejara objetivamente la realidad española de aquel momento' (1976: 141). Mockingly, Castellet sums up the decade of social realism as one of 'los *buenos propósitos* y las *mejores intenciones*'. He then expands:

> Estos 'buenos propósitos' consistieron en el intento de buscar toda una literatura—bajo capa de *realismo*—en los tradicionales buenos sentimientos de una izquierda tan inconformista como ingenua...Y por si fuera poco, el voluntarismo político convertía a la literatura en un instrumento de substitución de lo que no existía: una vida política consciente, de combate, de lucha civil eficaz contre el Régimen...los intelectuales firmábamos papeles—uno tras otro—protestando contra la arbitrariedades del Régimen: fueron unos bellos momentos de euforia que, en un momento dado, se vinieron abajo. Los escritores—excepto en su actuación cívica—no sólo no habían hecho política eficaz, sino que habían olvidado los medios y los fines de la literatura. (1976: 141, 142)

Once more, Castellet, in agreement with Goytisolo, sees the collapse of the realist project in its double failure: literary and political.[54]

It was with all these factors in mind that Castellet outlined a threefold programme for a new Spanish novel: (1) the renewal of literary language as Barthesian *écriture* ('an effort to destroy contemporary linguistic structures'), (2) the critical demythologizing of Spanish cultural tradition ('the history of Spain, which is a history of differences rather than *unity*, of indigence rather than *greatness*, of oppression rather than *liberty*'), and (3) the objective, non-dogmatic analysis of social reality.

Perceptive, self-critical and ironic, the Castellet of 'Tiempo de destrucción para la literatura española' echoes the destructive urges of both Goytisolo and Martín-Santos who claimed that: 'Prácticamente, en nuestra realidad espiritual española, está todo por destruir' (Martín-Santos 1976: 135).[55] The disavowal of social realism and a spirit of derision that accompanied it was shared by our protagonists by the mid-1960s, as seen in Goytisolo's comparison of this literary current to a bus ride: 'Si el autor, antes de iniciar la obra, conoce el punto de partida y el de llegada, lo suyo no es una aventura literaria sino un trayecto en autobús' (2005: 21).[56] Social realism, by this time, was perceived as politically ineffective and artistically moribund.

But a decade later, and with certain sense of historical distance and objectivity, Castellet once again placed value on his generation, naming them now 'a bridge generation' (*generación puente*) (Servià, 1975: 212). Castellet's latest reassessment of the role of the social-realist writers was echoed by literary heirs of the 1950s Generation. Manuel Vázquez Montalbán writes:

> El segundo referente que los escritores jóvenes de entonces teníamos a nuestro alcance era la existencia de una vanguardia real, de la única vanguardia real que entonces estaba a nuestra disposición: la de aquellos escritores que al margen de esta propuesta de cultura literaria oficial habían tratado de oponer un código de conducta como escritores y un código de expresión, un lenguaje de ruptura frente a esta propuesta. Es ese conjunto de escritores tan sumamente complejo y muchas veces tan falsamente esquematizado que se suele llamar la literatura social. Insisto en el carácter de vanguardia a pesar de que yo soy uno de los responsables de un intento de entierro de ese sector en mi juventud, en los años 60, cuando me alcé junto con otros escritores frente a lo que yo creía que era una pesadilla estética, la hegemonía que dentro de la cultura de vanguardia tenía ese sector. (1988: 128)[57]

Reevaluating his previous position and looking at the merits of this undervalued 'cabbage-patch generation' (*generación de la berza*) from a post-dictatorial vantage-point, Vázquez Montalbán lauds them for their avant-garde spirit. This acknowledgement clearly includes Castellet—an instrumental force of generational cohesion—and recognizes his critical role in articulating alternative literary and ethical practices in the insular world of 1950s Spain. His writing, true to his politico-ethical beliefs, was a form of acting in the world, in this case towards destruction of the dictatorial space that enclosed his critical trajectory.

Carlos Barral

In much the same way that Vázquez-Montalbán views the 1950s generation as being ahead of its time, Carlos Barral's avant-garde activity ushered in a new era of publishing that effectively refashioned Spain's book market. There are numerous parallels connecting Barral with Goytisolo and Castellet: the literary culture of Barcelona, the labour of writing as well as editing, participation as jurors of national and international literary prizes and anti-Francoist politics. But unlike Goytisolo and Castellet, Barral did not feel compelled to reconcile his aesthetic aspirations with his political commitment. Indeed, Barral's publishing activity and politics are somewhat divorced from his poetry. He published social-realist books while simultaneously acting as a standard-bearer of a new aestheticism that distanced itself from the approach of the *poetas sociales*. For example, his seminal essay 'Poesía no es comunicación'—a direct attack on social poetry—was published in 1953 while he still championed trends of social realism in his publishing business. These differences were for him a question of political strategy rather than a reflection of inner aesthetic turmoil: 'Los pioneros del social-realismo, eran la infantería ideal para las batallas destinadas a conquistar como grupo y como generación nuestro lugar al sol' (1978: 190).

Barral was a vibrant member of the Barcelona School, yet it was Barral the publisher who overshadowed Barral the poet. It is in his role as publisher that Carlos Barral most deeply influenced Spanish literary trends. Like Castellet and Goytisolo, Barral endorsed social realism in the mid-1950s. By the beginning of the 1960s, however, Barral was the main force in bringing Spanish literature and poetry out of its realist mode and back into the mainstream of European literature, a continuity that had been broken by the Spanish Civil War and post-war cultural and economic impoverishment.

The Seix Barral publishing house specialized in educational materials and was a joint venture created in 1942 by Barral's father (Gráficas Barral Hermanos) and Víctor Seix [in 1945 according to Barral (1978: 14)].[58] In 1957 Carlos Barral joined Víctor Seix on the board of directors of Seix Barral.[59] The publishing house that once specialized in pedagogical resources became, under Barral's lead, one of the most important presses in Spain's publishing industry.[60] Seix Barral's new publishing trends thoroughly changed the directions of Spanish letters. Barral often described himself as a cultural publisher who invested in new and often demanding literary products and presented himself as more devoted to artistic than to commercial values, yet his enterprise was a more complex union of art and commerce.[61]

Seix Barral became a driving force in the literary field through a strategic renovation of aims and methods. In the first place, Barral surrounded himself with the creative voices of his generation. His core team (*equipo de lectores de* Seix Barral)—Joan Petit, Jaime Gil de Biedma, José María Castellet, José María Valverde, Gabriel Ferrater and Jaime Salinas—led Seix Barral into a new era.[62] Second, Seix Barral's team created the *Biblioteca Breve* collection and Prize of reference, a vital instrument in the promotion of social realism. Thirdly, Seix Barral organized a series of annual international meetings of novelists, publishers and critics in Formentor on Majorca between 1959 and 1962, bringing international avant-garde writers to Spain.[63] In the fourth place, Barral was a major force in the creation of two international literary prizes, the Prix Formentor (1961–67) and the Prix International de Littérature. These prestigious prizes cemented Seix Barral's ties with larger European publishing houses. Fifth and last, Barral did market the Latin American Boom, yet did not regard Latin America simply as a place to sell books, but rather a source of renewal for domestic Spanish literature.

Barral's publishing strategies were essentially strategies of geopolitical realignment. Seix Barral broadened its theater of operation by focusing on three diverse geographical areas and becoming a publishing force beyond Spain's borders. This strategy was threefold: a renovation of Spain's literature and its dissemination abroad, bold marketing of Latin American writers globaly (Borges, García Márquez, Cortázar, etc.) and the translation and diffusion of European avant-garde writers in Spain.

Within the national context, the *Biblioteca Breve* Collection published Spain's vanguard writers: Juan García Hortelano, Jesús Fernández Santos, Luis Goytisolo, Luis Martín-Santos, José Caballero Bonald, Juan Marsé and Juan Benet among others. The intention behind this literary collection was again twofold: 'Se trataba de un instrumento de exploración de otras culturas vivas y, finalmente, de provocación de las propias' (Barral 1988: 78). In conjunction with the *Biblioteca Breve* collection, Barral also instituted the *Biblioteca Breve* Prize that became a vehicle of promotion of social realism. The prize was founded in 1957 and first awarded to Luis Goytisolo for his *Las afueras* of 1958.

The award of the 1962 prize to the Peruvian novelist Mario Vargas Llosa reoriented Barral's publishing activity towards the Latin American realm. The decision was symbolic on multiple levels: he was the first ever Latin American writer to be awarded the prize (which 'internationalized' the prize itself), but it also signalled the publisher's measured disengagement from social realism. Most importantly, it unveiled a politics of expansionism and 'discovery', or an attempt to reclaim Spain's cultural prestige on the international scene. Barral elaborates:

> A partir de la concesión del premio, por unanimidad, al desconocido Mario Vargas Llosa, aquella llamada editorial se convirtió en eje de una política de descubrimientos y de reconocimientos de escritores publicados en el secreto de la provincia y hasta entonces condenados al ergástulo de las estrechas glorias municipales. (1988: 79)

Barral's third angle of operation, the translation and promotion of avant-garde European literature in Spain, relied on a simple but effective strategy. Barral's team constructed a back-list of the most important recent European authors who might not have been of interest to their competitors (in this case Latin American presses) (1978: 139). They published Svevo, Pavese, Gadda, Doris Lessing, Böll, Robbe-Grillet, and Duras among others. The European enterprise was facilitated through alliances which Barral established with Claude Gallimard (France), Giulio Einaudi (Italy) and Les Éditions de Minuit under the direction of Jerôme Lindon and Alain Robbe-Grillet.[64] Besides connecting Seix Barral to other vital European publishing houses, these alliances were also a valuable source of publishing information. Barral had an ideal situation: business ties abroad and a hunger for novelty at home. The publishing void produced by a the cultural impoverishment of post-war Spain now became a factor in his favour: 'Un sector notable de la capa cultivada del país estaba realmente sediento de información literaria, deseoso de salir del *ghetto* virtuoso y ciego de la ñoñería nacional' (1978: 141). Barral, conscious from the start that his publishing house could be 'un activo instrumento de administración de la cultura', juggled these three publishing realms and leveraged immense profit (1978: 135).

Between 1959 and 1962, as noted above, Barral and his team organized a series of annual international meetings of writers, publishers and critics in Formentor on Majorca.[65] Its first assembly in May of 1959 can be seen as a crucial date in the history for Spanish post-war literature. Formentor, a literary agora of the 1960s, brought together writers from different languages, nationalities, literary orientations and political beliefs.[66] This first event counted with the presence of several Spanish writers such as Camilo José Cela who had just organized 'Las jornadas poéticas' in Formentor a week before (May 18–25) with Mercedes Salisachs, Juan Goytisolo, Jesús López Pacheco, Ana María Matute and Juan García Hortelano, among others. Barral's team and the jury of the *Biblioteca Breve* Prize numbered José María Valverde, José María Castellet, Juan Petit and Jaime Salinas. The gathering also attracted several European writers, as well as powerful European presses and their representatives: Michel Butor, Alain Robbe-Grillet, Marguerite Duras, Italo Calvino, Alberto Moravia, Octavio Paz, Gregor Von Rezzori, the Chicago author Nelson Algren and Henry Green. We have mentioned the Italian entrepreneur Giulio Einaudi. Italo Calvino was literary director for Einaudi and replaced Cesare Pavese who comitted suicide in 1950. From France came Claude Gallimard and Monique Lange, a writer and key figure in Gallimard's publishing house who was married to Juan Goytisolo (1978: 247). Carlos Barral thus joined the vanguard of the editorial world and became an active force in the global circulation of cultural capital:

> Formentor se tornó un signo literario, una cita de la literatura exigente y una marca de cohesión de la intransigencia editorial en una época de prosperidad general en la que literatura internacional con vocación de perdurabilidad parecía aún incorruptible, incluso en las zonas que lindan con el consumo. (1978: 293, 294)

Formentor, as Barral referred to it, became the crossroads (*encrucijada*) of literatures, travellers, ideas and commerce.[67] Barral aligned himself with an exclusive group of the most prestigious European editors and entered, as he phrased it, 'los intestinos de la gran edición europea' (1978: 256). This position of belonging to 'una reducida aristocracia del mundo literario y editorial' (1988: 28) gave him a great vantage point within the European publishing realm or 'descomunal intento de mercado común europeo de la alta literatura' (1988: 48). In a highly politicized and strategic move, Barral and Salinas affirmed *Biblioteca Breve's* national prestige and Seix Barral's international presence: 'satisfechísimos ante la perspectiva de institucionalizar los coloquios internacionales sobre narrativa y los premios Biblioteca Breve, potenciando ambas cosas a niveles internacionales como armas de afirmación y de presencia' (Barral 1978: 245).[68] Barral's strategy, successful within both a Spanish and Latin American context, put into international circulation writers 'ahora encerrados en los límites de cada literatura local o nacional' (1978: 253). In Francoist Spain the meaning of this gesture was clearly political: 'A mí me interesaba romper el cerco de aislamiento de la edición española, una de las murallas de confinamiento, desde el interior, de una literatura' (1978: 253).

García Hortelano is a good example of the brilliance of Barral's strategizing. His promotion, firstly through the *Biblioteca Breve* Prize for *Nuevas amistades* (1959) and secondly with the Prix Formentor for his novel *Tormenta de verano* (1962), put both

García Hortelano and Spain's social-realist wave on the European literary map. The timing was also impeccable. After all, a year between Hortelano's two prizes was the year of publication of *Veinte años de poesía española* (1960) in which Castellet also firmly endorsed social realism: 'la incorporación de García Hortelano a las conjuras que, paralelamente a la confección de la Antología de Castellet, servirían de arranque de la poética social-realista y de su rápida difusión' (Barral 1978: 201).

As stated, Formentor offered two literary prizes: the Prix Formentor and the Prix International de Littérature. The Prix Formentor was given to a previously unpublished work, while the Prix International de Littérature was awarded to works already in circulation. There were seven core editors involved: Claude Gallimard (France), Giulio Einaudi (Italy), Barney Rosset (Grove Press, United States), George Weidenfeld (United Kingdom), Heinrich Ledig-Rowohlt (Germany), George Svensson (Sweden) and Carlos Barral (Spain). The core group was joined by Scandinavian countries all represented by Svensson (Grieg from Norway, Otto Linhardt from Denmark and Erkki Rempaa from Finland). Together with Choukorow-Sha (Japan), Antonio R. Cruz (Arkadia Publishing, Portugal) and Willem Blumena (Meulenhoff Publishing, Holland) they formed an alliance of thirteen countries which were Formentor's 'cúpula política y financiera' (Barral 1988: 29).

The winning novel was translated and published into all thirteen languages. Significant monetary stimulus, visibility and prestige were inseparable in this literary-commercial enterprise. Given the powerful machinery behind the prize, it is not surprising that García Hortelano's *Tormenta de verano* (Prix Formentor 1961; published in 1962) achieved the highest level of international recognition attained up to that time by a new Spanish narrative. The first Prix International, a split between Samuel Beckett and José Luis Borges, had a similar effect, bringing Borges major international exposure.

The very creation of two prizes (rather than one) was part of a compromise between those publishers who harboured aspirations to literary prestige and those who sought economic gain. The Prix International offered distinction to the winners, since those works that received it already circulated in print, while the commercial interests were satisfied with the Prix Formentor. The format of the very voting procedure reflected this opposition. The Prix International was publicly debated by a revolving team of literary specialists, writers and critics. Similar in spirit to the Nobel Prize, it was sustained by the notion of 'quality' and did not necessarily bring economic gains to the editors. The Prix Formentor by contrast was decided by the publishers' secret vote and in closed session. Only the seven core editors listed above voted (*siete editores votantes*) and, as Barral emphasized: 'Todos llegábamos allí con ideas bastante claras sobre lo que queríamos premiar en el Prix International y con intenciones meramente tácticas y egoístas con respecto a cómo habría que operar en el Premio Formentor' (1988: 44).

Within the Formentor circle there were two publishing camps that seemed divided in their interests: 'el que pretendía un premio de prestigio, limpio de intereses, y el que deseaba un premio comercial con el lanzamiento de un libro a escala mundial o, por lo menos, en las principales lenguas occidentales' (1988: 487).[69] But this tenuous division, visible in the creation of two prizes, really points to an anxiety produced by the excessive proximity of cultural and economic interests. Barral saw both prizes as 'un instrumento útil a la circulación internacional de la literatura' (1978: 267). The mechanics of the Formentor prize, founded on the inseparability of art and market, opened up a unique opportunity for Barral's commerce in the contemporary literary avant-garde market itself.[70]

Barral's international editorial expansion was inseparable from his ongoing reevaluation of national literary trends. His trajectory of promotion and then disengagment from social realism resemble those of Goytisolo and Castellet. As seen, the confluence of Castellet's poetry anthology (1960) with their promotion of García Hortelano through Biblioteca Breve Prize and Prix Formentor prizes (*Nuevas amistades* [1959]; *Tormenta de verano* [1961]) set in motion the social-realist wave. The promotion of social realism depended moreover on a complex relationship between Barcelona and Madrid, Spain's two main cultural centres. While Madrid stood for a literary-political dimension, Barcelona represented the economic one.[71] Barral's commerical strategy can be seen in his administration of the two realms. Madrid writers had already formed as a 'group' before meeting with Barral, but they lacked any coherence in terms of the kind of publishing strategy he could offer. Conversely, Barcelona had devised a publishing strategy, but needed a product to export. The anti-Francoist struggle was their common ground, with the Madrid circle of writers belonging to a more dogmatic leftist tradition. Barral commented that

> en el curso de aquel año cincuenta y nueve, se hizo realidad una gran parte de mi proyecto…El Partido, colaborador imprescindible, se hacía cargo de la 'operación realismo' en la concerniente a los novelistas, al mantenimiento de su cohesión como grupo y a la vigilancia de su dedicación. Los poetas quedábamos libres bajo las alas del antólogo y crítico José María Castellet. (1978: 207)[72]

Barral insisted on a divorce between aesthetics and economic factors, yet it seems obvious that the underground Communist Party's political agenda was not that far removed from Barral's own politics of publishing or, for that matter, from Castellet's anthologizing politics in *Veinte años de poesía española*.

An international reception of social-realist novels was assured due to its political appeal:

> …lo que enfocaba la óptica internacional era una posible narrativa postfranquista, y los críticos y los editores estaban muy bien dispuestos a hacer concesiones, a pasar por alto las deficiencias que escudaba la incomodidad de esa literatura de renovación libertaria en un país tan descaradamente represivo y zafio en materia cultural. (1988: 59)

But the lack of the aesthetic qualities that was overlooked abroad for political reasons was harder to sustain in Spain. Barral disassociated himself from the social realism that he initially supported because of the movement's twofold shortcomings: its political ineffectiveness and its aesthetic naivete. Aesthetic shortcomings were especially noticeable in comparison with Spain's pre-war literature or the current Latin American contempory production:

> Una literatura que pasa generalmente de lo casi excepcional no diría que directamente a la basura ni pieza de organillo, pero sí a los terceros planos de banalidad uniforme. Una literatura, en fin, con muy pocos nombres propios y casi todos demasiado singulares hasta la llegada, la incorporación, de los novelistas latinoamericanos…(Barral 1978: 266)

Within this context, it is not surprising that Barral found a parallel between Spanish social realism and Latin American 'indigenous' writing (in contrast to the innovativness of Boom fiction). He perceived both to be lacking in literary value and marked by a 'poverty of style'. He proclaimed Spanish literature of the 1940s and 1950s to be 'un experimento indigenista español':

> La delgadez y la zafiedad de la llamada literatura social, que nacía precisamente por entonces, no sería facilmente explicable, por ejemplo, si las contemporáneas manifestaciones literarias admitidas, oficiales o no, no hubieran sido tan pobres y tan recalcitrantemente indígenas e indigenistas. (1978: 62)

'Indigenista' was clearly an inferior label as opposed to modern. Barral reinforced this idea by contrasting indigenous not only with the newly emerging Latin American avant-garde, but also with European Modernism from the likes of Joyce, Kafka, Musil, Proust, Svevo and Babel.[73]

But Barral's definite break with the movement stems from its failure to achieve real political transformation:

> Creo que se partió de un error; es decir, en primer lugar, los novelistas españoles de esa generación afrontaron el problema de creación literaria desde presupuestos históricamente falsos como una literatura de urgencia, de emergencia, una literatura pre-revolucionaria, a las puertas de una gran transformación del país, lo cual la historia ha demostrado que era absolutamente erróneo. Y eso dio lugar a una literatura que caminaba con las muletas de una poética inadecuada a su función. (2000: 59)[74]

The anti-Francoist struggle was displaced by an economic boom which, ironically, Barral chose to participate in as well.

Barral's editorial boom was inseparable from the Latin American Boom itself, each a product of the spiking economy crisscrossing the literary world. Besides, Barral's embrace of the Boom was directly related to the need for a new literary model (now that the testimonial force or informative function of the social novel was completely exhausted). The Boom was so successfully promoted in the 1960s by the very same people who championed social realism in the previous decade, because the Latin American novelists transformed literary practice and revitalized the idea of a committed literature. Their neo-Modernist writing found pleasure in an imaginary construction of the world and went far beyond the simple documentation of reality. As Mario Santana has shown, Latin American fiction was able to displace social realism at the centre of literary life because 'it was perceived as carrying on, in an updated and revitalized form, the same concerns for social transformations' (2000: 56). The Boom's writers had an ability to engage with politics without sacrificing the literature's aesthetic dimension. At the same time, they were not excessively formalistic or utterly lacking in human interest like their New Novel contemporaries:

> Se trataba de una novela rica, lingüística y estilísticamente. Era como el resurgimiento del Barroco. Frente a la novelística afectada de la misma época y frente al formalismo tecnicista de la novela europea, estos jóvenes escritores latinoamericanos parecían una excepción universal. (Barral 2000: 128)

Such acquisition of cultural capital also played a significant role in this turn to the Boom, as seen in Seix Barral's attempt to conquer the Latin American literary market. As Barral observed: 'España ha recuperado una cierta capitalidad, o una cierta posición central, en la difusión de esa literatura (Boom)' (2000: 58). It is useful here to call on French sociologist Pierre Bourdieu who distinguished a field of large-scale production (that submits to the laws of the market) and the field of restricted production which develops 'its own criteria for the evaluation of its products, thus achieving the truly cultural recognition accorded by the peer group whose members are both privileged clients and competitors' (1993: 115). Bourdieu's distinction is clearly articulated in Spain's move towards the Boom and New Novel and its break with the earlier narrative praxis. The move towards a 'field of large-scale production' is seen in Seix Barral's editorial policies that began to favour the distribution of the literary works of Latin American writers in the mid-1960s. Both Castellet and Barral were key figures in the field of the cultural production of the Boom and, as Barral observed, 'el llamado Boom no es un hecho de la historia literaria sino de la historia editorial de la edición en lengua española' (2000: 79). Latin American narrative was diffused internationally through the interaction of Latin American writers with the Barcelona intelligentsia of the 1960s. This interaction both benefited Latin American writers and the prominent Catalan publishing industry, an alliance symbolic of entwining literary and market forces in the 1960s.

Barral saw the Latin American novel as an injection of life into 'el aburridísimo y peinado mundo euronorteamericano de la postguerra' (1988: 58) and echoed the general sentiment that the European novel was moribund. He used his *Biblioteca Breve* collection and Prize as a mechanism to inscribe Spanish writers within Latin American modernity. He explains: 'Cuando el premio coronaba escritores españoles como Juan Marsé o Juan Benet, los inscribía también en la nómina de la modernidad hispanoamericana y los proponía a un desconocido lectorado extraterritorial' (1988: 79). But he also acknowledged a less fruitful outcome of this encounter as the explosion of Latin American writers onto the world literary scene silenced a great number of Spanish writers:

> inyección de una literatura más viva, más rica, más poderosa, anecdóticamente más atractiva, exótica y también más interesante estilística y lingüísticamente, es decir, en todos los aspectos, traumatizó a todos escritores de tan pobre armamento como eran los del realismo social, e hizo enmudecer a muchos. (2000: 150)

Barral's ambivalence parallels the more general ambivalence in regard to reception of the Boom by Spanish writers which produced anxiety around the question of origins, a common Spanish language, and the specter of neo-colonialism. As Mario Santana pointed out, 'it is precisely during the 1960s that the national conception of Spanish literature collapsed' (2000: 17). This anxiety was also perceived by Castellet, who remarked that: 'A partir de 1962 algunos escritores [españoles] empezaron a enmudecer. El estupor del fracaso esterilizó definitivamente a muchos de ellos' (1976: 142). As Mario Santana wrote, it was obvious that 'the reception of the Latin American novel was the "burning question" (*la cuestión palpitante*) of contemporary Spanish literature' (2000: 17).[75] A profound shift away from Spain to Latin America brought a major reevaluation of literature in the Peninsula. Significantly, 1962 was also a year of publication of *Tiempo de silencio*, which not only marked a break with the previous epoch, but also opened up a possibility for Spanish writers to explore fresh literary paths. Soon thereafter, the Spanish new novel—metaphysical, metafictional, and antidocumentary—emerged as an alternative to both politicized realist art of the 1950s and to Latin American fiction. This moment would also mark a new chapter for Barral, who continued—but now in a different context—with his winning streak as publisher.

Conclusion

Franco's ascent to power and his dictatorial regime was the historical motivation for the social-realist novel and the key to its existence. By the 1960s, however, and in the context of Spain's *apertura* it ceased to be operative. We can trace it to a demise of autarky, Spain's *desarrollo* or rapid economic development, consequent opening up of its borders, the political energy of the 1960s and the radically changing literary world trends (such as the emergence of various film and literary *new wave* movements). Alongside political ground giving way to economic boom, we have seen that the realist tradition, from its greatness in the nineteenth century to its evolutive modes of social realism, exhausted a rich vein of fictional possibilities and new modes of art and writing were more in harmony with the twentieth-century conception of human experience. The exhaustion of social realism, partially due to its suspicion of style, form and poetic language, prompted a search for a model that could subvert what by then had become the accepted novelistic forms and formulas. As Santana writes, 'the aesthetic devaluation of the hegemonic poetics of the social novel should not be understood simply as the reflection of the internal exhaustion of a literary model, but as a result of a new process of aesthetic evaluation' (2000: 54).

Historical responsibility and literature as an instrument of change gave primacy to linguistic experimentation and language games. Both fictional models examined in this chapter, social realism that lost historical validity (*vigencia*) and the New Novel or the Boom that displaced it do not stem simply from some 'interior mode' but are a reflection of a new political experience of age sensibility (Rancière). Significantly, the very crises that marked this passage from social realism to the New Novel is in itself a paradigm of modernization. Furthermore, the ascendency of new artistic and mass media, such as post-war cinema and television, suggested that literary fiction had to redefine its territory. In sum, political, economic and aesthetic changes of the 1960s, together with the technological development and optimism of modernization, called for a profound reexamination of the fictional space.

When we look back at social realism in 1950s Spain, it is not at all clear that the term 'social realism' designates a homogeneous production or that the social realists were sufficiently similar in their practice to be considered a coherent group. But, as we have seen, there were several reasons beyond pedagogical convenience or critical will for pigeon-holing these writers under the same label. The social realist writers formed a culture of the mid-century. Their symbolic power was sustained by a vast socio-cultural apparatus: publishing houses, literary journals, literary prizes, anthologies, *cine-clubs*, *tertulias*, the educational system, and other cultural expressions and institutions. What began as a generational strategy turned into a countercultural power when three forces converged: aesthetic ideology (realism), political ideas (Marxist thought) and publishing expansion (Seix Barral).

Nevertheless, only a handful of novelists from the 1950s are still read and taught today: Rafael Sánchez Ferlosio, Juan García Hortelano, Ana María Matute, Jesús Fernández Santos, Ignacio Aldecoa and Juan Goytisolo. They form Spain's social-realist canon. As Castellet mockingly puts it:

> De más de seis años de euforia no quedaban sino media docena de libros válidos—un par de novelas y algunos libros de poemas—y el resto había desaparecido para siempre o permanecía como objeto de tesis de algún estudiante norteamericano. (1976: 142)

Other novelists from the same period are mostly forgotten and can be loosely fitted into the following categories: authors with Falangist or Fascist leanings who continued writing into the 1950s in the post-war bombastic and messianic prose of the 1940s; Catholic writers mostly preoccupied with spiritual matters and embedded in the Spanish religious tradition; and radical socialists that were faithful to the spirit of Stalinist socialist realism rather than its diluted Peninsular version (as seen from the very titles of their work, from Jesús López Pacheco's *Central eléctrica* and Antonio Ferres's *La piqueta* to Armando López Salinas' *La mina* and Alfonso Grosso's *La Zanja*).[76]

Luis Martín-Santos's *Tiempo de silencio* (1962), celebrated as a radical narrative break with Spanish literary tradition, was the only Spanish novel that could truly compete with the Latin American Boom. *Tiempo de silencio* reflected a passage from social realism to (Latin American) avant-garde fiction, ended the so-called time of the reader (*la hora del lector*), and initiated the age of language and textual pleasures. It illustrated the turn to criticism

> tremendously wary of any literary work that 'means to say something' (that has a 'message')...The Sartrian dream of transparent language...has been replaced, in contemporary avant-garde criticism, by Mallarmé's dream of language as a mirror of itself...This substitution (where the pertinent opposition is not between prose and poetry, but between 'literary' language and 'ordinary' language, or between literature and communication) has had as one of its consequences the devalorization of a whole vast field of literature—a field that includes not only...the *roman à thèse*, but all the realist genres founded on the aesthetic (or as some of its attackers say, on the ideology) of verisimilar representation. (Suleiman 1983: 18)

Tiempo de silencio also shows, as John Guillory has argued in *Cultural Capital*, that any text is a sequence of mediations and what is at stake in its interpretation is not in the domain of representation, but in what is congealed in the work as social value—between readability and readership.

The mid-century evolution and exhaustion of *littérature engagée*, giving primacy to language, also illustrated the nature of cultural change as an interplay of concepts, institutions and practices. It illuminated ways in which the institutions of literature—editors, literary agents, scholars, readers, publishing houses and authors—interacted in the production of contemporary Spanish and Latin American narrative. Through the roles of Goytisolo, Castellet and Barral in the literary field we can formulate questions about Spain's national literature, literary tradition, canon formation, history and authorship. Their roles within the Spanish cultural milieu illustrate, following Bourdieu once more, that the cultural field is structured by the distribution of available positions and the consequent struggle between the 'position takings' of its members (1993: 35). Their critical activity points to a consensus of an 'interpretive community' (Stanley Fish), that is nevertheless challenged by those that are on the periphery of the communal space.

The movement from social-realist fiction, looking inward, to a globally circulated Latin American Boom was the strategic reinsertion in the European as well as the global circulation of cultural capital. European literary trends were now fashioned between Paris, Milan, Frankfurt, Barcelona and the once unknown Formentor. Like tourist masses that would shortly follow, seeking 'everything under the sun' on the Spanish shores, internationally renowned publishers gathered in Formentor, redrawing the map of the European literary scene. The peripheral village of Formentor on Majorca, until then removed from centres of cultural life, became a setting of major changes in Spain's literary and publishing industry as well as a tourist destination par excellence. The interweaving of literature and tourism in Majorca was also symbolic of other interlinked forces, such as economy (*desarrollo*) and politics (dictatorship). These—as we will see in the Epilogue—became a major force in the sloughing off of the old skin of dictatorial Spain.

This stress on crossing borders and on movement also parallels the 1950s Generation's reclaiming of their Modernist heritage and recuperating 'lost' cosmopolitan spaces. For Barral, it meant publishing world literature and moving through European editorial hot spots: 'uno circulaba de París a Londres, de Londres a Amsterdam, a Frankfurt, a Roma o a Turín o a Estocolmo' (1988: 29). For Goytisolo, it was his nomadic trajectory of existing somewhere between Spain and France (Barcelona and Paris) and his role as *consejero de literatura española* in Gallimard's new collection of Spanish novels in translation.[77] He stressed that

> El acto de renunciar al canon oficial para forjarme uno propio me proyectaba a un ámbito carente de territorio y fronteras: no al del país del que me había autoexiliado, sino al mucho más vasto e infinitamente más aguijador de la lengua. (2005: 46)[78]

As we have seen, the new spatial dynamic between centre and periphery was permeated by restlessness. Even for Castellet, in a more abstract sense, it was a movement of Spain into a newly rescued European theoryscape. The years discussed in this chapter were indeed *Años sin excusa* (Barral) and *Los años decisivos* (J. A. Goytisolo). Reincorporated into the post-war map of European modernity, Spain became a junction of trends and travellers. According to Barral, reconnecting to the wider European space was akin to reclaiming their emotional geography.[79] In essence, this was a gesture of refashioning local culture as universal, where 'universal' was interpreted to mean an escape from the narrow space of the nation. These cosmopolitan tendencies and global practices, though still haunted by the specter of social realism, irrevocably changed any vision of a post-war, 'Eternal' or Immobile Spain.

Notes

1. *La hora del lector*, p. 62.

2. The Barcelona School was both a cinematic and literary movement of the 1960s with an avant-garde tendency. Some of the most important participants of the literary Barcelona School were: Jaime Gil de Biedma, Gabriel Ferrater, Juan Ferraté, Esteban Pinilla de las Heras, Alfonso Costafreda, Goytisolo brothers and Jaime Ferrán. The label 'Escuela de Barcelona' was reinforced by Carme Riera's seminal study *La Escuela de Barcelona* (1988).

3. In a 2005 prologue to *Obras completas I* and with a sense of historical distance Goytisolo remarked: 'Lo que yo considero mi actividad literaria adulta, y de la que asumo la responsabilidad de sus faltas y méritos, arranca de *Señas de identidad* y de *El furgón de cola*, libros publicados respectivamente en México y Francia a causa de la censura franquista' (2005a: 12).

4. Notably, all three lived, wrote and published in Barcelona, more cosmopolitan yet politically peripheral vis-à-vis Madrid, a politico-cultural stronghold of Francoist Spain. Goytisolo's move to Paris in 1956 only accentuated further this literary and cultural dislocation.

5. Among other crucial differences was the atheism of the Mid-Century Generation in contrast to their predecessors' religious beliefs where 'el conformismo social va acompañado de un sentimiento religioso que, curiosamente suele coincidir con el dogma religioso oficial' ('Literatura y eutanasia'; 1976: 81).

6. In a similar vein Castellet writes: 'Mario Lacruz ha dado con *El inocente*—Premio Simenon 1952—, una novela pulcramente construida, en la que domina la inquietud técnica y una preocupación poética, lo que confirma la tendencia de los novelistas que como él, Ana María Matute y Goytisolo escriben—o se han formado en Cataluña, frente a los que como Aldecoa, Fernández Santos y Sánchez Ferlosio lo han hecho en Castilla y cuyas preocupaciones son más estilísticas y sociales' (1955b: 89, 90).

7. Goytisolo writes: 'Los periódicos y semanarios de izquierda subrayaban, como es lógico, su índole rebelde e inconformista, mi implícita pero indudable hostilidad a los valores oficiales. Pese a sus grandes defectos, limitaciones e influencias, el libro respondía a una espera y fue acogido con entusiasmo abultado: ninguna de mis obras adultas, de *Señas de identidad* a acá, recibiría después ni mucho menos tal aprobación masiva…' (1986: 15, 16).

8. Goytisolo's scholarship is extensive. To name just a few important works: Black (2001); Epps (1996; 2003); Labanyi (1989); Levine (1976); Pope (1995); Smith (1992); Sobejano (1975b); Ugarte (1982). All these works have been invaluable to my reading of Goytisolo and his complex opus.

9. *Juegos de manos* (1954) was followed by *Duelo en el Paraíso* (1955). *El circo* (1957), *Fiestas* (1958), and *La resaca* (1958) form the trilogy, 'El mañana efímero' (Machado). These were followed by *Para vivir aquí* (1960), *Campos de Níjar* (1959), *La isla* (1961), *La Chanca* (1962), and *Fin de fiesta* (1962). Critics often divide this period into 'fiction' and 'travelogues'.

10. According to Goytisolo's note at the end of the first edition of *Señas de identidad* he wrote it precisely within that period.

11. The writing of the Generation of 1898 and Ortega's ideas formed the basis of this debate. The 'Spanish Problem' 'monopolized political discussion in the first two decades of the Franco regime' (Labanyi 1989: 56). In the post-war years the leading antagonists in the debate were Pedro Laín Entralgo and Rafael Calvo Serer, the first one argued that 'the problems the 1898 writers had diagnosed still needed solving' and the later one 'insisted-in reply to Laín Entralgo-that any problems Spain might have had had been solved by the Civil War' (Labanyi 1989: 56). Laín Entralgo wrote *España como problema* in 1949 (Seminario de Problemas Hispanoamericanos, Madrid) and Calvo Serer published *España sin problema* in the same year (Biblioteca del pensamiento actual, Rialp) as a reply to Laín Entralgo. For a more detailed account on the debate see Jo Labanyi's chapter 'Fiction as mask: *Tiempo de silencio*' in *Myth and History*.

12. Machado wrote 'Seguimos guardando, fieles a nuestras tradiciones, nuestro puesto de furgón de cola' (Antonio Machado, 'La reacción', 12 de julio de 1916) (cited in Goytisolo 1976: 11).

13. 'Literatura y eutanasia' was first published in June of 1966 in Uruguay in *Marcha* 1307-8.

14. Goytisolo would defend the term 'generación del medio siglo' as 'algo más que una etiqueta o reclamo de propaganda' (1976: 78).

15. For more detailed information on Castellet's university involvement and collaboration in *Estilo*, *Qvadrante*, *Laye*, and *Revista*, see Salas Romo (2003) and Bonet (1988).

16. *Laye* has a complex history within the opposition culture of early Francoism that goes beyond the scope of this chapter. For a more in depth account on journal's history, see Bonet (1988). Also see Bonet (1994), Riera (1988) and Marsal (1979).

17. After the closure of *Laye*, Castellet started writing for *Revista. Semanario de Actualidades, Artes y Letras*. The journal was put in motion by a Catalan industrialist Albert Puig Palau in colaboration with Dionisio Ridruejo.

18. See Chicharro (1989).

19. Cited in an interview for *Ateneo* by Lorenzo Gomis. Gomis was Castellet's contemporary but belonged to a circle of Catholic writers.

20. See Ortega y Gasset (1971) and Marías (1949). Castellet writes: 'No ha de asustarnos el término "generación." Cuidadosa y sistemáticamente estudiado por Ortega, primero, y por Marías, después, el concepto de generación es familiar en la más genuina cultura española de hoy' (1955b: 83).

21. *Tener vigencia* (used in law): state of being in force (Ortega y Gasset's notion). See Castellet (1958b: 54). Castellet outlines the characteristics of the War Generation born between 1906 and 1921 in contrast to the Mid-Century Generation or authors born between 1922 and 1936.

22. However, Carme Riera in her seminal study *La Escuela de Barcelona* warned about the discrepancies between Peterson's postulates and Castellet's choice: 'Sin embargo, a nuestro juicio, ni la herencia ni la comunidad personal, ni siquiera

los elementos formativos son los mismos en todos; sí coinciden, en cambio, entre los miembros de la llamada Escuela de Barcelona o "grupo catalán" o "poetas industriales"' (1988: 207, 208). Above all, Riera's comment points to the differences in 1950s culture of Barcelona and Madrid, their cultural and aesthetic divergence despite considerable political affinity.

23. Bonet writes: 'Tono mental aún perceptible en aquellos años—al filo precisamente de 1950—cuando gente como Sacristán, Farreras, Viladàs, Núñez, García-Borrón, o el propio Castellet, estaban ya escorando hacia posiciones más críticas con la política y la sociedad españolas pero todavía parte de su lenguaje era hijo de tropos retóricos procedentes directa, o indirectamente, del Movimiento Nacional en su doble linde falangista y tradicionalista' (1994: 58). Bonet sees the ambiguity of their discourse due to the tension between what he terms 'el discurso mental' and 'el discurso lingüístico' (1994: 58).

24. Cela is an exception for Castellet. For him, a publication of Cela's *La familia de Pascual Duarte* in 1942 was an important mark that indicated the renaissance of the Spanish novel. Moreover, Cela's *Colmena* was seen by Castellet as a precursor and a model of objective narration because of its narrative point of view and its conversational technique, innovative at the moment of its publication.

25. They often presented themselves as a fatherless generation: 'no solamente nos marginamos del pueblo sino también de las castas intelectuales ya establecidas y más o menos comprometidas históricamente. Por ejemplo, en poesía esa situación nos hizo nietos de la Generación del 27, sin padres reconocidos' (Barral 2000: 133).

26. Castellet's importance for Spanish literature of the second half of the twentieth century was validated by the new edition of *La hora del lector* published in 2001 by Península, Barcelona.

27. Castellet's interest in the aesthetic of reception is shared by Carlos Bousoño, his contemporary. Bousoño's *Teoría de la expresión poética* (1952) parted from similar postulates to Castellet's, such as his emphasis on the dynamic function of the reader. Bousoño was the only other critical voice who attempted to systematize the reception theory in Spain, especially notable in the third edition of *Teoría de la expresión poética* (1962).

28. We can see Castellet's application of Ortega's ideas in 'Juan Goytisolo y la novela española actual' where he writes: 'Goytisolo, como novelista, prefiere mostrar. La interpretación debe correr por cuenta del lector' (1961: 139).

29. Until nine years of age Castellet studied in a French school. As he remarks: 'Esto fue determinante porque me dirigió hacia la cultura francesa que para mí ha resultado la cultura básica' (Marsal 1979: 83).

30. See Jordan (1990a: 115–128).

31. By this time he had published several articles on the subject which were a cornerstone of his early work, such as 'Faulkner y el lector' (1953); 'Cuatro características de la novela norteamericana actual' (1954); 'Prólogo para lectores europeos', prologue to F.J. Hoffman's *La novela moderna en Norteamérica* (1955); 'Notas para una iniciación a la obra de John Steinbeck' (1957).

32. Castellet explains: 'Creo que fue gracias a la 'Série Noir,' de Galimard, que descubrí a Dashiell Hammett y otros autores norteamericanos: Raymond Chandler, Horace Mac Coy, James C. Cain, etc. Todos ellos dan fe de la existencia de una literatura de singular calidad al tiempo muy crítica hacia la sociedad de su país. Bien, ambos aspectos—el técnico y el sociológico—fue lo que avivó mi interés por dicho tipo de novelística de gran importancia…' (Bonet 1994: 304).

33. In 1953, Les Editions de Minuit published *Les gommes* (*The Erasers*), Robbe-Grillet's first novels that launched a period of narrative experimentation, which is taken as a foundational text of the *nouveau roman*. Even though, the term itself did not appear in print until 1957 in an article in *Critique* by Maurice Nadeau. The year of the beginning of the *nouveau roman* is a matter of contention. Jérôme Lindon and his Editions de Minuit were fundamental in the promotion of the New Novel.

34. Clearly inspired by Robbe-Grillet, Castellet entitled the last chapter of *La hora* 'Hacia la literatura del futuro'. Theoretical and polemical essays by Robbe-Grillet were collected in 1963 in *Pour un nouveau roman* (*For a New Novel: Essays on Fiction*).

35. These question preocupied Castellet since the early 1950s. The subject was explored in Castellet's earlier writing. *La hora del lector* recasts most of the ideas already expounded in the two articles: 'Las técnicas de la literatura sin autor' and 'El tiempo de lector'.

36. Theorizing of *realismo histórico* worked especially well for Castellet when it was coupled with technical innovation, such as the objective narration techniques of Rafael Sánchez Ferlosio's *El Jarama*.

37. Sartre's thought, not credited here, but cited earlier by Castellet, in the same text. See Castellet (1957a: 65).

38. Castellet ties his preoccupations with Spanish context to a more universal *reivindicación* of the oppressed: 'Sin embargo, nunca como hoy (tiempo de reivindicaciones de los oprimidos: mujeres, negros, obreros, pueblos coloniales) se ha hablado tan justificadamente de la dignidad humana y de la justicia' (1957a: 95, 6).

39. *Colección Fe de Vida* was another poetry collection created by Castellet and editor J. Horta in 1956. See Castellet's prologue to María Beneyto's *Poemas de la ciudad. Colección Fe de Vida*, 1. Barcelona, 1956. Horta was a militant of PSUC from 1956 to 1964, and his promotion of realist poetry with strong ties to history, alligned well with Castellet's own agenda. Title is taken from Jorge Guillén, *Cántico* whose third edition is subtitled *fe de vida*.

40. Jaime Salinas points out that 'En su primerísima etapa *Biblioteca Breve* era una colección estrictamente formalista. Más tarde—con el cambio de la década—empezaron ya a introducirse en ella ciertos matices de tipo político...Decidimos pues, hacia el 58 o 59, ir incorporando novelistas y poetas *sociales* del resto de la península, vinculados a menudo al Partido Comunista. No obstante, este partido nunca tuvo una influencia directa en la programación de *Biblioteca Breve*, si bien nosotros—o sea, el comité de la colección—jamás rechazamos a escritores adeptos a dicha ideología, e integrantes buena parte de ellos de la Escuela de Madrid' [Bonet's interview with Jaime Salinas on 27 September 1992 (1994: 362 n.42)]. The first title published in the Collection *Biblioteca Breve* was F. J. Hoffman's *La novela moderna en Norteamérica* (1955), a text that exemplified *inquietudes formalistas* emphasized by Salinas.

41. The addressee of Goytisolo's essay 'Escribir en España' [*El furgón de cola*] is a French writer and the French public. Goytisolo highlights their inability to comprehend the Spain's oppressive political context and its limitations.

42. Barral recounts the conceptualizing of the *Antología*: 'Recuerdo la innumerables sesiones en casa de Castellet, discutiendo listas de autores, nombre por nombre, y datando poemas y libros, como si fuera una sola. Nos veo, a José Agustín Goytisolo, a Jaime Gil y a mí, sentados en el suelo, sobre la moqueta azul...' (1978: 192, 193).

43. The anthology signified Castellet's shift of interests from novel and cinema to poetry. Given the participation of Barral, Goytisolo and Biedma, it is not surprising that *Veinte años de poesía española* has been seen as a promotion or even manifesto of the Barcelona Poetry School.

44. It will turn out, as Goytisolo has already announced in his writing, that the 'violent social movement' was more due to entrance of international capital into Spain then to the antifrancoist struggle.

45. This point is reiterated throughout the introduction. For example, 'Como dijimos, en palabras de Cernuda, los jóvenes "encuentran ahora en la obra de Machado un eco de las preocupaciones del mundo que viven, eco que no suena en la obra de Jiménez"' (1960b: 101). Castellet also uses Jiménez's verse from *Piedra y cielo* to support his claims: '*Quisiera que mi libro/fuese, como es el cielo, por la noche,/todo verdad presente, sin historia*'.

46. It is in this spirit of 'misunderstanding' that Castellet proposes Machado's words as prophetic for the 1950s Generation: (las palabras de Machado resuenan hoy, como profecia cumplida) 'El mañana, señores, bien pudiera ser un retorno…a la *objetividad*, por un lado, y a la *fraternidad*, por el otro…Comienza el hombre nuevo a desconfiar de aquella soledad que fue causa de su desesperanza y motivo de su orgullo…El yo egolátrico del ayer aparece hoy más humilde ante las cosas' (cited by Castellet from *Los complementarios* 126, 127) (1960b: 55).

47. According to Castellet, witnessing of the Spanish Civil War, was a vital element of generational cohesion: 'En todos ellos late la inquietud de penetrar, de comprender y aun de asumir el sentido de una guerra civil en la que ellos no participaron más que como testigos mudos' (1960b: 103).

48. Around the same time Castellet would start writing in Catalan and about Catalan writers—a significant, new segment of his critical activity and identity, which goes beyond the scope of this chapter. In 1963, he published *Poesia catalana del segle XX* in collaboration with Joaquim Molas, an important figure in Catalan letters. Castellet has written before on Catalan writers, such as Pla, Riba or Espriu, although in Castilian.

49. See *Poesia, realisme, història* (1965), one of his last important works on historical realism, published only in Catalan. Significantly the second edition of *Poesia, realisme, història* included also Catalan version of *La hora del lector* and was published in 1987. Castellet also published some other articles informed by historical realism in this period, such as 'Veinte años de novela española (1942–1962)' in 1963 in the Mexican journal *Cuadernos Americanos.* Castellet writes: 'Creemos que por el recuerdo del pasado—en este caso, la memoria de la guerra civil—, por su disconformidad con el presente y por la esperanza puesta en un futuro constructivo, es decir, por su sentido profundo, vivido y sufrido de la

dinámica de la Historia, el *realismo* de la joven novela española puede calificarse de *histórico. Realismo histórico* que abre las ventanas de la novela española sobre un mañana presidido por la fe en una realidad democrática, de la que las obras de hoy no son sino manifestaciones de una esperanza' (1963b: 295).

50. The essay was published in the 1968 March–April issue in *Les Lettres Nouvelles* and in the May 29th issue of *Siempre*. It was not published in Spain until 1976 when it became a part of *Literatura, ideología y política.* All the quotes in my chapter are from that edition.

51. The congress took place from 16 January to 22 February, 1968 in conjunction with IX Premio 'Casa de las Américas' and Castellet's talk was published in 1971 in *Panorama de la actual literatura latinoamericana.*

52. Castillet defines more precisely the phases of historical realism claiming that authobiographical trait predominates in the period between 1954 and 1957 while the second period between 1958 and 1961 is marked by 'una cierta despersonalización y un enfrentamiento con los problemas de la realidad objetiva, desde un punto de vista predominante sociológico e histórico' (1963a: 53).

53. For example, around 1969 Castellet begins talking about the new generation of writers born from 1939 on—Terenci Moix, Eugeni Trias, Pere Gimferrer, Manuel Vázquez Montalbán, Joan de Sagarra—defined by camp sensibility and other postmodern tendencies.

54. To illustrate his point Castellet precisely quotes Goytisolo's 'Literatura y eutanasia': 'cuando, poco a poco, los escritores abrimos los ojos descubrimos que nuestras obras no habían hecho avanzar la revolución en una pulgada (en este periodo [1959–60], por el contrario, la habíamos heco retroceder (…) Los orígenes de esa confusión habría que buscarlos, tal vez, en nuestra acepción mezquina y esquemática del término "compromiso": no del compromiso total, admirablemente expuesto por Leiris, sino opción superficial y mecánica que nada nos dice acerca del escritor que la asume, ni nos comunica o revela intensidad de su experiencia' ('Literatura y eutanasia' cited in Castellet 1976: 148, 149).

55. Martín-Santos answering Castellet's questionnaire for a Seminar on the Contemporary Novel that was being organized in Barcelona, just before Martín-Santos death in 1964. Complete quote reads: 'Por el momento mi obra tiene un sentido claramente destructivo. Espero que en el futuro y por cierto tiempo, siga siendo destructiva. Prácticamente, en nuestra realidad espiritual española, está todo por destruir'.

56. Barral gives a similar evaluation of the movement: 'Pero, pese a que hacían literatura tan bien intencionada desde el punto de vista político y social, no supieron darse un adecuado instrumento expresivo, y se ha quedado la mayor parte como autores de una literatura mediocre, con esquemas fáciles, poco trabajados, sin complejidades psicólogicas. Cayeron en la tentación de una literatura didáctica y, salvo escasas excepciones, en esa tentación quedaron sepultados' (2000: 20).

57. Juan Benet, a representative of the aesthetic experimentalism of the next generation, was not as generous as Vázquez-Montalbán as he claimed that 'after the Civil War, almost all Spanish novels were Trojan horses' (1976: 99-101).

58. Víctor Seix inherited the business, created in 1911 by his father Victoriano Seix, a professional lithographer trained in France.

59. In 1970 Barral separated from Seix Barral, creating and managing Barral Editores.

60. See Herrero-Olaizola (2007).

61. See Rama (1981: 66–73).

62. Gabriel Ferrater is another important protagonist of the 1950s. An important literary figure, he wrote and published his entire poetic work between 1958 and 1968. He worked in Hamburg as a reader for Rowohlt Verlag publishing company, moving back to Barcelona in 1963 and accepting the job as literary director of Seix Barral. Later he also worked as a lecturer in Linguistics and Literary Criticism at the Universitat Autònoma de Barcelona. Gabriel Ferrater killed himself on 27 April 1972 in his residence in Sant Cugat. Both of the Ferreter brothers had a tumultuous relationship with Barral and Casetllet, vital for understanding of the period, but that goes beyond the scope of this chapter.

63. It is in his memoirs, a genre that Barral turned to in later years, during the transition to the democracy period, that he outlined his unique role in Spain's cultural and publishing trends of the 1950s. See *Años de penitencia* (1975), *Los años sin excusa* (1978) and *Cuando las horas veloces* (1988).

64. Barral fought on two fronts: for author's rights (*derechos del autor*) at book fairs such as competitive Frankfurt Book Fair and against censorship at home.

65. The Formentor group was active from 1960 to 1968. After being exiled from Spain for political reasons, they continued meeting in Corfu and later in Tunisia.

66. Barral writes: 'Formentor se convirtió en una referencia constante para la vanguardia de la edición europea y en ágora literaria más importante y famosa de la década de los años sesenta' (1978: 239).

67. Barral entitled the chapter on Formentor 'La encrucijada de Formentor' (1978: 239).

68. Barral points out that it was not an easy passage since 'Los editores extranjeros tenían que vencer el prejuicio de colaboración con la cultura del franquismo, ya que no franquista' (1978: 248).

69. Barral used George Weidenfeld as an example: 'Sus intereses dentro de la familia formentoriana eran claramente mercantiles. Era partidiario de reforzar el prestigio del Premio Formentor, puramente editorial, y dejar caer el costosísimo Prix International, que creía que era una desmedida competencia al Nobel—lo que empezaba a ser verosímil—y no tenía ninguna utilidad industrial' (1988: 40).

70. A mechanism that put Spain back on the map of modernity, such as the expansion of the publishing industry and literary prizes, had also a negative consequence, such as the loss of the cultural dimension and rise of the entrepreneurial imperative (that was obviously always already present in the cultural publisher). Only a few years after the first Formentor meetings, in 1965, Barral would denounce literary prizes that he himself put in motion: 'estamos dando anualmente una cantidad de premios realmente desorbitada'...'ello ha creado algo así como una raza de escritores de concurso.' On the book covers, prizes are listed as 'esquelas necrológicas de los periódicos' (2000: 27). Castellet had forseen this danger already in 1954, even though he himself was also instrumental in diffusing it. In his early essay, 'En vez de letras, números' he writes: 'sólo si nos apartamos del panorama de los premios y observamos a los escasos autores que no poseen ninguno de los 'tres grandes'—*Planeta*, *Nadal* y *Ciudad de Barcelona*—podremos encontrar a los novelistas *de verdad*—eso es, los que saben que escribir es un oficio serio y honesto y que, además, tienen el necesario don artístico y vocación para ejercerlo—que existen en el país' ('En vez de letras, números', 1955b: 37). He adds: 'llevados por el espejismo de los miles de pesetas que anualmente se reparten entre los aspirantes a novelista, es muy posible que dentro de poco tiempo esos aprendices a escritor escriban en números en vez de letras' ('En vez de letras, números', 1955b: 39).

71. Barral writes: 'En realidad, los escritores realistas de Madrid ya existían como grupo. Pero sus reuniones eran principalmente de intercambio social y citas políticas. Los encuentros del Suecia (hotel in Madrid) se hicieron, en cambio,

rápidamente operativos. Se hablaba de los libros en proceso, se establecían turnos de publicación. La edición Seix Barral, se entendía, iba a lanzar la ola realista' (1978: 203).

72. Spain's literary scene, Barral adds, 'giraba en dos niveles, uno en Barcelona, sobre un eje editorial-mi editorial básicamente-y otro en Madrid, por el tradicional sistema de tertulias...la rueda de Madrid era la que soportaba los proyectos político-literarios, proyectos que podían llegar hasta el reparto de temática para futuras novelas y, por supuesto, a la distribución de presencia en los premios y las publicaciones. La rueda de Barcelona, básicamente editorial, era la que conectaba esas conspiraciones, algunos libros y la prematura gloria de algunos autores con ese mecanismo internacional que habíamos ido poco a poco construyendo' (1988: 60).

73. Barral was always troubled with what he perceived as the 'Hispanismo provinciano' of the Madrid circle, such as 'el hecho de que ante ellos, una referencia a Baudelaire sonase a exotismo' (1978: 64, 65).

74. Barral's *Penúltimos castigos*, 'una especie de autobiografía moral', is a fictional account of these years. Carlos Barral, a novel's protagonist recalls 'la fatiga a los dogmas de la resistencia al fascismo, una vez el fascismo había muerto o estaba en fase avanzada de agonía'.

75. For Pardo Bazan's *La cuestión palpitante*, see note 15 in 'Introduction'.

76. Socialist realism, promulgated as the one essential literary and artistic method, was officially adopted as doctrine by the first (All-Union) Soviet Writers' Congress in 1934.

77. Goytisolo began working for Gallimard as *consejero de literatura española* (editorial adviser) in 1957. Maurice-Edgard Coindreau was a translator of the series and he proposed Goytisolo's novels to Gallimard. *Juegos de manos* was translated by Coindreau and published in French in 1956 in Gallimard's collection 'Du monde entière'. See Goytisolo (2005a: 36). Also see Castellet (1957b). Gallimards's politics of publishing, seen in their Spanish literature in translation series, mirrors Goytisolo's own confusion regarding his literary directions. Gallimard's collection of Spanish novels in translation, influenced by Goytisolo as editorial adviser, shows the erratic politics of translation as well as the inconsistent agroupation of writers. See Fortes (1988).

78. Goytisolo always emphasized that 'la condición ideal del escritor será la del nómada, a horcajadas sobre diferente lenguas y culturas, consciente de que sucumbir a los cantos de sirena de un renombre nacional o local le condena a subordinar la obra en cierne a unos valores que no responden a las exigencias innovadoras del campo artístico' (2005: 25). A tangible sense of exile existed in the beginning of Goytisolo's career: 'Argentina, México y Francia fueron mi patria editorial' (2005: 13).

79. Barral: 'Mi geografía emocional de París ha sido muy constante desde que la descubrí en un primer viaje en 1950.'

Chapter II

Television (Hi)stories: '*Un escaparate en cada hogar*'

> Hoy, día 28 de octubre, domingo, día de Cristo Rey, a quien ha sido dado todo poder en los Cielos y en Tierra se inauguran los nuevos equipos y estudios de televisión española. Mañana, el 29 de octubre, fecha del vigésimotercer aniversario de la fundación de la falange española, darán comienzo, de una manera regular, los programas diarios de televisión. Hemos elegido estas dos fechas para proclamar así los dos principios básicos que han de presidir, sostener y enmarcar todo desarollo futuro de la televisión en España: la ortodoxia y rigor desde el punto de vista religioso y moral, con obediencia a las normas que en tal materia dicte la Iglesia católica y la intención de servicio y el servicio mismo a los grandes ideales del Movimiento Nacional. Bajo esta doble instalación y contando con el perfeccionamiento técnico, artístico, cultural y educativo de los programas, que han de ser siempre amenos y variados, espero, con vuestra colaboración, que la televisión española llegará a ser uno de los mejores instrumentos educativos para el perfeccionamiento individual y colectivo de las familias españolas. Quedan inagurados los nuevos equipos y estudios de la televisión española. ¡Viva Franco! ¡Arriba España!
>
> – Gabriel Arias Salgado

The above passage is from the inauguration of national television in Spain in 1956 by Gabriel Arias Salgado, the then Minister of Information and Tourism.[1] As one sees, Christ in all His powers over Heavens and Earth and allied with the Spanish Falange will now also rule over public airwaves. Nevertheless, appearances may deceive and despite

Arias Salgado's association between God and Falange in the emerging television industry, the fusion of Church and State was eroding. Indeed, the ceremony took place only a few months before a sea change in the national government which would ultimately curtail Falangist political influence. The appointment of a new cabinet that promoted economic growth and technocracy emphasized development with foreign capital and widespread industrialization, which hastened the end of the dictatorship. The uneasiness and tensions that accompanied this rupture with the past were inscribed in the politics of television as well: managerial decisions regarding the start-up of television and the creation of national networks, as well as financial decisions regarding production budgets, scheduling, distribution, staffing and so on. Television became a microcosm of the larger contradictions and complexities that now afflicted all realms of culture, politics and economics. Anna McCarthy points out that besides

> small-scale politics of viewing—revolving around seating arrangements, lighting, authority over program choice, etc.—television images play out a broader cultural ideology of space as well. By appearing to make 'elsewhere' present in the home, the screen serves as a discursive and material figure for the ways in which family life is integrated into macrolevel issues of the nation, international politics, and the global marketplace. (2001: 2)

This alternation of micro- and macro-aspects of the family vis-à-vis national politics is probably true everywhere, but in Spain, it was much more pronounced. The reason stems from the fascist obsession with family and nation and the fuzzy boundary between the two. For the Falangist Spain would become a crucible in which the concepts of nation, of family and of culture would be forged. The founder of the Falange, José Antonio Primo de Rivera, would even call for the disappearance of political parties since 'nadie ha nacido nunca miembro de un partido político, en cambio nacemos todos miembros de una familia' (cited in Rodríguez Puértolas, 1987: 106).[2] Franco would view himself as an alloy in the national metal but the popular trope was that the dictator was entrenched in the entrails of the country.[3] The evolution of television in Spain would not only be buffeted by these countervailing forces but would ultimately internalize them in the projection of a national imaginary.

Television studies

Given that the penetration of television coincides with a crucial shift in Spain's political and economic framework, it is somewhat surprising that more attention has not been paid to the medium. The absence of research may owe to the belated impact of cultural studies on Hispanism. Such lines of inquiry have advanced considerably since 1995, when Helen Graham and Jo Labanyi declared that 'Spanish cultural studies are in their infancy' (1995a: v). Cultural studies journals now exist and several conferences have been held that centred on debate of the future directions of Spanish cultural studies.[4] Unfortunately gaps still exist due largely to the 'institutional compartmentalization' and 'little attempt at interdisciplinary co-ordination' (Graham and Labanyi 1995a: v). Thinking along similar lines, Paul Julian Smith proposes 'changing the object of contemporary Hispanism, by incorporating new media, such as photography, town planning, and popular music...' (2000: 1). Television would also integrate well into any such approach by hispanists and be especially promising in as much as the development of television studies is closely linked to the development of cultural studies.

The changing landscape of academia has meant shifting borders which, in turn, increase interdisciplinarity and decompartmentalize institutions. The emergence of cultural studies in general and television studies in particular is evidence of having bridged the 'Great Divide', 'which insists on the categorical distinction between high art and mass culture'. No longer would there be 'institutional separation of literary studies, including the new literary theory, from mass culture research, or the widespread insistence on excluding ethical or political questions from the discourse on literature and art' (Huyssen 1986: viii).

The debut of television studies in the academy was met with the disrespect that once greeted cultural studies. Was the topic really worthy of studying? Would it lend itself to serious analysis and research? How would television studies be taught? Despite these misgivings the line of enquiry struggled into existence and eventually emerged as a legitimate field within the academy. Like cultural studies, television studies has benefited enormously from the recognition of popular culture as a topic worthy of a place in university curriculum. Moreover television studies were already positioned as an hybrid between journalism, mass communications, critical theory and film departments. By having secured its status in academy, the concept of television studies is no longer questioned. The old concept of television entertainment as a cultural waste product was suddenly outdated.

Although television studies is new as a field, television as object of organized research goes back to the 1950s where the focus was on television-the-technology rather than television-the-driver of popular culture.[5] Infiltrating modern culture, the medium became 'inseparable from the modern experience it has both reflected and created' (Smith 2002: 311). The earlier television of the social sciences had disregarded this positive feedback mechanism by which, as John Corner points out, television 'ingests selectively from the wider culture with voracious energy and disseminates images, often with high impetus, across the full range of public and private life' (1999: 127).

What television selects is an obvious nexus for cultural studies. With a methodology already in place, cultural studies can enable television studies to focus on the textual analysis of programmes and explore generic interests (news, game shows, drama, soaps, comedies). One can shift the focus from production to reception (audience, fan culture) and engage questions regarding television pleasure. Furthermore, cultural studies can foster interest in analyses of television as a domestic medium and its role in the reconstruction of domestic space. In short, by complicating the television of social sciences current television studies discourses became centred on 'a television of sitcoms, soaps and crime series, rather than a television of playwrights, a television of ideology rather than aesthetics' (Brunsdon 1998: 105).

Just as television of popular culture would eventually impact how culture is studied, the new digital technologies foreshadow perhaps another re-organization of thought. The reality of a digital culture has already impacted TV studies as scholars revise and redefine theoretical constructs as well as question their own epistemology. History, however, is not repeating itself. Unlike the television studies of the 1950s that obsessed with the technology, the new digital studies is fully aware of the local-national-international interplay and the globalization of media industries.

This thumbnail sketch of television studies can help one evaluate the Spanish experience. The cultural studies approach to Spanish television is fairly incipient and only begins in the early to mid-1990s. For example, in 1992 José Maria Baget i Herms published *Historia de la televisión en España 1956–1975*, and Ignacio Rodríguez Márquez and Juan Martínez Uceda launched *La televisión: historia y desarollo (los pioneros de la televisión)*. By 1996 the *Archivos de la Filmoteca* issued a special edition *Televisión en España 1956–1996* (eds. Barroso and Tranche) which was crucial in tying cultural politics of Francoism and television history. During these years Valeria Camporesi worked on television and cinema and Juan Carlos Ibáñez on early TV and its implementation.[6] To date, the most prominent Spanish television historian seems to be Manuel Palacio who authored *Una historia de la televisión en España. Arqueología y vanguardia* (1992) and *Historia de la televisión en España* (2001). Among U.S. and British Hispanists, Richard Maxwell worked mostly on post-dictatorship television in work such as *The Spectacle of Democracy. Spanish Television, Nationalism, and Political Transition* (1995). More recently Paul Julian Smith has reassesed Maxwell's contributions to the field, which Smith terms 'a near apocalyptic institutional history' (2002: 317). Smith's major contributions of late have passionately affirmed the existence of quality TV in Spain (Smith 2002, 2003, 2006a, 2006b, 2007a, 2009).

The scarcity of research on Spanish television may have much to do with logistics. Access to primary sources has always been difficult and since its beginnings, television was characterized as a medium without a memory. There was no ethos of archiving or preserving TV programmes since broadcasts were considered ephemeral. Indeed, the fleeting nature of television programming militated against any archival value. Most of Spanish early programming, beginning in 1956 and lasting into the early 1970s, is gone: even records that would help us reconstruct an historic outline, such as annotated scripts, memoranda, contemporary reviews, studio plans and so on, are missing. The loss of their archive is also due to a technical deficiency in transmission,

> en los primeros años la mayoría de los programas se emitían en directo sin que se hiciera un 'kinescopado' de la señal. Más tarde, con la introducción de los primeros magnetoscopios con formato de 2 pulgadas, se empiezan a grabar, aunque únicamente como procedimiento para diferir su emisión. (Barroso and Tranche 1996: 6)

The most comprehensive source, the Documentation Center of RTVE (Centro de Documentación de RTVE), houses an excellent photographic archive. Another source which offers some clips of a few of the lost programmes is NO-DO (Noticiarios Documentales).[7] This is irony that does not escape media historians Jaime Barroso and Rafael R. Tranche:

> no deja de ser paradójico que las pocas imágenes conservadas de los primeros años correspondan a un género con el que, años más tarde, acabaría la propia televisión: el noticiario *NO-DO* y la revista de actualidades *Imágenes* que formaban parte de la programación y ocasionalmente tomaban la televisión como noticia, al tiempo que se exhibían en las salas de cine. (1996: 9)

Another primary source that may shed light on the nature of Spanish television are the industry trade journals; published by TVE, that discussed programming, advertising, customs and the role of TV in society. Personal recollections and memoirs of the pioneers of the media were also subject of articles and letters-to-the editor.[8] Although the reconstruction of the incipient television history in Spain is possible, it is nonetheless fraught with problems. Any reconstruction will rely heavily on in-house accounts, personal anecdotes and interviews with TV veterans, all of which may bias an accurate portrayal. Also problematic have been empirical approaches to audience research such as the many surveys that measured size of audience, gender ratios and so on. These instruments were not standardized and the statistical methodology appears flawed. Even the basic information regarding the number of households with a TV set vary considerably according to methodology used. Manuel Palacio shows that the data discrepancy is enormous. For example, while TVE estimated that in 1966 there were 2,125,000 television sets, Sindicato Vertical (Plan de Desarrollo) reports a number smaller by almost a third (1,500,000)! Palacio also reminds us that, however bizarre, one of central sources for reconstructing early television history and the expansion of the medium was Manuel Fraga Iribarne's commentary during the inauguration of the new TV station Prado del Rey on 18 July 1964. The Minister of Information and Tourism exaggerated the population of TV sets fifteen-fold (from 600 to 10,000).[9]

In light of these problems, it seems wise to follow Lynn Spigel's advice and look at the available sources and studies as simply a 'kind of machine for the production of discourse on television rather than as a repository of social facts' (1992: 6). This is my approach. This study draws on a variety of sources and a diverse array of textual and visual materials, including the following: a historical and photographic archive from the RTVE, *TeleDiario*, a valuable weekly publication; debates in the specialized press such as José Maria Baget's articles for *La Vanguardia*; advertisments and other filmic representation of television; and film journals and women's magazines that debated incessantly the arrival of the new medium.[10] While the discursive context of television will never replace the lost programmes, the intertextuality of the television texts can reveal a lot about the phenomenon of television, its historical specificity, and the everyday tensions and worries surrounding the new medium. Finally, an overview of diverse sources can show that 'while the media discourses do not directly reflect how people responded to television, they do reveal an intertextual context-a group of interconnected texts-through which people might have made sense of television and its place in everyday life' (Spigel 1992: 2).

The approach outlined above departs from the traditional institutional character of television studies which 'rather than focusing on the social and domestic context…has continually framed its object of study around questions of industry, regulation, and technological invention' (Spigel 1992: 5). The approach outlined above also integrates with recent attempts by television historians to bridge the gaps that divide researcher in the social sciences and humanities. John Corner emphasizes that the obsession of the humanities approach on textual analysis and reception lacks 'specific analysis of formal structures' (1999: 69). It also does not engage sufficiently with broadcasting history and its institutional dimensions are often overlooked. The social studies approach adopts a pseudoscientific methodology, tends to dismiss the domestic component, and overlook the scopic appeal of television, '[ignoring] the ways in which television programmes generate meaning and produce knowledge and pleasure' (Corner 1999: 6). Nevertheless, the two approaches are not mutually exclusive. Anna McCarthy reminds us that 'the two scales of analysis-the macrolevel of the political economist and the microlevel of the cultural researcher-are not really incompatible after all' (2001: 15). TV binds space and constitutes, simultaneously, an intensely local and global phenomenon which invites pluralism.

This chapter centres on delayed implementation of television in Spain with all its attendant political consequences. At the macro-level of the political economist, one looks at the industrial regulations, structures and organization that complicate any easy institutional description. At the micro-level of the cultural researcher, one looks at television's multi-faceted impact on people in the domestic space. So, TV goes from being a physical object or household fixture to an intangible force in the reconstruction of domestic space and national culture.

After fleshing out the difficult birth of television in a post-war and autarkic Spain, the study moves on to the accelerating rate of change in the country as it entered a capitalist technocracy. This expansion of Spain's economy outward was accompanied by television's own expansive politics of space. Saénz de Heredia's 1965 film *Historias de la televisión* captures the Spain's tumultuous passage to modernity with its discourse of progress and consumerism that is both inscribed into and problematized by the text. The two main characters, Tony Leblanc (a *concursante profesional*) and Conchita Velasco (an aspiring pop singer, chica *ye-yé*), enable exploring such complex themes as the connection of TV to modernity, the commodification of culture and the reason for the immense popularity of contest shows. All this is tied to the consumer frenzy and the emergence of the *generacíon ye-yé* with concomitant rise of a star system and the fascination of all things televised. *Historias de la televisión* can be understood as 'a refraction rather then a reflection' of the troubled birth of television in Spain (Spigel 1992: 7).

This study considers the sense of urgency that makes television an affective space-binding technology. It will then look at the notion of intimacy that enables TV to generate powerful imaginative and affective relationships. Thus, what emerges is 'the lack of a sharp differentiation, in everyday experience, between the para-social encounters of broadcasting and the "network of actual social relations"' (Corner 1999: 39). The chapter concludes looking at the role of TV in relationship to modernity.[11] Women of the time were caught in the conflicting demands of domesticity and the work place, provincial loyalties and the celebration of national mobility. The complex interplay of motherhood and sexuality, household chores and wage income, traditional economizing and frivolous consumption implies an evolving process of conflict resolution—both internal and external. As the epitome of modernity and progress, TV became a rhetorical figure for that contradiction. This takes on a complex dynamic when one considers that private advertising was financing public television.

Screens and spaces: *el mundo reducido*

As can be gleaned from the opening quote, the inauguration of TV on 28 October 1956 did not mark the first experiment with television in Spain. Since the 1940s, television broadcast was intermittently attempted.[12] Several historians of the medium attribute the late start of Spanish television to Spain's politics of autarky in the post-war period. As Juan Carlos Ibáñez makes clear,

> en el heróico y espartano imaginario de los defensores de la autarquía, la TV carece de objeto social, y su imagen se halla enormemente alejada de los principios rectores que marcaron la reconstrucción económica y social del Estado en el periodo 1939–1956. (2001: 62)

Not only was TV perceived as lacking social objective, but there was also absence of ingenuity on how to proceed with its implementation. The ambivalence of the government to such a powerful medium was remarkable, all the more so given state intervention in other forms of mass media such as radio, press and cinema.

After this initial period of indifference the government, clumsily, attempted to involve itself with television. Authority was delegated to the perceived expertise needed. So, some aspects of TV's implementation were left in the hands of engineers as evidenced in the Plan Nacional de Televisión, issued after the First National Congress of Telecommunication Engineers in December of 1955. Other aspects were left in the hands of enthusiastic amateurs as evidenced by Luis Guijarro, a naval colonel, who proposed that the first TV station be located in a building adjoining his own house in Paseo de la Habana de Madrid. The appearance of conflict-of-interest to the contrary, the space was indeed acquired and served as a home of Spanish television until its move to Prado del Rey in 1964. Luis Guijarro recalls: 'Lo primero que hice fue mandar hacer una puerta en el tabique que separaba ambos chalets, para poder pasar directamente a él desde mi casa en cualquier momento' (Martínez Uceda and Rodríguez Márquez 1992: 32).

Despite the government's initial bungling, television was gaining importance before its official inauguration on 28 October 28 1956. Nevertheless, the inaugural ceremony itself reflected the government's general mismanagement of the medium. On 27 October, the day before the ceremony, it was still not clear whether television would be financed through state or private enterprise, what the length of programming day would be, and what the broadcast station would be named (Palacio 2001: 37, 38).[13] After Catholic mass held at the altar installed at the station, followed by brief addresses by David Cubedo, José Ramón Alonso and Jesús Suevo, the Minister of Information and Tourism, Arias Salgado, made the speech, that metaphorically served as a benchmark for incipient decline of Falangist influence.[14]

The new government of February 1957 revealed a radical downgrading of Falangists and renewed emphasis on technical expertise (see 'Introduction'). The autarkic Spain was becoming technocratic; 'the three key technicians in economic affairs and state administration were all members of Opus Dei (Laureano López Rodó, Alberto Ullastres, and Mariano Navarro Rubio)' (Payne 1987: 450, 451). 'Progress' became the buzzword of the technocrats. Their entry into the economic sphere and celebration of post-war capitalism were contrary to Franco's earlier economic ideals. Therefore, the implementation of television not only corresponds to a moment in Spanish political and cultural history, marking the transition from autarky to capitalism but, as I will argue, augmented that transition.

No longer insistent on self-sufficiency, Spain could re-orient towards open trade and assume a more significant position in the larger geopolitical space. With the advent of live global broadcast, Spanish TV became not just a window onto a wider world but a portal through which to enter it by means of initiatives such as the US Wide Wide World and Eurovision in Europe. With its aura of immediacy, television was an ultimate space-binding technology. Lynn Spigel points out that such an interpretation is not as novel as it may seem: 'the image of television as a "global village," which media critic Marshall McCluhan spoke of in the 1960s, was already suggested in the popular discourses of the postwar period' (1992: 104). In Spain, José Julio Perlado wrote that '[e]l mundo se ha podido reducir, igual que aquellos cráneos deformados, hasta empequeñecerse en la pantalla y en el ritmo de estas imágenes que se suceden incansables' (1959: 3).

The 'reduced world' of a global village was being mapped out by the industrial western nations. However, within those nations, networks of power were shifting and re-aligning. The military–industrial complex was emerging and it was only logical that the implementation of television would reflect power struggles over institutional turf in the aftermath of the Second World War. The Cold War also helped to explain how power shifted within the broadcast media.

Ironically the Cold War which is associated with jingoism in the United States and the United Kingdom, actually contributed to ending of the Spain's isolation. To be on the side of the West, Spain sought admission into various international organizations, which in turn opened up possibilities for foreign investment further cementing Spain's 'entry' into the 'West'. The economy was on an irreversible path to modernization with Spain's admission in 1958 to the Organization for European Economic Cooperation (OEEC), the Export-Import Bank and the International Monetary Fund. The creation of the Common Market in 1958 had a tremendous impact on Spain and as Payne points out,

> the achievements of west European economic integration were already apparent to most Spanish administrators, and the development of the Common Market almost immediately exerted strong influences on many of them, who were soon convinced that the road to Spain's future prosperity could not lie apart from the rapid economic growth of the western economy as a whole. (Payne 1987: 468)

With a growing membership, the Common Market was absorbing culturally diverse countries into its sphere and sought identity in being European. So the name was changed to the European Economic Community (EEC). It was now something much more than taking down trade barriers. Just as the government was interested in joining the EEC, so too was Spanish TV eager to join the European network, Eurovision. Spain's anticipated entry into the network was met with optimism,

> dentro de poco Europa no será algo que queda al otro lado de los Pirineos, y que hay que salvar de salto aéreo o periplo marítimo o ferroviario. Europa estará en casa, junto a la chimenea, debajo del cuadro preferido, porque TVE la traerá a domicilio. (Sueiro 1959: 6, 7)

Spain did not confine its economic hopes to the EEC. It also looked towards the United States for economic aid. Thus, it was not surprising when

> on July 22, 1959, after Ullastres had arranged a $544-million loan in Washington, a new decree law was issued for a '*plan de estabilización interna y externa de la economía*.' Its goal was retrenchment, deflation, and above all a liberalization that would open the economy to the international market. The peseta was devaluated from 42 to 60 to the dollar, and by the end of the year, eighteen government control agencies had been abolished and a wide variety of items freed from regulation in both domestic production and foreign trade. (Payne 1987: 470, 471)

As the Spanish economy was evolving away from a poor, 'have-not' nation, foreign economic interests started to coincide with Spanish ones, thus marking Spain's gradual entrance into the limited world of the 'haves'. Predictably, the new economic order could not accommodate the provincial obsession with 'real' roots, 'authentic' character and 'lo español'. How would one insulate Spain and, at the same time, indulge in seeing the world, all without leaving one's parlour. The paradoxical experience of 'night out at home' became feasible as mobility was no longer physical but mental. Other tropes such as 'la ventana maravillosa', 'ojo mágico' and 'la supersónica alfombra mágica' revealed a perceived demand by television to bring the 'world' into the home. Juan Emilio Aragones states that 'la pantalla televisora brinda a todos la posibilidad de hacer turismo sin moverse del hogar y en zapatillas' and an elderly spectator in 'Gracias a la televisión' writes:

> He visto cosas muy curiosas que no había visto ni oído nunca, a pesar de mi edad: prestidigitadores, cantantes célebres, músicos españoles y extranjeros, etc. Me enteré, casi al día, de las más importantes noticias industriales, etc. En fin, sin gastarme ni cinco céntimos en medios de locomoción, ni en automóvil (porque carezco de él) he presenciado más actos y he visto más cosas agradables en este año que en los diez años anteriores. Y todo por mucho menos dinero y con mucho menos esfuerzo que cualquier persona gasta en un mes. ('Gracias a la televisión' 1)[15]

Television became a vehicle of exploration. The viewer had seemingly endless access to faraway places with their exotic cultures and distinct realities. In slippers and without a penny spent on transport all the corners of Spain as well as the world were now easily accessible. So, the introduction of television redefined the notion of time while complicating spatial scales since 'television technologies are at once "global" in their scope and infinitesimally "local" at the point of reception' (McCarthy 2001: 10). The world now shrunken appeared in the midst of Spanish living rooms proving the point that TV is, on one hand, 'a site-specific apparatus of spectatorship and on the other hand a figure for the modern collapse of space' (McCarthy 2001: 10). José Julio Perlado captured this phenomenon colourfully with the trope of television screen as 'una pupila sin fondo, una cuenca vacía, que se llena imprevista, diabólicamente de imágenes' (1959: 3). Suddenly ubiquitous in the social landscape, television enabled powerful meeting of the global and local; of worldly images and domestic spaces; of outside events and domestic activities. Images flooded living rooms and were received with both wariness and excitement; to some TV was diabolical, to others sacred, but to few was the TV inconsequential.

Speed and the fleeting nature of the image were features of the new medium of which the public took note: 'The piece of domestic furniture with the electronic picture tube in which staged and non-staged facets of the world were transformed into images at an incredible speed, pixel by pixel, and evaporated just as quickly once they have been visible...' (Zielinski 1999: 12). Through its very speed and omnipresence, perception of reality was blurring with that transmitted electronically. Very tellingly cartoons would depict spectators in front of TV sets, intrigued, frightened, confused and perplexed by the images. For example, a man, slightly frustrated by not being able to access the giraffe he sees on the TV. In next strip he takes a saw, makes a hole on the top of television, while the giraffe, now disconcerted, pokes her head out of the TV and looks at the man. Still holding the saw, he looks on with much satisfaction. Another cartoon will show a whale in the sea splashing water onto the viewer sitting in his living room or a women frightened by a rat jumping up on a chair. Often the interaction is violent. A man is stretched on his living room floor pierced by an arrow. The cartoon then shows an Indian, with bow and arrows, running away. Fusion of the spaces can also carry sexual connotations. For example, while the phonograph is playing, a man, dressed in a suit, is dancing, cheek to cheek with the TV image of a beautiful woman. Another man with magnifying glass in hand is lustfully examining a women on the TV. Besides attesting to the tensions and interplay between the real and electronic spaces, a theme of the cartoons is often the novelty of TV and its intrusive nature in the home. TV had not yet become integrated with everyday life. In the editorial 'Yo ante las cámaras' Ángel Ruis Ayucar points out that TV had not yet become commonplace 'las familias se movilizan todavía para 'ir a ver la televisión...[que] constituye un pequeño acontecimiento, que se prepara, por lo menos, como el plan para ir al cine o al teatro' (1959: 3).

Such examples complement the rising use of the trope of 'invasion' to describe the relationship between spectators and images. Ruis Ayucar illustrates further the confusion and new articulation of 'electronic' and 'real realms':

> Los personajes de la televisión tienen la curiosa particularidad de su capacidad invasora. Los personajes de la televisión tienen una capacidad vital que se manifiesta en su aptitud para la invasión. Hablábamos de que sus personajes parecían liliputienses, pero unos liliputienses con algo de vikingos milimétricos-y algo de termitas también-que no se limitasen a reaccionar encadenado a Gulliver que les invadía, sino que hubiesen invadido ellos el hogar propio de Gulliver. (1958: 9)

Considering the cartoon depictions, along with the ritual of collective viewing, one can say that the television screen was an arresting feature of the living room in the early era of TV. Even the texture of the TV screen seemed permeable, both penetrated and penetrating at the same time.

The heads of giraffes were sticking out of television sets, beautiful women were stepping outside the TV box and into one's living room. In the heady days of early television, hosts were thought of as 'pequeños intermedios entre reales y fantásticos' and stardom emerged as the real and electronic spaces achieved coexistence. Intimacy was carefully cultivated and became a defining trait at the core of the symbolic function of the new medium.

In the ever-shifting landscape of media, television was at first classified as not-quite-radio, not-quite-cinema and not-quite-theatre. Drawing on McLuhan's notion of 'the rear view', Paddy Scannell explains the public's attempt to classify TV under old rubrics: 'it is tempting to suggest that the ways in which new media were thought of at first defined them in terms of the characteristics of older forms of public address which they appeared to displace' (2000: 7). One can say that intimacy was the quality that helped define the medium and set it apart from radio, cinema and theatre. Intimacy was also key to the ideological function of the televisual apparatus.

The ability of TV personalities to generate powerful imaginative and affective relationships with anonymous audiences resulted in 'a lack of a sharp differentiation, in everyday experience, between the para-social encounters of broadcasting and the "network of actual social relations"' (Corner 1999: 39). The rising fame of Spanish TV hosts, such as Laurita Valenzuela, Blanca Álvarez, Jesús Álvarez, David Cubedo and Ángel de Echenique, all depended greatly on establishing a parasocial function with their viewers. So they would enter Spanish homes on a first name basis, and offered audiences 'the mise-en-scène of friendly, solid, and decent intimacy' (Zielinski 1999: 107). Enrique de las Casas has jestfully called this the intimacy of bathrobe and slippers or *la intimidad de la bata y de las zapatillas*:

> La T.V. impele inmediatamente al tuteo con la imagen, al diálogo personal con esa figura o con ese rostro que muestra la pantalla. Es un tuteo natural, sencillo, como de algo amigo y conocido de siempre, y

> producido, más que por ninguna otra razón, por el modo peculiar en que esa imagen es recibida: En la intimidad, y con absoluta y plena intimidad. Esa intimidad que, en cada uno, es la de la bata y la de las zapatillas. (1958b: 3)

Not surprisingly, the spaces of early television often simulated the home even though the staging was obviously *faux*: fake living rooms, fake kitchens or even fake canteens. For example, we read in the 1958 March issue of *TeleDiario* that Pedro Chicote, the owner of Museo del Pedro Chicote, a meeting place for Francoist culturati was hosting a popular show 'Imagen de una vida' and had invited 'un buen número de primeras figuras de cinematografía española'. Those that missed the show could be consoled by two stills of the broadcast in *TeleDiario*:

> En la primera, Chicote, detrás del mostrador, junto al actor Joaquín Pamplona, cuenta algunas curiosidades de su conocido museo. La otra foto muestra a Luisa Ortega, Fernando Rey, Virgilio Texeira, Ana Mariscal, Carmen Sevilla y Angel de Andrés haciendo una pequeña tertulia en la falsa cafetería.

The job of constructing 'television personalities', to be received into living rooms as one would receive personal friends, was constantly reinforced by the programs themselves. For example, *Caras nuevas* emphasized that '[u]na cara para televisión debe poseer cualidades especiales: telegenia, cultura, buena voz, dominio del gesto', adding that, 'en esto como en todo, también solicitamos su colaboración crítica. Al fin y al cabo, se trata de "su intimidad," a la cual llegan' ('Caras nuevas' 1958: 8).[16] With its focus on intimacy, it is also not surprising that *Caras nuevas* was staged in a simulated living room. Behind the furniture was a giant papier-mâché TV screen with large question mark. An oversized sign read: fotogenia + naturalidad + improvisación = ¡¡ÉXITO!!

Besides the frequency of tête-à-tête's in simulated living rooms, snack bars and kitchens, there were also repeated visits to the homes of other television celebrities. The reports would focus on the intimacy of the celebrities as well as on their relation to television and the impact of the new machine in their homes and in their lives. Viewers would learn inane trivia about the constructed stars: at what time Bobby Deglané watched TV; which brand name of TV Conchita Velasco received for Christmas; which programmes Tony Leblanc's family prefers, and so on. This relentless exposure of the personal details of the celebrities helped to blend their off with their on-screen personae. John Corner claims that a fan culture developed around newsreaders, weather presenters and game-show hosts based on pleasure of intimacy:

> ...considerably reinforced by the appearance of stories about celebrities in popular newspapers and magazines, where aspects of their backstage life can be revealed and their self-presentation to the viewer thus gain more depth and resonance. The regular appearance of television personalities at public events (charity shows, fêtes, dinners) shows them being playfully invited into the real social spheres of specific groups of strangers, not primary to do anything but simply to *be there* and generate for participants the pleasing and privileged experience of seeing them in real life. (1999: 95)

There were various technical conventions used in creation of this new space of intimacy. These included speaking directly to the viewers and addressing the camera as well as the use of close-ups. A unique tone was carefully cultivated for each programme. Facial expressions, gestures, personal idiosyncrasies would take on the role of trademark. Above all, TV would distinguish itself through a direct address to its viewers:

> [R]ather than pretending the viewer isn't there (as in the cinematic mode of address), the rhetorical mode simulates face to face encounter by directly addressing the viewer. The anchor recruits people as viewers...persuading the actual person watching at home that he or she is the 'you' to whom the addresser is speaking. (Allen 1992: 117)

The relationships generated by 'television personalities' helped to create an imaginary universe. To many viewers, this universe was not perceived as fictitious, but very real:

> El gran camino de la T.V. no está en lo espectacular, que se sitúa en lo ficticio, como en los otros espectaculos, sino en lo real, donde los hombres se presentan a los otros tal y como son, tal y como están siendo, pese al largo y complicado camino de electrones que tienen que recorrer hasta llegar a nosotros. (De las Casas 1958a: 7)

Other strategies also existed that intensified viewers familiarity with the TV personalities. Prominent among them were fan mail and magazines. Not only would correspondence with fans play a crucial role in solidifying the intimacy, but the correspondence with some of those fans would actually be televised. Soon after its appearance, *TeleDiario* created a special column entitled 'Laurita contesta' geared to augment the popularity of Laura Valenzuela. Letters to the TV hosts were perceived as 'cartas de amigos, preguntando e interesándose siempre por cuestions reales y sensatas; cartas personales de quien convive a distancia pero continuadamente, con nosotros' (De las Casas 1958a: 7).

The two traits that defined the early televisual experience (televisual apparatus' ability to produce a highlighted sense of the intimacy and an alienating feeling of being bombarded by relentless, incessant pixels) inhabited the new electronic landscape with equal intensity. They were symptomatic of modern experience itself, imbued with the contradictory desires of intimacy together with the spectacle of the world in the midst of one's living room. Coexistence of alienation and intimacy is also reminiscent of the debut of TV which stirred both anxiety and excitement, leading to endless debates in public fora. This disquiet manifested itself in debates of the genre 'what is TV?', and the tone was always suspicious: '¿Saludaremos a esta ventana con optimismo, o saludaremos a esta ventana con recelo?' (Martín Abril 1958: 3).

A dystopian discourse on television, emphasizing its dehumanizing effect, became standard fare. Highlighted was the potential of television to bring discord into both the home and the nation. Accordingly, gender dynamics and traditional ways would be first to feel the impact. The diatribes harped on the invasive nature of television and its tireless penetration of everyday life. Nevertheless, the innovative aspects of TV were also very much present in the debate. On the positive side, TV was portrayed as a potential for uplifting culture through high-brow entertainment and as a harbinger of technological utopia.

Thus, television was, on the one hand, a sinister invention and a 'giant eye on life itself' filled with inane chatter and fake settings.[17] On the other hand, it was a window to an exciting world that promised specifically televisual ways of seeing and new and different pleasures. Despite the dystopian discourses, the optimism generally prevailed and TV was seen as both 'la fabulosa facilidad de ser "nuestros ojos" y "nuestras miradas"' (Melero Melero 1958: 16) and 'un gran ojo de buey prehistórico que se clava calmoso pero fulminante sobre estas largas y entreabiertas praderas de los siglos' (Perlado 1959: 3). In 'El rostro de los escritores' Eugenia Serrano calls the TV 'la pantalla de la sinceridad' (1959: 3) and Francisco Javier Martín Abril 'una especie de cátedra complementaria a domicilio' (1959: 3). Jesús Fragoso del Toro would find a patriotic and patronizing metaphor in the antenna: 'un soldado en descubierta…que puede suponer una tremenda conquista en el avanze cultural de nuestros campesinos…No se necesita ahondar para convencer a alguien de lo que puede hacer la T.V. en ese campo ancho y fecundo que son gentes campesinas' (1958: 3).

Television was both a marvelous toy and a pleasure machine that everyone seemed to want. In the beginning, it was also a status symbol that would lose its snob appeal as prices fell. TV as an accoutrement of modernity was accompanied by the other 'must-have' big-ticket items. Households seemed deprived if they did not also house refrigerators and washing machines. Finally, cars would also pass from being a luxury to a necessity and were soon brought within economic reach through mass production. Consumerism gripped Spain and would work its way into the cultural fabric:

> Las aspiraciones de los nuevos burgueses y de sus hijos, de los cuales se había de hacer cómplice la publicidad, se orientaban hacia la consecución de los pequeños placeres materiales que propicia la sociedad de consumo, desde poder veranear hasta adquirir un cochecito funcional, una nevera o una lavadora. Los conceptos autárquicos del nacional-sindicalismo, con su perenne referencia al heroísmo y a la tradición, empezaban a sonar como una música anticuada, aburrida e inoperante. (Martín Gaite 1987: 213)

Television would become a linchpin to the emerging culture as it demonstrated to the masses what could be bought and what pleasure consumption would bring. Becoming also a more familiar object television increasingly blended into the rhythm of everyday life.

Un anuncio en T.V.E. es un escaparate en cada hogar

Television held a singular role: it was both a new commodity and a means to advertise other new commodities. Its potential as advertising tool found fertile soil in the Spain of the 1950s. For purposes of business, Spanish Television crafted a slogan which ironically was a metaphor for the new social role of television: *Un anuncio en T.V.E. es un escaparate en cada hogar* (or its variation *UN ESCAPARATE EN CADA HOGAR, al servicio de las empresas*). Connoting the technical marvels of television with magic, the advertisers promised likewise magic in sales:

> como una supersónica alfombra mágica vuela por los espacios y, sutilmente se introduce, primero, en las casas de los espectadores, y, luego, también de forma mágica, en las mentes de grandes y pequeños… más o menos imperceptiblemente, en el domicilio del espectador, sin tener éste que deambular por calles y plazas. ('Publicidad' 1958: 8)

The use of television as an advertising medium was more prevalent in Spain than other European countries because of the formal ties between the government-run Spanish Television and the advertising industry. Spanish television stood out as one of few public enterprises in the world that were privately financed. This arrangement arose from both convenience and necessity: advertising *pesetas* were to be easily had and government budgets proved inadequate to finance the new technology. While it was clear that the successful integration of television into global capitalism was connected to a vital decision regarding its financing, it was nevertheless approached in a similar manner to the other crucial features of television's implementation in Franco's Spain (left to the hands of scientists, amateurs, or simply chance). At first there was an attempt to finance it by taxing the owners of TV sets (*los ingresos del canon*) but that attempt failed, and, as Manuel Palacio observes, 'sin dinero público y sin contar con el canon lo más cómodo, y quizá lo único, que se podía hacer en TVE era lanzarse a los brazos de la industria publicitaria' (2001: 45).[18]

Palacio's metaphor of television 'hurling itself into the arms of advertising' was no hyperbole; the income from advertising skyrocketed:

> Ya en 1958 TVE ingresa por inversiones publicitarias unas 4.400.000 pesetas; en 1959 van a entrar en las arcas de TVE unos 16 millones de pesetas y en 1960 algo más de 33 millones. El servicio televisivo español podía asentarse, crecer y ser prácticamente autosuficiente con los ingresos de la publicidad. (2001: 46)

Turning to the advertising was also a logical step since it fit perfectly the moment of incipient consumerism in the rapidly developing Spain.

Even though most of the programmes had relied on some form of sponsorship, the marriage of entertainment and consumerism in 'UN ESCAPARATE EN CADA HOGAR' was most prominent in TV contests or give-away game shows called *concursos*, kind of quintessence of the bond between television and the advertising industry. Immensely popular, TV *concursos* dominated the airwaves: *Hacía la fama*, *Telemímica*, *Caras nuevas* (¡Su cara puede valer!), *Gran parada* ('El personaje y su frase'), *Primer aplauso* and so on.

Carmen Martín Gaite introduced a taxonomy of post-war personalities ranging from *eternal girlfriends* and *patient secretaries* to *topolino* and *swing* girls. To her taxonomy, one can add a professional contestant (*concursante profesional*), a personality evolved from the 1950s obsession with concursos. This figure is incarnated in Felipe Carrasco played by Tony Leblanc in Jose Luis Sáenz de Heredia's 1965 film *Historias de la televisión*.[19] *Historias de la televisión* was Sáenz de Heredia's unsuccessful sequel to much praised *Historias de la radio* from a decade earlier.

In a film, Felipe Carrasco first appears on a mechanical horse. Donned in a cowboy hat, he competes with another contestant for the prize of 5,000 pesetas:

> Ya conocen en qué consiste nuestro concurso. Aquí tenemos las ruletas que nos han de dar los temas y la letra sobre la que ustedes tienen que disparar. Tan pronto como se enciendan las dos sus dos caballos comenzarán a galopear y ustedes alternativamente habrán de ir disparando nombres uno tras otro. Cinco segundos sin replicar al otro son suficientes para que el caballo se pare y las 5000 pesetas de este combate pasen a engrosar la cuenta del que sigue galopando. (*Historias de la televisión*; my transcription)

Unable to respond to subject category of vegetables starting with the letter A and bullfighters with the letter S, Felipe Carrasco loses again which elicits his father's (Faustino) glee: 'cada vez que le cascan me alegro, alguna vez comprenderá que el dinero se gana trabajando' (*Historias de la televisión*; my transcription).

Despite this initial failure, Felipe perseveres with the same enthusiasm participating in two more contests: 'De la fama y algo más' and 'La unión hace el hogar'. In the first one he is *El Gran Fu, el genio de ilusionismo* and in the second contest he plays the ersatz boyfriend of Katy (Conchita Velasco), the protagonist of the next story competing for alluring 85,000 pesetas. Tony Leblanc's real life mirrors Felipe Carrasco character in *Historias de la televisión*. In the *TeleDiario* of July 1959 Leblanc 'lamenta de que pese a querer trabajar en televisión no encuentra casa de publicidad que lo patrocine' (Palacio 2001: 48).

Felipe Carrasco's fixation on contests is reminiscent of the radio show host Bobby Deglané. Deglané had become a famous post-war personality with the creation of *Cabalgata fin de semana*. Spanish companies sought Deglané to promote their products and in 1959, at the height of the contest frenzy, he created an exceptionally successful contest, *Operación Felicidad*.[20] Just as Deglané perceives that 'el español aspira a felicidad', Carrasco satisfies that aspiration in *Historias de la televisión* which has a happy ending. The fortune and fame that changed lives of so many average people in this contest obsessed society finally did not escape Felipe Carrasco. Felipe Carrasco, an 'antihero of advertising' at the end of the film, acquires both fortune and fame. In a strange turn of luck, his lack of talent gets interpreted as endearing. His failure flips into accidental success. Signified and signifier merge and Felipe becomes the commodity itself (in a slapstick comedy mode his body literally becomes a watch that he is promoting) illustrating perfectly that [even if] 'at first glance, a commodity seems a commonplace sort of thing, one easily understood. Analysis shows, however, that it is a very queer thing indeed, full of metaphysical subtleties and theological whimsies' (Marx 1976: 163).

Felipe Carrasco's tumultuous path to success and fame is tied to the rise of the female protagonist, Katy, a lead singer (*chica ye-yé*) of a pop band 'Katy and her horses'. She is also the star of the second episode 'Una chica de Fortuna' and co-star of the third and last one which interlinks her destiny with that of Felipe Carrasco. After a long run of failures, Felipe also reached stardom as a member of the band.

'Una chica de la Fortuna' is an endearing story which centres on Katy's internal conflict between living the small-town life and aspiring for a singing career beyond her limited horizons. The monotony of her life unexpectedly changes when one of her songs is selected to represent Spain at a *Eurovision* contest. However, the policy of *Eurovision* is that the song can only be performed by someone who is already famous. Carlos Aguilar, a famous pop star, will sing Katy's song and she, indignant by the unfairness, decides to seek fame in Madrid and perform the song herself. In her pursuit of fame, she ends up fighting a bull, assuming the persona of someone already famous and so on and so forth.

After many vignettes in this screw-ball comedy, Katy realizes that the song she thought was hers and the object of her indignation actually belonged to another.

The pursuit of fame and material wealth is what brings Felipe Carrasco and Katy together, and is what also presages their frustration and disappointment. The moral of the story implies that modernity, imbued with dangers and ambition, should be measured. Delusional, Felipe and Katy use their future fame as collateral and borrow money from a loan shark and, at the end, are pressed to payback the principal at usury rates. Felipe realizes that the last chance of paying his debt is through wining a considerable sum at yet another game show! Katy, not seeing another solution, agrees to do likewise. They meet in the last episode, desperately trying to raise the money they owe. The game show is *Unión hace el hogar* which joins them together in a pretense that they are engaged to be married.

The film comments on easy money, imprudent investments, untrustworthy business deals and material ambitions. *Historias de la televisión* reminds us of *¡Bienvenido Mr. Marshall!*, where among other themes García Berlanga viciously comments on duplicitous foreign aid (Marshall Plan, economic aid to the post-war Europe, capitalist development and so on). In García Berlanga's film the Americans (that were supposed to bring prosperity to Villar del Río) remain purely imaginary. The villagers' own real transactions leave them even poorer than they were before because they have to return all the things they purchased on credit in order to appeal to what they imagine is the American image of Spain. Before they realize that the Americans and their economic aid will never arrive the Spanish hosts put in a request for anything they could possibly lack. The town's mayor, Don Pablo, records the requests, allowing each person one thing. The compilation would resemble a taxonomy from the Chinese encyclopaedia used by Borges and quoted by Foucault in *The Order of Things*. The villagers thus requested: a watch, a mule, a clarinet, a cart, racing bike, weights for bodybuilding, a pair of cows, chocolate, a large mirror, an embroidered bedspread, church bells, field-glasses, sawing machine, a Sunday suit and so on. Earlier metaphors of economic prudence on the part of villagers are now replaced with images of wanton expenditure.

The role played by the cheap hats and outfits purchased on credit by country people in García Berlanga's film is substituted for urban paraphanelia in *Historias de la televisión*:

> La olla laster con capacidad para cuatro litros, dos espléndidas hamacas plegables para bien gozar de la primavera al aire libre, un ramo de rosas de plástico, tan naturales que hasta exhalaban su poquito de perfume, una caja de bombones artísticamente decorada a mano, un colchón de muelles FLEX.[21]

Thus, the villagers in *¡Bienvenido Mr. Marshall!* as well as Felipe Carrasco and Katy in *Historias de la televisión* end similarly. Their venture into modern capitalism terminates in debt.

Unión hace el hogar

Besides the obvious critique of consumerism, the last part of *Historias de la televisión* also illustrates the problematic and contradictory role of women in modern society. The third and last episode is the game show *Unión hace el hogar*. Explicitly linked to gender and consumerism, the humour of this episode lies in inverting gender roles. Thus, Katy, *chica ye-yé*, is incapable of whipping eggs into a mayonnaise, gives absurd answers of how to prepare *bacalao al pil pil* and does not know how to remove a tomato stain from clothing. Lacking even the most basic homemaker skills, she is in every aspect unfit for marriage or any other kind of union based on the requirements postulated by the show.

Katy's life becomes an allegory for the profound changes that the country itself was experiencing. Katy is torn between traditional ways and seductive new options: should she continue living in sleepy Fortuna or depart for cosmopolitan Madrid?; should she marry her good-hearted but lackluster boyfriend Antonio or take-up with debonaire men that she will encounter on her journey to fame? In sum, should she stay in Fortuna as a simple newspaper vendor or become a pop star, a famous chica *ye-yé*?

Each of Katy's boyfriends will represent a distinct type of the times. Tony Leblanc, her on-stage boyfriend for the game show *Unión hace el hogar*, has achieved the status of *concursante profesional*. His personality reflects the times with its emphasis on mass-produced goods, material comfort, increasing purchasing power and so on. The second boyfriend is a music composer, and the third, a journalist, who capture different aspects of modernity. Finally, Antonio, her original boyfriend from Fortuna, will be regarded by Katy as 'un bicho raro' ('Siento tener que decirte que empiezas a parecerte a un bicho raro'). Antonio's character, played by Alfredo Landa, is indeed *un bicho raro*, uprooted from tradition but not yet integrated into modernity. The profile will resound with the audiences of the 1970s as it is a by-product of emigration and tourism. The character can also be found in Spanish comedy (known as *comedia sexy celtibérica*, *la comedia desarollista de los años 60*, or *cine de reprimidos*). Antonio endlesly repeats: 'Yo aquí pinto algo, ¿no? Vamos, digo yo'. To the same extent that Antonio is out of step with the times, Felipe Carrasco, a *concursante profesional*, is in sync.

Katy leaves Antonio behind in provincial Fortuna, embarks for the big city to rightfully perform her Eurovision song. Amusingly, Katy's character echoes Lolita Garrido's song *La televisión* from the 1940s 'La televisión, pronto llegará/yo te cantaré/y tú me verás…'. Katy's relation to the new entertainment juggernaut is complex. Although it opens up avenues for the broader recognition of her talent, it also means her exploitation and humiliation by the television industry.

Historias de television holds both textual compromises and ambiguities, it shows simultaneously the allures of female mobility as well as its dangerous consequences. The move towards modernization was never smooth, though inexorable.[22] Like the fictional Katy, the women of the times were caught in conflicting demands of domesticity and mobility, tradition and modernity, motherhood and sexuality, house chores and work outside the home, and so on. The complex interplay of these factors entailed an ongoing process of struggle and negotiation. The TV became the rhetorical embodiment of the multiple struggles facing Spanish women. Almost simultaneous with the implementation of the TV was the identification of women as a target audience for shows, ads and columns. So, early texts would express gratitude to their female audience for 'una arribada de consuelos epistolares que cien manos femeninas han trazado para nosotros con indecible y apretada bondad...Ellas nos dicen: Tengan ánimo. Estamos con ustedes...' (*TeleDiario* 56, March 1959: 2). The gratitude was in and of itself the recognition of the consumer power of women, reflecting shifting economic structures. So, the politics of television financing, contingent on advertising revenues, were tightly linked to the purchasing power of the female audience.

Soon after the inauguration of television the possibility of an exclusively female-oriented programme was prioritized:

> *La hora de la mujer* puede convertirse en un programa fuerte desde el punto de vista publicitario. El hecho de que cada día de la semana abarque un tema distinto, desde la 'Belleza en la mujer' hasta la 'Muñequería,' pasando por las secciones de 'Modas,' 'Cocina,' etc., abre un campo inmenso al patrocinio por firmas comerciales dedicadas al ramo de que se trate. La identidad entre la casa patrocinadora y el género de programa ha demonstrado ser de una gran eficacia publicitaria; crea una especie de recuerdo subconsciente en el telespectador, predisponiéndole a un encadamiento lógico de ideas que redunda en la mayor venta de los productos anunciados. ('¡TVE presenta!' 1958: 5)

Of all the products advertised over the airwaves, household appliances were the most prominently featured. Television was saturated with images of Laurita Valenzuela and Jesús Álvarez, smiling next to countless refrigerators, washing machines, irons, toasters, vacuum-cleaners and so on. While advertising offered women 'technological fantasy worlds that promised to reduce the time and energy devoted to household chores' (Spigel 1992: 46), it also resolved a paradox: spectatorship would counter-intuitively enhance useful labour at home and watching TV would not compete with doing chores, but instead TV advertising could communicate the existence of labour-saving technologies suggesting more time could be liberated through appliances advertised. Nevertheless advertisers and networks were reluctant to air daytime programming, 'assuming that, unlike radio, television might require the housewife's complete attention and thus disrupt her work in the home' (Spigel 1992: 76). Thus prompted by a comment of Conchita Velasco's mother who 'me lo aseguró, no da golpe a la hora de las emisiones' Álvaro López Alonso cautions his readers that '[L]as mujeres, antes, con la radio, podían hacer punto, coser los calcetines e incluso hacer la sopa. Con la televisión se crea un problema de economía y producción nacional' (*TeleDiario* 60, February 1959: 16). Álvaro López Alonso's reservations reduced to a question of TV time versus chore time. Trying to adapt to the rhythm of domestic duties in turn created eleborate rhythms of reception and a complex interplay between programming and women spectatorship. Flexibility was the goal. *Hora de la mujer* was divided and structured around various segments, thematized according to women's interests ('Belleza en la mujer', 'Muñequería', 'Modas', 'Cocina' and so on) and conceived as 'a series of fragmented consumer fantasies that women might tune into and out of, according to the logic of their daily schedules' (Spigel 1992: 83). Worries about the domestic duties and disruptive ability of television were addressed headlong. In today's lingo, women could compartmentalize and do chores while watching television. Programmers accepted that 'there was something taboo about the sight of a woman watching television alone' (Spigel 1992: 95). Ironically, no such demand was made of men. The men portrayed in the advertisements were always relaxed and in 'a posture of repose…watching in undisturbed passive comfort' (Spigel 1992: 95).[23] These mixed signals were summed up in a column of *TeleDiario* 60 (February 1959) entitled '¿Eres una chica moderna?' Constructing image of the Spanish woman became a balancing act: valued aspects of tradition would have to be simultaneously meshed with emerging cultural habits, sometime seemingly mutually exclusive:

> Nuestro test de hoy es sobre la mujer moderna. No esa falsa mujer moderna que no es más que una frívola, una 'snob,' que va por el mundo de aquí para allá, hablando un lenguaje varonil y sin saber que es peinar a un niño o hacerse un jersey. Nuestra mujer moderna no es esa. La nuestra es la que posee las manos y la dulzura de su abuela, pero esta no sólo toca el piano, ha salido a la calle. Sabe lo que es la Universidad, lo que es un amigo, conoce la psicología de un niño y ha recorrido quizá medio mundo. A veces nuestra mujer moderna ha ido lejos, a esquiar; otras han hecho su propia comida después de venir del trabajo; pero, sobre todo ha tenido como denominador común el gran carácter de la mujer frente a la vida y no se ha olvidado nunca de Dios ('¿Eres una chica moderna?' 1959: 10)[24]

Being modern was not easy; however, if one could master all the competing demands for one's time and score the maximum number of points, a warning popped up: 'Si has puntuado más de 90, ¡enhorabuena!, eres una chica excepcional y habrás hecho feliz siempre a los que te rodean; tienes carácter y sabes afrontar la vida; pero cuidado…, ¿no serás un poco impulsiva?' So it was a no-win situation. This warning closely resembles *Historias de la televisión* where Katy (*chica ye-yé*) was also reprimanded for being a little too impulsive and just a bit too modern.

In addition to these frustrating messages geared towards women there were 'expert' columns focused on a variety of themes concerning the new medium. The columns ranged from the traditional, entrenched voices of authority (church and medical experts) to the more experimental voices (pedagogues, educators, child psychologists, range of social science experts). Their advice was in keeping with the times when traditional norms were now clashing with an emergent culture. These regulating forces were tied to anxieties that television brought into the household with profound changes in social and gender structures. In the TV show *Unión hace el hogar* the title word 'union' is precisely one of the central issues of debate surrounding family and TV viewing habits. Unity and disjunction as well as other spatial tropes between the nation and the world were also used in describing the dynamics of the family. This topic appeared almost in every issue of *TeleDiario*, starting with the very first one from December 1957 that optimistically attributed family peace and unity to the arrival of the TV:

> Papá no sale de casa. El programa de la Televisión le ha reconciliado con la tertulia familiar que sigue a la cena. Ante el receptor, y entre programa y programa, conversa con mamá, aclara preguntas a los niños, se ríe de las ocurrencias de la abuela y se permite algún comentario ingenioso cuando la locutora es bonita o el actor un tanto feo...La Televisión es el único invento de la técnica que ha hecho posible que absolutamente todos los miembros de la familia asistan a un espectáculo sin que papá proteste del traje de mamá, los niños protesten de que ellos han de quedarse en cama, la abuela proteste porque se gasta demasiado. Venga en buena hora, pues, la Televisión al hogar, que con ella llega la paz a la familia. ('La televisión en el hogar' 1957: 1)

All the regulatory mechanisms together with the unending discussions regarding men's, women's and children's viewing habits showed that

> ...when the TV set becomes part of the family living room, it not only adapts to the conventional spatial or sensorial arrangements of its location, but it also enters into, and takes up a position within, the immaterial networks of power that characterize family life...TV activates, and embodies, the gendered struggles that lie beneath the surface of domestic space. (McCarthy 2001: 2)

Unexpected configurations and sometimes tense moments arose in the relationship of women to television. A fundamental gap lay in the discrepancy of networks ideal images of female viewers...rooted in abstract conceptions about women's lives and the heterogeneous experiences and situations of real women. Women developed intricate strategies of resistance and accommodation to the new machine and

> [p]opular media presented women with opportunities to negotiate with the modes of spectatorship that the television industry tried to construct. It is in these texts that we see the gaps and inconsistencies-the unexpected twists and turns-that were not foreseen by networks and advertisers. (Spigel 1992: 86)

Hence, the very act of struggle with and re-elaboration of the industries' prototypical female viewer contributed to a departure from the traditional gender role. Television discourses and debates would now create a cultural space through which women could negotiate their relationship to the media. After all, when '¿Eres una chica moderna?' asks '¿Tienes en tu equipo unos pantalones, un traje de fiesta y unos guantes para la cocina?' the elaborated strategies of resistance and adaptation allowed one to choose the most desirable item and disregard the rest, thereby embodying the notion of 'culture as a form of struggle' (Graham and Labanyi 1995a: vii).

The insistence on progress as indistinguishable from globalization meant women would be incorporated almost immediately into the modern configurations of Spanish society. So, it became harder to sustain the traditional discourse on womanhood by the existing ideological apparatus. As suggested in a Philips TV ad, entitled *En marcha hacia el futuro*:

> **PUEDE SER QUE ALGÚN DÍA** [original capitalized in bold letters] esta avispada jovencita vaya a una famosa universidad con la esperanza de conseguir uno de los más preciados títulos académicos...Por ser mujer puede gustarle especializarse en zootecnia o en los espectos cientificos de la agricultura. En estas ramas de la biología encontrará numerosos productos Philips. Es muy posible que los descubrimientos de Philips sean un arma de paz en las manos de esta inteligente mujercita (1958: 8).

Phillips's 'idealized, invented' woman, a consumer of their products and a potential specialist in, say animal husbandry or agronomy would clash with the previous model of womanhood still entrenched in social psychology.

Epitomizing the change that was clearly paving the way to consumer capitalism, the end of *Historias de la televisión*, unites Tony Leblanc (a *concursante profesional*) and Conchita Velasco (*chica ye-yé*) thereby marrying modernity, commodification of culture and consumer frenzy with the public's fascination with television and the emergence of the *generacíon ye-yé*.

Hence in reality, even though TV was inaugurated by Gabriel Arias Salgado, the development of the medium was very much marked by the more liberal Manuel Fraga Iribarne. Technical advances in Spanish television were still being contrasted to a spiritual dimension, as seen in César Gonzales Ruano's article 'Televisión y castillos'. Gonzales Ruano reminds his readers that

> nuestros progresos en la televisión nos vayan poniendo a la altura de otros mundos superiores al nuestro sólo en eso: en las formas aparenciales del progreso. El ideal sería tener lo que ellos tienen y además, lo que no pueden tener. Televisión y castillos. (1958: 7)

Thus the massive and planned introduction of TV from 1956 on went hand in hand with 'la voluntad, ahora claramente explicitada, de integrarse plenamente al concierto capitalista internacional' (Ibáñez 2001: 62). Between its own disorganized and unplanned beginnings and its inscription into the discourse of progress (together with other novel mass-produced goods) television was located at the core of a changing society, oriented more and more towards consumer values.

Franco, less and less in touch with reality, increasingly drifted into his hobbies such as 'hunting, fresh water and deep-sea fishing, golf, watching endless westerns in the private cinema in El Pardo, painting, and developing his large estate at Valdefuentes, where he grew wheat, potatoes and even tobacco' (Preston 1994: 627). Preston writes that 'a further contributing factor to [Franco's] isolation [from the world around him] was the manic enthusiasm of both Franco and his wife for television' (1994: 719). Fascination with the dazzling images of television did not bypass the Dictator either. He was becoming a TV junkie: 'having been delighted by the introduction of television into Spain, he also spent increasing numbers of hours watching the many sets placed around the Pardo' (Preston 1994: 700).[25] Ironically, Franco embraced the same technology and mass media that would ultimately undo the ideological and moral underpinnings of his regime.

Notes

1. Gabriel Arias Salgado, the Minister of Information and Tourism from 1951 until 1962, was a critical figure in curtailing the airs of change, 'La continuidad de Arias Salgado supone, para los sectores inmovilistas del régimen, una garantía de ortodoxia y de firmeza en la censura, y para los núcleos más activos de la disidencia cultural, una barrera en contradicción con los impulsos hacia la liberalización económica y con la imagen de España que se pretende proyectar hacia el exterior' (Heredero 1993: 28).

2. Quote comes from José Antonio Primo de Rivera's 'Discurso fundacional de Falange española' given on 29 October 1933 in Madrid's *Teatro de la Comedia*.

3. As Giménez Caballero tellingly suggested, '¿quién se ha metido en las entrañas de España como Franco hasta el punto de no saber ya si Franco es España o si España es Franco?' (quoted in Martín Gaite 1987: 19).

4. *Arizona Journal of Hispanic Cultural Studies* and *Journal of Spanish Cultural Studies.*

5. This phenomenon closely resembles 'the modernism/mass culture dichotomy [that] has been gendered as masculine/feminine' (Huyssen 1986: x).

6. See Camporesi (1999) and Ibáñez (2001).

7. The acronym NO-DO stands for Noticiarios y Documentales Cinematográficos (Cinematographic Newsreel and Documentaries), the newsreel shown in all cinemas. It presented the official view of Spain to the outside world.

8. The most important publication was *TeleDiario* published weekly in Madrid (publication of RTVE). The first issue came out on 31 December 1957. Later on it was renamed *Tele-Radio.*

9. See Palacio (2001).

10. Barroso and Tranche write that 'conviene recordar el papel que la prensa especializada ha jugado al hacerse eco de los entresijos de producción y financiación de nuestra televisión. Su importancia ha sido tal que prácticamente puede decirse que se ha convertido en la única fuente reconocida' (1996: 9).

11. One of the important issues in Spanish television that this chapter does not cover is, for example, issues of regionalism. This element is indispensable in the case of Spain where 'the tension between centralism and regionalism was decisive in shaping the organization, and orientation, of Spanish radio and television throughout the twentieth century' (Maxwell 1995: 12).

12. For early television history, see Palacio (2001).

13. Palacio adds: 'Un asistente, arquitecto jefe del Ministerio y con el tiempo responsable de la creación de la antena conocida como de la Bola del Mundo, confiesa que "ignora si habrá en el nuevo servicio una tendencia estatal o de monopolio o si derivará en empresas de cáracter privado"' (2001: 38).

14. For more information on Inaugural Day, see Palacio (2001).

15. Another similar text reads: 'La TV es como una mágica ventana que permite al hombre asomarse desde la muelle comodidad de su sillón predilecto a las

realidades distantes, a los paisajes más exóticos, a las existencias de otros hombres de quienes jamás hubiera sabido nada verdadero sin ayuda de este admirable medio de aproximación' (Aragones 1959: 3).

16. It is interesting to compare desirable features of Spanish TV anchors with BBC ones. BBC's applicants were required to possess: 'charisma, charm, tact, a voice in the mezzo-soprano range, a good memory, acceptable to both men and women, photogenic, not red-haired, and unmarried' (Zielinski 1999: 109).

17. Spigel points out that in the 1950s 'television's threatening aspects were represented not only in terms of surveillance per se, but also in terms of a more generalized fear of technologically perfected vision that rivaled human eyesight' (1992: 119).

18. Palacio writes: 'Entre noviembre de 1957 and abril de 1958 se elabora una minúscula reglamentación para atender a los aspectos administrativos y ecónomicos de la Administración Radiodifusora Española (ARE), en la que se encuadra el servicio televisivo. En ella se autoriza que Televisión Española recaude dinero a través de la publicidad' (2001: 45). Palacio also cites a comment made by Jesús Aparicio Bernal, a General Director of Spanish Radio and Television from 1964–1969: 'Televisión no podría sostenerse si no fuera por la publicidad. El problema es: o jugar a la televisión o tener una televisión' (2001: 48).

19. Sáenz de Heredia is not easily classifiable as a filmmaker, even though thanks to his film *Raza* (with script by none less than Franco), political inclination, and kinship with José Antonio Primo de Rivera, he is often pigeonholed as cineast of the regime. Instead of classifying him as such, it would be more productive to see him as a chronicler of the *Zeitgeist*.

20. Bobby Deglané explains the inspiration behind his popular game show in the following terms: 'Consciente de mi gran responsabilidad, dejé mi coche y durante tres días y tres noches me lancé por esas calles a hablar con las gentes de toda condición, inquiriendo sus apetencias, sus necesidades, sus gustos...La vieja que vende periódicos, el abogado, el militar, el limpiabotas, el padre de familia, el ingeniero, el empleado, la chacha, el ama de casa, el inquilino, el casero, el banquero, el taxista, el portero, el artista de cine y el de teatro, el empresario, el sereno, el guardia, el comerciante...En una palabra, todos los estratos sociales fueron diciéndome sus cuitas y llegué a una conclusión: así como el nórdico quiere tranquilidad y el inglés comodidad, el español aspira a felicidad. De ahí surgió mi *Operación Felicidad*.'

21. This example comes from *TeleDiario* 80. The list closely resembles other countless prizes offered at the time.

22. In the post-war period preceding the economic boom discussed here the woman situation was as problematic. Gender politics of the Francoist state demonstrated deep inconsistencies between the ideals of femininity and domesticity and the realities of post-war experience since 'the regime's project for Spanish "womanhood" scarcely functioned as its ideological progenitors had intended' (Graham 1995: 193, 194).

23. On feminine and masculine viewing practices see Spigel (1992: 93-96).

24. Some of the twelve questions were following: '¿Escogerías un hombre de tu propia profesión que te gustara aunque fuera más pobre que aquel ingeniero que conociste este verano?; ¿Practicas algún deporte al aire libre?; ¿Conoces hasta cinco movimientos culturales modernos?; ¿Tienes en tu equipo unos pantalones, un traje de fiesta y unos guantes para la cocina?; ¿Tienes en la vida un puesto digno e independiente?; ¿Sabes algún idioma extranjero?; ¿Crees en el cine como uno de los mejores descubrimientos al servicio de la cultura?'

25. Franco's love affair with TV continued and deepened with the arrival of the colour television: 'When not away on hunting trips, he watched television and movies. He was captivated by the arrival of color television' (Preston 1994: 735).

Chapter III

Voces de oro: Spain, modernity, and the child-star system

After panning valleys, rivers and mountains the camera focuses on a remote village, zooming in on a lonely figure walking down empty, cobblestone streets. The scene is accompanied by sacred polyphony reminiscent of Palestrina.[1] The figure is that of a woman carrying a suitcase. Her modern style is incongruously at odds with the rural surroundings. She continues her descent until a church bell-tower comes into view. At this moment, the streets are suddenly filled with an eerily magical voice singing the *Ave María*. The woman is enthralled and the overpowering *Ave María* also sweeps up the audience. As if out of nowhere the voice is heard offscreen, and no specific source can be attributed to the sound.[2] A few moments later, however, the voice becomes attached to a body. Somewhat surprisingly, the penetrating voice is that of a small boy in the church tower. His petite stature is accentuated by his posture: he is teetering on a chair and can barely reach the bell that he is tolling.

The boy-soprano is José Jiménez Fernández in the 1956 film *El pequeño ruiseñor*. This was his début on the silver screen. He would become known as Joselito (*el pequeño ruiseñor* or little nightingale) and from that moment forward his real-life persona would become inseparably blurred with his screen persona. His diagetic success likewise transcends the confines of the frame, becoming an object of endearment first in rural Spain, then in the Spanish capital, Madrid, and finally being reinvented as an export throughout Latin America.

The second Spanish junior to achieve child stardom would be Josefa Flores, known to her public as Marisol. Her first appearance was in *Un rayo de luz* in 1960. Like Joselito, Marisol first startled the audience through song. In a well-appointed salon in an Italian country villa, Marisol sings the popular Italian classic *Santa Lucia*. Suddenly, she switches from the melody and atavistically turns to her 'native' flamenco. The reaction of the governess and her paternal grandfather is one of horror and condescending disapproval.

To the Spanish public of the 1960s Joselito and Marisol would be inescapably associated with children's cinema (a Shirley Temple cinema). What distinguishes them from their under-age predecessors is that Joselito and Marisol would be subjected to the making-of-a-star system. Such a system demanded exclusive contracts, the morphing of personal life with their star personae, as well as the multiple marketing ploys aimed at promoting their image, such as fan clubs, franchises, merchandise endorsements and carefully scheduled 'impromptu' appearances.

Because of Joselito's and Marisol's success, modern audiences can easily forget that there were many child actors that came before. To mention a couple, there were Alexia Ventura and Alfredo Hurtado. To quote Carlos Heredero:

> In 1915 Hispano Films (la productora catalana) intenta hacer de Alexia Ventura el epígono local de Mary Pickford y en la década siguiente es Alfredo Hurtado, alias 'Pitusín,' quien se convierte en el primer 'niño prodigio' del cine español desde la temprana edad de los cuatro años y deviene luego el equivalente de Jackie Coogan. (1993: 226)

Alexia and Pitusín were followed by Antoñito Cabero, Alicia Nuri, Valeria de la Fuente, Beringola and so on. The Second Republic had its own stars such as Mari Tere, Arturito Girelli and Miguel Ángel Navarro. During the early years of the Franco regime there was no lack of children on the screen either and Spanish audiences enjoyed the performances of Carlitos Larrañaga, Eugenio Domingo, Olvido Guzmán and Fernando Galiana, among others.

A consensus among critics has emerged that the 1955 film *Marcelino, pan y vino* débuting Pablito Calvo, represents a landmark moment in the history of Spain's star system. The sucess of *Marcelino, pan y vino* was somewhat unexpected: '...el éxito desmesurado sorprende a la propia [compañía] productora' (Heredero 1993: 226). But the film's clever recombination of tried and tested devices appealed to the affective make up of the audience. The melodrama of an orphan adopted by friars captivated audiences and *Marcelino, pan y vino* created a formula for success which would be exploited in subsequent films.

Now Spanish audiences were ready for yet another screen orphan. A year later, *El pequeño ruiseñor* would open in Madrid's Cine Rex and Muñoz Seca. Although only mildly successful in the capital, it was a smash hit in the outlying provinces and rural areas. Besides lifting elements from *Marcelino, pan y vino*, says Heredero, '...el esquema de la película fagocita y redefine en beneficio propio varias fórmulas extraídas del cine confesional, del cine folclórico...y del folletín decimonónico' (Heredero 1993: 231). The film also incorporated *Campanera*, a highly popular song of the times, as the central focus of its diegesis.

Of all recurring traits from child-exploitative cinema, the choice of orphaned protagonists was the most prominent and persistent one. *El pequeño ruiseñor* would revitalize the genre.[3] The writer and film critic Terenci Moix dubbed a piece on Joselito precisely 'Joselito: de profesión huerfanito'. Even though Heredero claims that '... la pobreza, la orfandad o cualquier otra desgracia que les amenace [a los niños] son producto de coyunturas estrictamente melodramáticas o, como mucho, de causas bien abstractas o bien ajenas a la diégesis del relato fílmico', in Joselito's and Marisol's first films, the issues surrounding abandonment are indeed central (1993: 230). They are tied above all to the question of voice and linked to fundamental issues of origin. In their subsequent films both child stars will again and again embody screen orphans, be vehicles of family reunion, and search for surrogate and/or real parents. However, the first film of each actor is really arresting in its 'quest for origin'.

As stated, in *El pequeño ruiseñor*, Joselito first appears singing the *Ave María*. The hymn is praised by the child's grandfather, who emphasizes: 'Esto es cantar como Dios manda y no lo que te enseña el sacristán'. To which Joselito replies: 'El sacristán no me enseña nada; me sale sin querer'. In the next scene, the singing voice springs from the child's body without consent of his will. It is not the inspirational *Ave María* but a popular song of prohibited love. The spectator is affronted by the incongruity of the scene. The story of passion, adultery and illicit love emerges from the unlikely body of the child. This incongruity persists until Joselito admits that the irrepressible voice is that of his father, whom he had never met but whom he mystically knew via the father's singing:

> José: Así dicen que cantaba mi padre. De allí me viene el cante.
> Era un maestro.
> Don José: Un maestro...de granujas.
> José: ¿Por qué habla usted así de él siempre?
> Don José: Tienes razón. Tu padre murió. Dios le haya perdonado.
> José: ¿Y mi madre? Nunca me habla usted de ella.
> Don José: Tu madre es la Virgen Santísima. Ya lo sabes.
> José: ¿Por eso le cantamos todos los días?
> Don José: Sí. (*El pequeño ruiseñor*; my transcription)

It seems as if Joselito discloses his innermost self, the most intimate sphere of his being, through singing; 'he publicly reveals the object in himself, the *agalma* or hidden treasure that supports his identity' (Žižek 1991: 130).

In a similar fashion, Marisol's voice in *Un rayo de luz* is linked to her innermost self.[4] Her aristocratic, Italian grandfather repeatedly tells her: 'Tu profesora Elizabeth educará tu voz para que el día de mañana te luzcas en las fiestas de la sociedad. Debes pensar que has nacido aquí y que aquello no lo has visto nunca' (*Un rayo de luz*; my transcription). But Marisol's voice, nevertheless, suddenly and involuntary forsakes *Santa Lucia* for flamenco. This gesture is also linked to a parent, but in the second case to her mother who is a popular singer struggling for recognition in common taverns and night clubs or 'una figura de segunda fila' (Barreiro 1999: 43).[5]

The notion of an 'errant voice' is vital to linking the vignettes within each film and to binding the two films as a sub-genre. As we have already seen, *El pequeño ruiseñor* begins with *Ave María* resonating over the cobblestone streets. We are fascinated by '*la voix acousmatique*, the voice without bearer, which cannot be attributed to any subject and thus hovers in some indefinite interspace' (Žižek 1991: 126). Michel Chion, who introduced the concept of *la voix acousmatique* to film studies, emphasizes further that for the spectator

> the filmic acousmêtre is 'offscreen,' outside the image, and at the same time *in* the image: the loudspeaker that's actually its source is located behind the image in the movie theater. It's as if the voice were wandering along the surface, *at once inside and outside*, seeking a place to settle. Especially when a film hasn't yet shown what body this voice normally inhabits. Neither inside nor outside: such is the acousmêtre's fate in the cinema. (Chion 1999: 23; Chion's emphasis)[6]

Once the voice finds a home in Joselito's body, it still continues to wander but from then on the restlessness will be driven by the trauma of abandonment and the search for essence, truth and origin. In both films, the tension is created by errant voices which contain that which is hidden, unknown and should not be articulated. The true origins are manifested in songs that unwillingly spring forth from Spanish roots: immemorial popular tunes and flamenco. For example, Joselito the altar boy and *cantor religioso* will sing troubled stories of unrequited love at weddings and baptisms. In *Un rayo de luz*, the exotic melos (in this case Italian) is seen as sophisticated (high class) and is contrasted with homegrown flamenco, which is seen, in this case, as common and prosaic. *El pequeño ruiseñor* can be read as the story of a renunciation of the father's voice. Joselito loses the voice and ability to sing once he is adopted. His adoptive father turns out to be the man his mother was supposed to have married before she eloped with his biological father—the flamenco singer. In contrast, there is reconciliation and negotiation between the two voices in *Un rayo de luz*. The mother is incorporated into the upper-class family towards the end of the film by marrying the brother of her prematurely deceased husband.[7]

This diagetic obsession with quest for origins and the institutionalizing of a 'stardom machine' coincided with Spain's tumultuous passage to consumer capitalism in the 1960s with all the political and economic complexities that entailed. The films reflect a crisis of meaning and a search for new parameters, marked by the vacuum left in the wake of abandoning the Nationalist-Catholic discourse with its rhetoric of Spanish essence, destiny and so on. Joselito's and Marisol's early films span from the last year of Falangist grip on power and the technocrats' entry into the cabinet (*El pequeño ruiseñor*, 1956; *Saeta del ruiseñor*, 1957) to the so-called *Plan de estabilización* and subsequent *Plan de desarrollo* (*Escucha mi canción*, *El pequeño coronel*, 1959; *Un rayo de luz*, 1960; *Ha llegado un ángel*, 1961; *Tómbola*, 1962).[8] Economists aptly named this period the Hinge Decade (*el decenio bisagra*).[9] Juan Goytisolo captures this difficult passage to capitalist economy well by describing a faded inscription on the wall that reads POR EL IMPERIO HACIA DIOS that is still visible under the vivid and brilliant poster of the blond woman marketing BEBA COCA-COLA (*Fiestas*; see 'Introduction'). Marisol is actually nicknamed by Terenci Moix 'flamenquilla de coca-cola' and Joselito's cinema, marked by faith and belief in God, is filled with religious and moral traits reminiscent of autarky.

The milieu of the first two films starring Joselito and Marisol is so distinct that it belies the fact that the two stars are cast as contemporaries. *El pequeño ruiseñor* is entrenched in provincial Spain while *Un rayo de luz* takes place in a sophisticated upper-class Europe. Heredero points out that:

> la paradoja consiste en que las películas de Joselito se remiten a un escenario ya periclitado (las coordenadas morales y económicas de los años cuarenta o los primeros cincuenta), mientras que se despliegan y triunfan en las pantallas de una sociedad que pretende escapar, precisamente, de aquella coyuntura, de su oscurantismo y de su miseria, para acercarse a nuevos modelos culturales y económicos. (1993: 232)

Alberto Elena disagrees claiming that 'la saga del pequeño ruiseñor constituye una muy precisa radiografía de una España profunda que probablemente se encontraba en puertas de una gran transformación, pero que todavía se reconocía sin ambages en obras como *El ruiseñor de las cumbres*' (2001: 53). Jean-Claude Seguin (*Joselito: la voix inhumaine*) would support Elena's claim by regarding Joselito as a 'Fenómeno del cine de barrio' at the cusp of a mass migration of country to city. Although seductive, Seguin's assessment would be difficult to corroborate as there are no empirical studies that establish a statistical profile of exhibition, circulation and consumption of Joselito's films.

Their careers can be understood as inhabiting the gap between the two historic periods, autarky and incipient capitalist development. Elena's, Heredero's and Seguin's disagreements converge at the same issue. The two stars seem to project two distinct realities: Joselito, the old autarky, and Marisol, the new capitalist consumer society. However, Joselito's films, like the autarky itself, were 'afflicted with a kind of sclerosis—the living content escapes from them and only the rigidity of '"pure form" remains' (See 'Introduction'). Marisol's films were *dans le vent*, reflecting the material aspirations of the times but with challenges and frustrations. The child's absent parents were not truly a phenomenon of the times, rather they fit into the earlier circumstances of the 1940s. In *Ha llegado un ángel*, one of the characters comments on the endurance of the role of orphan ('no serás una huérfana de tiempos de mi abuelo') even though, some twenty years after the Civil War, orphans were no longer common in Spain.

The gap afflicted with sclerosis functions as an empty signifier concealed by the presence of fantasy, that is, anachronistic worlds of Joselito and Marisol. Like their wondering voices, neither Joselito nor Marisol were able to find a 'proper' place (especially in their early opus). Both Joselito's and Marisol's films are generally disregarded as representative of the Francoist cultural and ideological agenda. Far from being some sort of pedagogical tool of indoctrination, films reveal tensions between tradition/modernity and immobility/movement. By illustrating a crisis of representation (brought by changing epistemes) the films are as familiar as estranging. They distinguish themselves by conflicts and uneasy relationships. Joselito's and Marisol's images as stars are hard to reconcile; at first glance they are distinct, at other times coincident and even complementary.

Joselito and Marisol were part of the same milieu. They frequented the same places, had some of the same screen writers, and even some of the same producers.[10] Marisol first met Joselito while doing her screen test in studios CEA and their paths would repeatedly cross. In an article entitled 'Joselito nuevamente en España' we can read:

> Al aeropuerto fueron a recibirle los productores don Cesáreo González y don Benito Perojo, la juvenil Marisol, acompañada del señor Goyanes; personal de Suevia Films, Televisión Española, periodistas, fotógrafos, emisora de radio y un gran número de admiradores y amigos, que le dedicaron grandes aplausos al descender del avión que le traía de Venezuela. (*Radiocinema*, March 1962)

This airport encounter contains all of the elements crucial in the construction of the stardom of Joselito and Marisol. No doubt, the encounter was carefully staged to seem 'impromptu'; a shameless marketing ploy aimed at promoting their image. Three influential producers were present: Cesáreo González held an exclusive contract with Joselito; Goyanes considered Marisol his discovery; and Goyanes' father-in-law, Benito Perojo, another powerful figure in the film circles would also lay claim to the profits of their stardom. Indeed, it was Benito Perojo who was behind Marisol's first film with *Producciones B.P.*, a coproduction between Guión Films and Perojo; in the second film Perojo would participate with Cesáreo González and Suevia Films. By 1963, Perojo had also identified twin child actors, Pili and Mili and launched an unsuccessful replica (*Como dos gotas de agua*) to Marisol's hit *Marisol rumbo a Río*, exploiting the doppelgänger theme, inspired by successful American *The Parent Trap* (1961) (*Tú a Boston y yo a California*). With Pili and Mili, Perojo also produced *Whisky y vodka*, the twins playing the role of a Russian and an American girl. Profit drove all three producers' art form rather than artistic expression. The modernized forms of production and circulation were tied by the industrial and ideological linkages and rendered the child stars a cultural commodity.

Joselito's and Marisol's discovery also attests to the moment in which 'la ascención hasta la fama y el reconocimiento artístico desde los estratos más humildes de la sociedad' appealed to an audience that was emerging from years of deprivation (Heredero 1993: 232). The tale of childhood poverty struck a chord with public consciousness and was crucial in cementing the success of children as actors. The 'vocation for poverty' (See 'Introduction'), so ingrained in the Spanish psyche, now found a venue in child stardom.

Both Joselito and Marisol hail from desperately poor homes. Joselito's father lived precariously as a day-labourer. He was a migrant from Jaén who moved to Valencia in search of employment; Marisol's family lived in el barrio de la Victoria (de Capuchinos), perhaps the poorest sector of Málaga. The families were both large and struggled to survive. Joselito's and Marisol's musical talent became apparent at an early age. Through radio and television programmes, their images quickly became diffused and fixed in the public mind. In other words, 'discovery' itself was a reflection of mass media. After performing on radio, Joselito travelled from Valencia to Paris under the tutelage of Luis Mariano and the singer Antonio Fernández ('El Chaqueta') before being discovered by Antonio Guzmán Merino for the film industry.

Marisol's father and paternal grandmother were talented amateur singers and dancers. She recalls that her early years were filled with music. At the age of six, she was already a member of *Coros y Danzas de la Obra Sindical de Educación y Descanso* and later joined the touring troupe *Los joselitos del cante*. Stardom required a relentless schedule as the troupe moved from city to city. After her debut in Madrid in the theater María Guerrero, Boby Deglané invited Marisol to perform on his radio show *Cabalgata, fin de semana*. There she sang the song 'María Belén Santajuana' that had already gained fame thanks to an interpretation by Lola Flores. In 1959, she then joined Casa de Málaga en la Feria del Campo, and drew the attention of NO-DO's and TV's cameramen, who were so attracted by her verbal wit and spontaneity that they focused almost exclusively on her. Soon she and her group *Los Coros y Danzas de Málaga* were invited to the Tico and Yale. Impressed by her talent, Tico and Yale interviewed her the next day. The rest of the story accords with the script for TV 'discoveries' of the times. She was seen on the television programme by Mari Carmen Goyanes, the daughter of producer Manuel Goyanes. Encouraged by Joselito's meteoric rise to stardom, Goyanes realized that Marisol had similar potential. This trajectory from a provincial dancing troupe to the most highly regarded radio and TV shows in the capital was just the beginning of commodification of Marisol.

Impromptu events were anything but. For example, at the Barajas airport in Madrid, personalities from the press, radio and television, along with admirers and friends, were waiting to greet the disembarking Joselito. In other words, the child stardom was carefully calculated as would be the production of any other high-priced commodity. Marketing became progressively more aggressive with the success of each film. Not surprising the cinematic relationship of the children stars to the popular audience would become more complex.

The scene at the Barajas Airport encapsulates the cultural and social trajectories that were merely mirrored in the lives of the children stars. As seen from Joselito's return from Venezuela, stardom was a product of economic interests feeding on existing cultural practices. The story of children becoming stars is the story of producers: hitting upon a new 'hot' commodity. Child stars were fabricated, exploited and revered while their producers created a new form of cultural capital. This did not escape the children. Joselito, looking back, would later remark: 'Tenía una voz excepcional a una edad prematura y me convertí en una máquina de ganar millones' (*El País*, 8 September 1991).

Joselito: *Saeta del ruiseñor*

> 'Cantar también es rezar'.
>
> – Alicia, *Saeta de ruiseñor*

Joselito was enlisted into the film industry by Antonio Guzmán Merino, a screen writer who was previously involved in the world of folkloric musicals. As Alberto Elena remarks: 'Joselito no podía pasar desapercibido para el mundo del cine en un momento en que las películas con niño se encontraban claramente en alza' (2001: 50). Antonio Guzmán Merino proposed the 'Joselito project' to Antonio del Amo. Antonio del Amo was chosen to direct the newly found prodigy partially because of his successful launching of Antonio Molina, another legendary voice, a few years earlier in *El pescador de coplas* (1953). *Campanera*, the song that contributed to Molina's fame was a central part of diagesis in *El pequeño ruiseñor*, and from then on 'constituyó [la] carta de presentación [de Joselito]' (Moix 1993: 271). Nine of Joselito's fourteen feature films were filmed by Antonio del Amo. Del Amo, with his leftist past and political views, considered directing Joselito a parenthesis in his career.[11] Antonio del Amo was an independent producer/director struggling with his own projects and production company (Producciones Cinematográficas Argos). He accepted the job in order to finance his future, more socially engaged films. This never happened, and his career became inseparable from that of *el niño de la voz de oro* (a boy with the golden voice). In a letter to Román Gubern he laments:

> He cometido muchos errores de los que se llaman 'de estómago,' para sacar adelante a la familia, y no hay nada que yo odie más que lo que me he visto obligado a hacer, porque lo he hecho a costa de haber renunciado a mis ideas y a mi programa. (2001: 12)

The choice of Del Amo also points to a certain 'de-ideologizing' of the regime (See 'Introduction'). Although directed by a filmmaker of leftist background and other

Figure 3.1. Child star Joselito in late 1950s.

artistic aspirations, ironically, Joselito's films are read as the classic expression of Francoist ideology.

Antonio del Amo continued directing Joselito's films, but after *Saeta del Ruiseñor* (1957), still a co-production between Argos and Suevia Films, Joselito signed a contract with Cesáreo González, becoming his exclusive product. This move was extremely profitable. Due to elaborate marketing strategies *Saeta del ruiseñor* was an instant success. Cesáreo González, one of the most ambitious and powerful producers of the times, became Joselito's tireless promoter: circulating releases, organizing media extravaganzas and conducting publicity campaigns. He was known as down-to-earth, practical and unscrupulous. While González was looking for quick returns on his investments Joselito was undisputedly becoming the biggest child star that Spain had ever known.

El pequeño ruiseñor (1956), *Saeta del ruiseñor* (1957) and *El ruiseñor de las cumbres* (1958) loosely form a trilogy, and as already mentioned, cleverly synthesize and refashion formulas already successful with Joselito's predecessors. Drawing from different models, Joselito's opus dissolves the boundaries between genres, skillfully blending together the *folletín*, religious cinema and *melodramas folclóricos*.[12]

The first three films set the tone for most of the Joselito's opus. There is an obsessive replaying of certain themes: (1) real or apocryphal orphanhood; family discord; restoration of the broken familial ties; (2) maternal and paternal oedipal dramas; (3) absence of the erotic and sexual elements; (4) profound religious sentiment; (5) disinterest in the material and elevation of the spiritual realm; (6) lack of social conflict; (7) social and rural immobility of the traditional Spain accompanied by the virtual nonexistence of the outside world. A detailed reading of all Joselito's films is beyond the scope of this chapter, so it is limited to some motifs and repetitious fantasmatic scenarios which provide a common thread between the films.

As Terenci Moix observed, it seemed as if Joselito was a professional orphan ('Joselito, de profesión huerfanito'). This role was his second skin and was so inseparable from his screen persona that the second film, *Saeta del ruiseñor*, where Joselito lives in a 'normal' family, is quite conspicuous. His films' elemental affective charge stem from real or apocryphal orphanhood. Regardless if one reads orphanhood as a traumatic replaying of the post-war devastation or a cleverly manipulated formula with charged melodramatic potential, what is impressive is its insistent repetition. It was replayed and exploited for over a decade, persisting throughout Joselito's entire opus, even his Latin American odyssey and later 'urban' films.

Besides absent parents, another key affective charge of Joselito's opus comes from maternal and paternal oedipal dramas that enable cathartic restoration of the symbolic order at the end of the films. *El pequeño ruiseñor* is illustrative of this scenario. To recapitulate the plot, *El pequeño ruiseñor* is modeled on the protagonist of *Campanera*, the eminent song of the period and a central part of film's diagesis. The song is about a 'fallen' woman and functions as the driving force of the narrative that tells the story of Joselito's mother, an adulterous woman carried away by a passion that leads her to abandon her child. Eloping with a flamenco singer, she has left Joselito into care of her father. Joselito's grandfather renounces the daughter, raising Joselito to believe that his mother is a Holy Virgin. After her lovers' death the mother attempts to return to the village, but her father is unforgiving and does not accept her back. Years pass by, and she is finally forgiven and reunited with her son. Even Gonzalo, the man she was supposed to have married before she eloped with Joselito's biological father, forgives her and offers once again to marry her. The only condition is that Joselito be sent to study with priests, since he is a reminder of her 'infidelity'. Despite being torn about the decision the mother nevertheless consents. Not being able to bear the 'second' separation from his mother, Joselito runs away from the monastery to return home. He overhears a violent discussion between Gonzalo and his mother and learns the whole truth. Running away in distress, he is run over by a herd of bulls. In the last scene, Joselito, virtually on his death bed can only be saved by a blood transfusion. In the film's climactic scene Gonzalo has a change of heart; his blood miraculously matches the child's, and the transfusion is successful. After his recovery Joselito is accepted and reintegrated into the family.

Maternal and paternal dramas are tightly woven together in Joselito's opus, even in *El ruiseñor de las cumbres* where, as Elena claims, 'las relaciones paterno-filiales emergen a primer plano' (2001: 51). Joselito is reintegrated into the family only after his adoptive father's blood literally flows through his veins. The moment Joselito is integrated into the family and symbolic order he stops singing. The 'loss of voice' enables him to utter 'father, father, father', the last words of *El pequeño ruiseñor*. The filial (melo)drama is the emotional high-point of the film as well as its closure. The moment of blood transfusion and the loss of voice also symbolizes the rift induced in the hypothetical mother–child unity. In the transfusion scene it is clear that the reconfiguration of the family is enabled by maternal sacrifice. The mother, haunted by the loss, is confined to the melodramatic register. The scene is charged not because of the reinstating of the family but because of the mother's agony of knowing and accepting renunciation of her passion as a price to pay for the restoration of the symbolic order. Joselito's entry into language (father, father) is accompanied by the mother's double loss: of her son and of the flamenco lover, her true passion.

Despite the 'final' loss and sacrifice the mother is the only character who has access to emotional excess, pleasure and desire throughout the film. Joselito is told that his mother is the Holy Virgin, but her expansive passion is obviously incongruous with the virginal frame that she is given. The mother's very desire is the arresting detail in the film, 'an element which rises from the scene, shoots out of it like an arrow, and pierces [the spectator]' (Barthes 1981: 26). In the historical period in which, as Carmen Martín Gaite remarks, two key words of the Francoist lexicon, restriction and rationing, suffered a semantic displacement into other realms (gender relationships), the erotic force itself was the ultimate taboo. In the film where there is no explicit erotic force the voice itself is most eroticized, displaced onto Joselito's passionate singing. The son's voice maps out the mother' erotic passion. The audio fetish; that is, the mother's bond to the son's singing is evocative of her true love, the flamenco singer. Joselito's singing is also an attempt to grasp what is essentially indecipherable in the mother's (other's, mOther's) desire. Despite its conservative lesson, narrative closure and the final reintegration of mother and the son into the symbolic order, the film allows a multiplicity of identifications and readings. Especially since 'heavy censorship made Spanish audiences adept at the art of resignification' (Labanyi 1997: 216). Privileging of the attachment between mother and son explodes the family framework and the conventional song becomes a subversive element that can undermine the very ideological machine to which it belongs.

The visual claustrophobia of Joselito's films mirrors a matrix of the immobility of the rural and the static social relationships idealized by Francoism. The establishing shot sutures the spectator in the immobility of Joselito's world, and it seems as if the very same footage was used for the first three films. There is a virtual non-existence of the outside world, and everything occurs within the boundaries of the village and the path between the village and surrounding pastures. Profoundly tied to this immobility, Joselito played essentially the same character: simple, humble, honorable and religious. On the other hand he was also a voice of desire, being a locus of tensions as much as resolutions. His songs seem to 'exert pressure on time itself, generating an affect of temporal anamorphosis, extending the dragging of time well beyond what we perceive as justified by the requirements of narrative movement' (Žižek 2001: 102). Multi-layered text and Joselito's singing disturb and explode the framework of the Francoist monolitic project. The tensions burst out in songs. Affective charge of flamenco and melodramatic imagination interlock powerfully. The excessive pathos and emotions of flamenco fit well with the excessive traits of melodrama, one of the key genres of Joselito's opus. This configuration has a subversive potential. Even though it 'may not set out to subvert or undermine conventional values…in its fascination with power, eroticism, and violence, melodrama inevitably unleashes a host of cultural antagonisms' (Landy 1998: 28).

The conflictual scenarios described above are tied to the profound religious sentiment of the rural communities, the exclusive settings of Joselito's early cinema. The films are best understood when seen within the context of what Timothy Mitchell terms, 'passional culture', that is; Andalusia's cult of Passion, rituals of Semana Santa (Holy Week), '[Andalusian] powerful and heterodox retelling of Christ's ordeal', elevation of poverty, and 'Andalusia's penitential concept of philanthropy [that] endowed [the poor] with an almost magical role' (1990: 1; 99).

One of the obstinate traits in most of the films, the disinterest in the material and elevation of the spiritual realm, is deeply grounded in 'passional culture'. Joselito's relationship to money is never self-serving or instrumental. It is always geared towards charitable affairs: in *Saeta del ruiseñor* money is needed to recuperate the eyesight of his blind friend Alicia; in *El ruiseñor de las cumbres* Joselito consents to Pepino's 'show business proposal' only after he witnesses the scene of his drunken, abusive father stealing money from his mother; in *Escucha mi canción* he takes money from the wealthy impresario who manages him in order to share it with the troupe of impoverished travelling performers. The films are full of popular sayings and clichés about the poor. Tied to the Francoist ideological project of sublimation of poverty, they function to rationalize the socioeconomic inequities.

The sublimation of poverty goes hand in hand with concealment of the social conflict. The social status quo is justified and there is a lack of conflict even among the most obvious antagonistic elements: between a poor musician performing for the wealthy landowner (*Ruiseñor de las cumbres*), a town's major and its poor (*Saeta del ruiseñor*) and between the wealthy impresario and Joselito (*Escucha mi canción*). In its portrayal of social relations Joselito's cinema mirrors 'Holy Week in southern Spain [that] represents the canny symbiosis of rich and poor, oppressors and oppressed' (Mitchell 1990: 7). The constant presence of the figure of 'the sacrificial Christ has been the perfect catalyst for the rich-poor symbiosis, for He is simultaneously Lord and Master, poor and defunct, a powerful judge, an obedient Son, and a model prisoner' (Mitchell 1990: 82).

Joselito and his companions perform for the wealthy and entertain them. The wealthy on the other hand 'collect' their poor, take them into their homes to perform and patronize them. (*Ruiseñor de las cumbres*, *Saeta del ruiseñor*, *Escucha mi canción* are just a few obvious examples.) The poor and the rich are tied together by 'an emotional consensus' (Mitchell 1990: 7) since 'upper-class interest in under-class expressive styles goes back a very long way in Spain, especially in southern Spain, where the symbolic and religious aspects of poverty played a key role in the ideology of aristocratic Catholics' (Mitchell 1994: 99).

Joselito is always demonstrating his religious devotion: he carves saints, baptizes lost animals, takes care of an abandoned hermitage, prays for the reconciliation of his parents, takes vows to cure the blind girl, asks humbly for the Virgin to protect him on a voyage across the Atlantic, and so on and so forth. The second film, *Saeta del ruiseñor*, illustrates well the ways in which Joselito's films derive emotional charge from religious elements. As the title indicates, Joselito (*el pequeño ruiseñor*) sings *saetas* in his village celebration of Semana Santa. The *Saeta* (a Passional *copla*), a main narrative vehicle of the *Semana Santa* (Holy Week), narrates the Passion: arrest, torture and execution of Christ.[13] Flamenco professionals monopolized the public singing of *saetas* in the early twentieth century, replacing its sacred character by the *siguiriya*.

Saeta in particular and flameneco in general, as Mitchell has shown, is an offshoot of modernization with profound ties to both religious sentiment and marginalized 'underclass' culture: 'musical forms of great emotional expressiveness, perfected in the hothouse environment of an ethnic drinking subculture came back to the larger culture to offer emotional salvation to all' (1994: 142). *Saeta* (flamenco) is thus a musical style marked by hybridity and negotiation between religious sentiment and modern forms.[14] The presence of flamenco in Joselito's opus is therefore not a question of entertainment, but an articulation of the passage from the traditional to secularized society; 'not one that has simply left the religious elements of its tradition behind, but one that continues to live them as traces' (Vattimo 1992: 40). The passage between autarky and rapid capitalistic development of the times is both marked by accommodation to the new and imbued by nostalgia since '[o]n the one hand, capitalism entails the radical secularization of social life...[but] this reduction of all heavenly chimeras to brutal economic reality generates a spectrality of its own' (Žižek 2001: 103). Joselito's cinema did not appeal because of its faithful depiction of reality but because the audience itself, confronted with challenges of modernization, emigration to the city and urban life, responded above all to this spectralization that was embodied in Joselito's uncanny voice.[15]

Marisol: *La vida es una tómbola*

La vida es una tómbola, tom, tom, tómbola.
La vida es una tómbola, tom, tom, tómbola.
De luz y de color.
De luz y de color.
Y todos en la tómbola tom, tom, tómbola.
Y todos en la tómbola tom, tom, tómbola.
Encuentran un amor.
¡Tómbola!

(*Tómbola*; my transcription)

After Goyanes' daughter Mari Carmen called her father's attention to Marisol's performance on Tico's and Yale's celebrated television programme, Manuel Goyanes did not wait long before signing an exclusive contract with her. Goyanes belonged to the Francoist elite and was a producer with high connections in powerful places. Nevertheless, as seen in the eclectic nature of the films that he produced, the profit was more important for him than ideological loyalty. By the time he signed a contract with Marisol, Goyanes had already produced several films by 'leftist' director Antonio Bardem: *Muerte de un ciclista*, *Calle mayor* and *La venganza*. He was also interested in José Luis Borau's and Jesús Fernández Santos' script: *Cien dólares al mes*, a project that he dropped upon Marisol's discovery. She was his sole project from then on and a major source of his profits.

Goyanes did not only have an exclusive contract with Pepa Flores/Marisol but he also 'adopted' her, bringing her from Málaga to live with his own family. Abruptly taken from her roots and family, she was transposed from the poorest section of Málaga (el barrio de Capuchinos) to the fanciest one of Madrid (la calle Serrano). As Francisco Umbral would sarcastically remark: 'Marisol era un ángel con rebequita que había llegado del barrio de "Tira y chupa" de Málaga, un rayo de sol financiero que hizo millonario al señor Goyanes' (1991: 19). Her real name, Pepa Flores, was too plain for a future star, and Goyanes, her 'adoptive' father, named her Marisol. The naming was just a first step in her 're-fashioning'. Marisol herself recalls: 'se ocupaban de comprarme la ropa, los calcetines que tenía que usar, la forma del peinado y todo…Me enseñaron hasta cómo tenía que comer. Me pusieron profesores de cante, de baile y de ballet' (Morales: 1979a: 27). Class differences and tensions were an underlying theme during her stay with the Goyanes. Marisol resented her mother's tratment: 'A mi madre, cuando venía a verme de Málaga, los Goyanes la ponían a comer en la cocina, con las criadas' (Morales 1979a: 27) and felt like a lower class entertaining toy forcefully incorporated into Goyanes' upper-middle-class family.

Once re-fashioned, renamed and refined, Marisol starred in 21 films in a career that lasted from 1960 to 1985. Luis Lucia directed the first three films that became the core of the Marisol myth. In film circles Luis Lucia's name was associated with entertainment and

Figure 3.2. Marisol in her hit film *Tómbola*, 1962.

popular cinema.[16] After graduating from law school he was a legal consultant for CIFESA (La Compañía Industrial Film Española S.A.) in Valencia.[17] Soon thereafter he moved to production and direction. CIFESA was losing markets and tried to substitute historical epics with comedies and popular films that gave quick returns on the investments. Lucia was a welcomed addition to CIFESA since his preference for popular cinema fit the company's own reorganization in times of changes and crisis.

After his 1943 debut *El 13-13*, Luis Lucia was steadily gaining reputation: *La princesa de los Ursinos* (1947), *Currito de la Cruz* (1948), *La duquesa de Benamejí* (1949), *El sueño de Andalucía* (1950), *Lola la piconera* (1951), *Jeromín* (1951), *Gloria Mairena* (1952), *Cerca de la ciudad* (1952), *La Hermana San Suplicio* (1952), *Morena Clara* (1954). As these films show, Luis Lucia was skillfully moving from one to another genre; equally comfortable directing folkloric films, melodramas, religious cinema, films with child protagonists, light comedies and espionage films. He directed many stars of Spanish cinema: Amparo Rivelles, Ana Mariscal, Luis Mariano, Marujita Diaz, Lola Flores and Fernando Fernán Gómez among others. He also had experience directing child actors, having worked with both Pepito Moratalla and Jaime Blanch. However, after Marisol's debut in *Un rayo de luz* (1960), his career was exclusively oriented towards three female child stars: Marisol, Rocío Dúrcal and Ana Belén. Goyanes could not have made a better choice for Marisol's director since Luis Lucia was extraordinarily able: responding to the ever-changing directions of commercial cinema, skillfully blending eclectic mixtures of genres and always keeping his audience entertained.

Marisol's first three films, directed by Lucia, established a matrix that remained a crucial part of her later films. Again, a detailed reading of all her films is beyond the scope of the chapter, but I will single out some significant underlying fantasmatic scenarios that tie the films together. Some recurrent themes are: (1) real or apocryphal orphanhood; family discord; restoration of broken familial ties; (2) class mobility; (3) Marisol as the epitome of modernity; (4) secularization of religious values; (5) presence of the erotic and sexual elements displaced on the child; (6) lack of social conflict; (7) emphasis on fantasy and pleasure.

While some of the above scenarios closely resemble ones from Joselito's opus, others perfected and modernized his successful formulas. They were both on-screen orphans, but they embodied this role quite distinctly. Joselito was ridden by melancholic longing, as Moix remarked, 'ofrecía un aspecto desvalido, un aire de patetismo…' (1993: 270). Imbued with the heaviness that seemed to engulf the spectators, Joselito dwelled 'in a kind of uncanny "massiveness"…and [his] spiritual dimension stems from the damp heaviness of earth' and his cinema is a cinema of loss and lost objects (Žižek 2001: 102).[18]

While Joselito was stranded in the melancholic mode, Marisol occupied a space of future possibilities: she confronted life with ebullient wit, *desparpajo* (self-assurance) and *simpatía*. Marisol's optimism was contagious. In the spirit of Bobby Deglané's 'Operation Happiness' she assured her audience that the life is indeed a raffle. *Tómbola*, one of Marisol's most popular musical hits, is illustrative of both the spirit of her films and the spirit of the times. The song is reminiscent of other light songs that swept Europe in the early 1960s. It was the time of pop hits and Eurovision song contests, and 'los gustos del público estaban evolucionando hacia la modernidad, personificada en la música ligera con sus victorias sobre la copla, antes dominante' (Moix 1993: 275).

Marisol's striking appearance contributed to her becoming an icon of modernity:

> Rubia y de ojos azules en un país latino en que predominan las morenas, pero preservando su identidad y gracejo andaluz, ofrecía un *look* muy personalizado en nuestro *star-system*…resultaba exótica y próxima a la vez, reuniendo el atractivo y las ventajas de ambas condiciones… (Gubern 2001: 13)

Her image was carefully fashioned and deliberately distanced from the stereotypical images of the Andalusian stars that preceded her. Like her fictional double in *Un rayo de luz* and *Búsqueme a esa chica*, she was 'sophisticated' and rid of her lower class Andalusian traits. She was carefully tutored: her accent was de-andalusionized, she was given musical lessons, piano, English, and so on and so forth. Detached from her roots she was put through intense exercise of cultivation, sophistication and modernization. She was an antecedent of postmodern simulacra and pure outwardness.

Marisol was a teenage idol and an icon of popularity. Her roles were seductive; she generated order and disorder as if by caprice; fantasy and imagination were crucial elements of her films. An entire industry was put to use exploiting every facet of her fame: records, dolls, magazines, comics, scrapbooks and toys. Records from her films were designed as vehicles for promoting and furthering Marisol's career. She fit everywhere: equally comfortable in aristocratic households (*Un rayo de luz*, *Tómbola*), middle-class milieu (*Ha llegado un ángel*) and in struggling working-class families (*Marisol rumbo al Río*). Even though some of Marisol's films would epitomize the *arriviste* material aspirations of the Spanish middle class during the economic development of the 1960s, her first and third film are aristocratic in tone (the first one is an adaptation of *Little Lord Fauntleroy*). She also epitomized devastating poverty: in *Marisol rumbo al Río* she lives in a *corrala* (tenement) reminiscent of her own childhood spent in the poorest section of Málaga and *Cabriola* is set in a shanty town on the outskirts of Madrid. She was equally loving to servants and aristocrats but would often seek alliance with the former since they were complicit with her goals to change and restructure the family and integrate all the antagonistic social elements into an harmonious community. The social immobility of Joselito's films was replaced in Marisol's opus by porous boundaries and continual movements between different social strata. The erroneous impression that Marisol exemplified solely middle-class settings comes from her ability to swiftly move from one milieu to another.

Marisol also exemplifies progressively secularized culture. *Tómbola* is illustrative of this phenomenon. Even though the film is a girl spy/mystery movie, the plot is embedded in religious background. The plot revolves around a painting stolen from El Prado: 'La Madona de las Rosas'. While trying to convince thieves to return the painting Marisol gives a tearful speech on TV:

> Y si, en vez de reíros como estáis haciendo, devolvierais el cuadro, la Virgen María de las Rosas y el Niño Jesús regordete se pondrían muy contentos. Y a lo mejor [yo] convencería al juez de que hiciera la vista gorda. (*Tómbola*; my transcription)

During her adventure she is protected by the Virgin and Jesus. She also seeks a priest's alliance in 'recovering' the stolen painting. However, even when Marisol's films 'promote' Christian values they are abstracted and embedded in entertainment. As if the message of her films aligned with Opus Dei's mission of 'disseminating of spiritual values through secular venues and the sanctification of the secular world' (Payne 1987: 437, 438). Like Joselito, Marisol is not attracted to the material but while Joselito's rejection of the material is grounded in deep religiosity Marisol's is in pop psychology. Despite the morality of the story even priests and thieves are figures of entertainment, bursting into songs and choreographed dance numbers. The religious matrix is a stage for mis-en-scène of Marisol's musical and dancing talent.

Dancing, music, optimism, entertainment, effortless moves between social classes, lack of conflict and exaggerated happiness were tied to their repressed underside: the presence of the erotic and sexual elements displaced onto the child. This underlying sexual tension did not escape the two emblematic intellectual figures, Francisco Umbral and Manuel Vicent, who are known as chroniclers of 'Marisol's decade'. Román Gubern also noted that Marisol had 'un cuerpo elástico que podía invitar a paidofilia' (Gubern 2001: 13). Umbral, who often focuses on apparently 'insignificant' details, was especially attentive to Marisol's sexualized figure. Just as he will later focus on Ana Torrent, Umbral obsesses over Marisol's adolescent, growing body and describes Marisol 'como Lolita de Nabokov, "a las doce era una adorable criatura y a los catorce una lamentable anciana"' (1991: 17).[19]

While Umbral 'plays the part of the paedophile' Manuel Vicent is less ironic and conscious about his own libidinal involvement in writing about Marisol's body. His article denounces Marisol's explotation but is also problematic in itself since he finds pleasure in detailed and sadistic descriptions of Marisol as an animal:

> Debe de ser terrible que a una niña le apunten las tetitas en la rebeca bajo la mirada espesa de un país entero, estar consciente de que treinta millones de contribuyentes miden cada mañana en su memoria el crecimiento de tu culo…la alzada que va tomando la grupa, la densidad de los muslos, la tripita colgada de bantú que crece bajo la camisa, el hocico que se hincha…Goyanes le fajaba el pecho a Marisol, hacía con ella una especie de afeitado taurino con esparadrapo para que a la novilla no le asomaran las puntas. (Vicent 1981: 144, 145)

The infantile sexuality persistently protrudes from the seemingly innocent scenarios of Marisol's films. The deceptive surface of her films is imbued with surplus meaning, and the domain of unsaid and prohibited produces lasting tensions. The idyllic moments that Marisol ('the sunbeam') exemplified so well were disturbed by the effect of the *point de capiton* (the quilting point). The effect of the *point de capiton* is manifested when

> a perfectly 'natural' and 'familiar' situation is denatured, becomes 'uncanny,' loaded with horror and threatening possibilities, as soon as we add to it a small supplementary feature, a detail that 'does not belong,'

> that sticks out, is 'out of place,' does not make any sense within the frame of the idyllic scene. (Žižek 1991: 88)

The quilting point resides in a tension between the idyllic surface and the concealed infantile sexuality that cannot be voiced but is imbedded in the very materiality and subtext of Marisol's films and her relationship with various characters: Mr. Morrison (*Búsqueme a esa chica*), a group of rowdy students (*Ha llegado un angel*), three thieves (*Tómbola*) and an aging torero Ángel Peralta (*Cabriola*).

España es diferente: The new direction

As Marisol matured, a conflict arose between the established image of a child star and the reality of adolescence, so childhood would be arrested as long as possible. Joselito was likewise not allowed to grow up. Both were forced to linger in an indeterminable space so as not to shatter the image so dear to their audience, and so profitable to their producers. Age was retarded in stages. Joselito 'se hizo de un adolescente un niño, y de un adulto un adolescente' (Heredero 1993: 231) and with Marisol 'una legión de consumidores anónimos haya cometido un estupro psicológico con una niña que no podía ser adolescente, con una adolescente a la que no dejaban ser mujer porque se venía abajo el negocio' (Vicent 1981: 144).[20] Marisol would complain that well into her late teens, producers were bounding her breasts and forcing her to wear braids (Morales 1979b: 28). Despite the multiple optical illusions to make Marisol and Joselito look like children, at some point, the producers would have to accept their adolescence. So by 1963 and 1964 both had finally abandoned their infantile roles. To capitalize on their name recognition, the producers searched for a different star image that would entail a modern look, a taste for pop music and sexual interests. However, Joselito's attempt at transition fared poorly, due in part to the loss of his signature voice: 'Empezó a cambiarme la voz a los dieciocho años, pero creo que Cesáreo González había ganado tantos millones que no le preocupó demasiado. Aunque, eso sí, hicieron todo lo posible para que el cambio no me afectase, sin traumas' (Moix 1993: 275). Despite these shortcomings, Joselito played Johnny in his first *ye-yé* film *Loca juventud* in 1963.[21] He sang: 'Me llaman loco porque anhelo/Robar estrellas en el cielo/Para tenerlas en tu pelo/Loco por ti/Chico loco/A mí me llaman chico loco/Y me lo llaman por quererte a ti'. Johnny was discordant from Joselito's earlier role. As an urban adolescent, Johnny was flip and spoiled in contrast to Joselito's simple and good nature. Despite the new persona, Joselito somehow continued representing 'la imagen de una España pasada de moda, que no era de buen tono recordar' (Moix 1993: 275). The audience rejected '[u]n Joselito inverosímil subido a un coche *sport* y alentando a toda una panda juvenil mientras cantaba con acentos *ye-yés* un *twist* titulado *Chico loco*' (Moix 1993: 275). The discordance was so great that Moix adds that this image 'queda mucho más ridículo hoy que todos sus folletines rurales de infancia' (Moix 1993: 275).

In the transition from child to adolescent, Marisol had an inherent advantage. Because she was a child at the beginning of modernity, her transition did not entail a cultural shift. Her first film, as an adolescent, *Búsqueme a esa chica*, came out in 1964 when she was 16 years old. Goyanes had paired her up with *Dúo Dinámico*. Manuel Arcusa and Ramón de la Calva made their debut as *The Dynamic Boys* in 1959 at a Mediterranean music festival with the promising song *Quisiera ser estudiante*. In 1961 they took the second place in the Benidorm music festival with their hit song *Quisiera ser* and in 1965 *Dúo Dinámico* would fill the niche equivalent to Beatle-mania. Not only did Marisol team up professionally with *Dúo Dinámico* but during the filming of *Búsqueme a esa chica* emerged a romance with Ramón de la Calva. Regardless of its truth, the rumour itself was highly effective in marketing the new image of the former child star. Indeed, a liaison with a rising pop star epitomized modernity and pop (*cultura ye-yé*).

Búsqueme a esa chica is set in Palma de Mallorca and also reflects Spain's comparative advantage in the modern world economy: tourist destination. The mobility of Marisol was not confined to Spain. In October of 1965 Marisol went to Germany to sing for audience that were guest workers. She toured Göppingen, Düsseldorf, Möenchengladbach, Darmstadt, Hannover, Grossheim, Wiesbaden, Frankfurt and Bad Godesberg. The event was organized by Instituto Español de Emigración and sponsored by the Ministry of Information and Tourism.

> Tras proyectarse su última película, interpretó *La luna y el toro*, *Cabriola* y dos o tres cantes aflamencados que susicitaron el entusiasmo entre una concurrencia de procedencia mayoritariamente andaluza…aparece en una boda entre dos emigrantes para rubricar y prestigiar el suceso, cena con los diplomáticos y el director de la orquesta del restaurante la invita a llevar batuta mientras los músicos le dan pasodoble…antes de la actuación en Göppingen, donde trabajan cinco mil españoles, visitó dos hospitales, donde se encontraban sendos emigrantes que no podían asistir a la actuación. (Barreiro 1999: 80)

The visit to Germany was in keeping with the country's new role in Europe, indicating the rising economic importance of Spanish emigrants and their continual identification with Spanish culture. The careers of Joselito and Marisol were now reflecting the confluence of emigration, tourism, and the changing global economic flows and patterns.

Both stars in mid-career converge on a similar image of youthfulness, modernity, and a Spain that is able to offer 'everything under the sun'. Even though it may have disappointed the fans of Joselito-the-child star, Joselito-the-adult ditched his peasant *boina* (beret) and donned chic outfits, not to dance flamenco but the *twist*. Similarly,

Marisol leaves behind the white socks and braids for smart clothes and pop tunes. After breaching the void of signification, Joselito and Marisol will gradually embrace Western-style commodification of culture. Errant voices that hovered in a gap of *decenio bisagra* would continue resonating in the air but would be articulated in different fashion. The *Zeitgeist* marched on. The pair would come to symbolize the Spain of *desarrollo*. Gone were the Imperialist pretentions and the National-Catholic moralizing. The National-Catholic discourse was reduced to a simple and catchy slogan: 'España es diferente'. By this time, Franco, who now excercised a power that he no longer truly understood, had himself become a simulacrum. Thus, one can say that the rise and mid-career of Joselito and Marisol corresponded closely and curiously to Franco's virtual downfall.

As their mid-career advanced, both Marisol's and Joselito's films were becoming more and more predictable. The ambiguity that once made them fascinating was disappearing. Ironically, Marisol, always the 'modern' girl, was being identified with flamenco and the corrida de toros (*Solos los dos*, *Cabriola*) and other clichés of 'Spanishness'. Joselito and Marisol went on 'marketing' Spain abroad, almost as if employed by the Ministry of Information and Tourism, appropriating whatever was popular, be it toros, fútbol or music. But this reduction of their filmography to demonstration of Spanish difference had lost the subversive quality of being the voice of intrusion; 'pinning down the voice to the letter, limiting its disruptive force, to dissipating its inherent ambiguity' (Dolar 1996: 22).

The traumatic awakening

The effect of saturation was induced by the repetition of overworked formulas and it eventually led to a traumatic awakening of the child stars. First of all, they discarded the pseudonyms and claimed their original names. Reclaiming one's name is also repudiating the child-star system since the stage name was a trademark of their commodity status. Reclaiming their names destroyed the illusion that the person and the performer were one and the same.

In 1963, 20 years old and nine films later, Joselito finally left the 'Joselito role' behind, and became successively Tony, Tomy, Johnny and Marcos. Rather than denouncing Cesáreo González, and the system that profiteered off him, he would emphasize that he was not the classically exploited child star:

> A mí me han dado lo que quería, inclusive a veces me han dado mucho más de lo que pedía y me han tratado de verdad con una generosidad y una amabilidad y un cariño enormes, inclusive los que estaban haciendo negocio conmigo. (Moix 1993: 276)

Nevertheless his last film, *Prisionero en la ciudad*, can be read as denounciation of the world of entertainment. Marcos Villena (Joselito) feels stranded in sophisticated urban environment, and returns to his village and his origins. The film is a Spanish version of *Splendor in the Grass*. Joselito, in his very last film, returns to the origin that were from the beginning always already invented. Thus, the last film is reminiscent of the quest for origins, so prominent in the earlier works, but even more displaced, functioning as the citation of the post-war films promoting idyllic, rural Spain in contrast to the troubled modernity, urban decay and corruption.

Marisol was not so charitable in reflections on her past. After years of mending fictional families on film, she broke with her film family in life. She denounced her producer Manuel Goyanes, divorced his son Carlos, and exposed the details of her exploitation. Perhaps in protest to her own commodification, she embraced leftist causes in the transition period, and started to work exclusively with the filmmakers who directed social commentary. Finally, in 1977 in Mario Camus' *Los días del pasado* she reclaimed her identity and accent, erased since childhood, by playing the role of an Andalusian teacher. In short, Marisol repudiated the image of the white muse of Francoism and exemplary child of Francoist times. Umbral colorfully phrases it:

> Pepa Flores asesina a Marisol, con el cuchillo de desescamar besugos, en un apartamento oscuro de Capitán Haya, sobre la moqueta color rata. Pepa Flores, madre madrasta de Marisol, asesina su adolescencia cursi y vendida sobre la moqueta color abandono, color vacío, color tiempo. (1991: 19)

Both Joselito and Marisol, each in their own way, participated in a symbolic settling of accounts. Their voices emerged in the clamour between autarky and the rising consumerism of the 1960s. At times, they resonated with progress, as they illuminated the problematic course of modernity. However, ultimately, they turned into wounded voices of the transition. Since their first appearance on the screen, where Joselito's sweet voice filled the village cobblestone streets and Marisol's equally sweet voice gave life to a lifeless mansion in Italy, both children remained tied to the construction of a national image. Their singing voices and careers projected special effects onto a screen designed by the dictatorship. However, they were also a nation's recalcitrant remainder, resistant to the signifying operations. Like an *acousmêtre* in film, they were a talking and acting shadow of the dictatorship. The body of their work is alluring because of our fascination with errant voices. Both Joselito and Marisol haunted the foundation of the dictatorship and later could be heard exposing its structural flaws.

Indeed, their uncanny voices were haunting since 'haunting belongs to the structure of every hegemony' (Derrida 1994: 37). Marisol and Joselito were the voices that addressed Spain through 'the enigma of the otherness of a human voice that cries out from the wound, a voice that witnesses a truth that [they] cannot [have] fully known' (Caruth 1996: 3). In as much as the nation, a fictional or enunciated construct, 'in addition to being "narrated" is also insistently sung and danced' (López 1997: 310). For years afterward Spaniards would persist in re-evaluating the past and coming to terms with it. Paradoxically then, the voices that were supposed to epitomize what is national were the very same voices that would finally point out what lingered buried in the national narrative.[22]

Notes

1. Performed by the Coro de Real Monasterio de Guadalupe.

2. The intensity of the voice is related to its source offscreen. Michel Chion points out that 'so-called synchronous sounds are most often forgotten as such, being 'swallowed up' by the fiction' (1999: 3).

3. Joselito is not really an orphan, since his mother is alive, but he is made to believe so.

4. Discussing folkloric musicals of the early Franco period Jo Labanyi points out that '1940s *folklóricas* dramatize the superior oral immediacy and authenticity of folksong, represented mainly by the female voice, by comparison with male written culture' (1997: 224). However, in 'Musical Battles: Populism and Hegemony in the Early Francoist Folkloric Film Musical' she also points out that in those films "'the people" are constructed not as "natural" but rather as "natural or born performers"' (1997: 219).

5. In the mother's own words her only success in life was being a good 'wife' to Carlos. She renounces the child in order not to interfere with her ascendance to a higher class. Thus, Marisol, like Joselito is only symbolically the orphan.

6. Chion also writes: 'When the acousmatic presence is a voice, and especially when this voice has not yet been visualized—that is, when we cannot yet connect it to a face—we get a special being, a kind of talking and acting shadow to which we attach the name acousmêtre' (1999: 21). He adds that 'Apollinaire, who loved rare words, wrote a poem in 1913 entitled 'Acousmate', about a voice that resonates in the air' (1999: 19).

7. Jo Labanyi points out that 'the vast majority of early Francoist *folklóricas* dramatize a fantasy of miscegenation through the surrender of the low-class, usually gypsy, female singing lead to the higher-class, white male hero' (1997: 224).

8. Their careers continued during the First Development Plan (announced in 1963 and introduced in 1964) and by the end of the so called 'la década Fraga' (1962–69) Joselito will retire and Marisol will start working exclusively with the politically engaged directors Antonio Bardem, Mario Camus, and Carlos Saura.

9. See García Delgado (1986).

10. Jaime García Herranz, who adapted *Little Lord Fauntleroy* for Marisol's first film, also worked on Joselito's third one, *El ruiseñor de las cumbres.*

11. Commenting on Antonio del Amo's trajectory and the ideological clash between his ideals and his films Heredero writes: 'La filmografía de este hombre (crítico y ensayista de *Popular Films* y de *Nuestro Cinema*, colaborador de *Mundo Obrero*, responsable de la sección de cine en la Brigada Líster del ejército republicano y autor de varios libros teóricos) gira ya definitivamente, desde que tropieza con Joselito, hacia una producción de consumo y de mera supervivencia profesional, después de haber realizado antes ensayos tan interesantes como *Día tras día*, *Puebla de las mujeres* o *Sierra Maldita*' (1993: 232).

12. A *folletín* is a 'trabajo literario publicado por entregas en un periódico, novela de enredo de gran simplicidad sicológica, suceso o acontecimiento melodramático' (Pequeño Larousse, 1998).

13. In the glossary of *Passional Culture saeta* is defined as a Passional *copla*; *saeta afectiva*: a Passional *copla* whose primary purpose is to evoke emotion rather than narrate; *saeta carcelera*: any Passional *copla* sung by a prisoner or sung in a gruff or mournful prison house style; *saeta narrativa*: a Passional *copla* whose ostensible purpose is to narrate some moment or event of the Passion.

14. Demystifying flamenco and its association with the pure racial (gypsy) origins, Mitchell stresses its hybridity and ties to various underprivileged 'subcultures' of southern Spain. Some of the examples that Mitchell gives are: 'urban subproleteriat made up of poorly assimilated groups like moriscos, gitanos, beggars, peddlers, pícaros, criminals, and drifters' (1994: 67).

15. Since *saeta* is not accompanied by music the singer arrests the audience by the sheer power of his voice.

16. For a discussion of Luis Lucia and his film career see Labanyi (1997, 2002).

17. *Alba de América* (1951) was one of the famous CIFESA films. Despite its 'success' in obtaining national interest, 'cierra, con gran fracaso de público, la serie histórica de Juan de Orduña y marca el principio de la crisis y decadencia de CIFESA' (Ballesteros 1999: 63). CIFESA was closely related to the regime's ideological interests. Heredero points out that the *Alba de América* failure is 'el comienzo de la agonía para el ciclo historicista desarollado al amparo y para justificación de la autarquía' (1993: 16).

18. This is just one predominant trait of his music. I am not trying to suggest that there was no diversity to his musical opus since, as Terenci Moix points out 'las ilustraciones musicales de aquellas películas pasaron al disco en un *pot-pourri* que alternaba géneros diversos, para escándalo de los puristas y fascinación de los adictos' (1993: 273).

19. On Umbral and Torrent, see Smith (2000). Smith writes: 'The child actress Ana Torrent overwhelms Umbral: his forty years cannot withstand her pubescent thirteen, cannot bear to bear witness to the maturity which he had anticipated when first he saw her on screen' (2000: 17). Smith also adds that 'if journalist [Umbral] plays the part of the paedophile then the child herself is cast as "Lolita"' and that 'in the figure of the child...Umbral saw the body of the adolescent she was to become coming towards him: "nicely grown up, reader. Nicely grown up"' (2000: 36).

20. Heredero is citing from Jean-Claude Seguin's doctoral thesis *Joselito: la voix inhumaine. Du genre au corpus, du corpus à l'acteur.*

21. For the reading of exaltation of the working class in the film see Vidal Estévez (1999).

22. Writing about the contemporary postmodern performance *Cegada de amor*, which is a take on Francoists child prodigies, Paul Julian Smith remarks: 'For the void above which *Cegada de amor*'s flashy structure is constructed is the dictatorship itself, as invisible and as all-pervasive in the nightingales and sunbeams of the past as in the *mancheguita* who so uncannily and perilously persists in the present' (2000: 65).

CHAPTER IV

Spain's mass tourism: *Condenada belleza del mundo*

> Si la belleza de la corrida supone un régimen de latifundio responsible de la miseria del bracero andaluz; si el brillo del sol sirve de justificación a nuestra pereza y nos incita a cruzarnos de brazos, en buena hora desaparezcan sol y toros.
>
> – Juan Goytisolo, *El furgón de cola*[1]

The abundance of sunshine and the bullfight, symbolic of the landed gentry that Gotyisolo descries, became the elements that created the mass packaged tourism of the 1950s and 1960s, which put Spain on the map as a destination. The sun, a plentiful asset, in an otherwise struggling economy, would become central to Spain's dramatic rise as a world tourism power. Its commodification, together with the development of long stretches of virginal coastal land, became an essential force in carving Spain's place in the post-war European leisure industry. The marketing of sun, *torros* and other exotics such as *flamenco*, *el piropo* or *el donjuanismo* differentiated dictatorial Spain and irrevocably changed its direction, which at that time was already opening up to outside economic and social forces.[2] Simultaneously, the increasing arrival of tourists into Spain that had begun in the late 1950s was paralleled by Spanish emigration to northern Europe. The emergence of the tourism industry was concurrent with Spain's signing of bilateral emigration agreements with Switzerland, Germany and France.

Tourism and dictatorship, as Sasha Pack pointed out, 'the two prevailing emblems of the age, scarcely could appear more discordant' (2006: 1). Pointing to a main paradox of what he has called 'Europe's peaceful invasion of Franco's Spain', Pack adds:

> Franco, owing to his association with the fascist dictators, his austere Catholicism, and his contempt for liberal democracy, appeared anachronistic and isolated, the antithesis of reconstructed Western Europe. The tourists, by contrast, represented the hallmarks of postwar European civilization—consumer entitlement, transnational mobility, efficiency, comfort, and permissiveness. (2006: 1)

Pack signals the unresolved tension between the dictatorship's impulse to modernize and its lack of democratic institutions. However, the attempt to modernize while holding in abeyance negative forces of change, as perceived in Spanish context, eventually failed since modernization irrevocably compromised even the most resilient political and economic dictatorial structures. Franco's dictatorship and tourism programme, symbolic of two seemingly opposed worldviews and political systems, found ways to coexist throughout this period of intense socio-economic change; dictatorship and tourism were at once in profound disagreement while at the same time allied in an unlikely coalition. In the words of Justin Crumbaugh, 'the phenomena of tourism, in many ways, helped the regime stave off democracy paradoxically by articulating surprising continuities between the Franco dictatorship and the industrialized West' (2009: 6).

A historical overview of Spanish tourism

Spanish tourism has a surprisingly long history, dating back to 1905, at the creation of the Comisión Nacional de Turismo (State Tourism Commission) under Alfonso XIII, Spain's Bourbon monarch (1886–1931). The Comisión was the world's first such institution and it signalled the beginning of the growing importance of tourism and tourist revenues for the state. At this juncture, Spain had recently lost the last four remnants of its empire (Cuba, Puerto Rico, Philipines and Guam) and was underdeveloped by comparison to most other European industrial powers. It is significant that the creation of the Comisión, ahead of its time and symbolic of modernity, coincided with a traumatic colonial loss and crisis for Spain—a crisis that would only continue to intensify in the years to come. Nevertheless, in this initial period Spanish tourism parralleled broader European development in some areas, while lagging behind in others. The most acute problem was a considerable lack of infrastructure that limited the operational scope needed to take advantage of the abundant cultural and historical attractions Spain could offer foreign visitors.

The Comisión regulated the quality and prices of hotels and inns and promoted Spain's rich cultural heritage. This oversight and protocol for developing tourism was transferred to the Royal Tourism Commissariat, directed by Marqués de la Vega Inclán, that replaced the National Commission in 1911. This period, represented by the works of the State Tourism Commission and Royal Commissariat, as Pack emphasized, was 'heavily weighted toward promotion rather than industrial planning' (2006: 27).

In contrast, the subsequent period, under Primo de Rivera's dictatorship (1923–30), was devoted to massive public work projects with more attention paid to the modernization of the country. In 1928 a new tourist bureau, the Patronato Nacional de Turismo (PNT), replaced the Royal Tourism Commissariat. PNT was created to tackle problems related to the lack of basic infrastructure. Spain had to battle its inferior reputation abroad in regards to lack of necessary amenities, poor hygiene, insufficient water supply, inadequate roads and quality of tourist itineraries. This acute lack of infrastructure that still plagued most of the country was furthermore reinforced by an image of economic and cultural backwardness that was carried over from Romantic travelers of the nineteenth century. PNT was formed to mend deficiencies listed above such as 'highways for motorcoach excursions, tourist itineraries, custom and frontier crossing for tourists, lack of good hotels in some cities of renowned artistic interest and absolute scarcity of publicity abroad' (Pack 2006: 30).[3]

The years of the Second Republic (1931–36) brought a radical restructuring to the tourist sector led by the establishment of yet another entity: the Dirección General de Turismo (DGT). The Republican government housed it within the Ministry of the Interior and reduced the PNT to 'a small subdivision of the new bureau responsible for the Paradors program' (Pack 2006: 31). Furthermore, this government 'pursued a decentralized model, permitting local tourism initiative societies to carry out many of the functions previously performed by state appointees' (Pack 2006: 31). These innovative reforms were halted by the military uprising in July of 1936 and the consequent outbreak of Spanish Civil War, which brought an end to ambitious tourist projects of the Second Republic.

Until the beginning of Spanish Civil War, Spain was mostly in step with other European tourist development trends, but its path departs considerably during the Spanish Civil War. This understudied period has a remarkable history that goes beyond the scope of this chapter, such as the creation of battlefield tours (*Rutas de Guerra*) during which 'clients were transported to battle sites in chartered busses and subjected to politically charged narrations' (Pack 2006: 33). Regardless of these attempts to salvage tourism, war-torn Spain was not a fertile ground for the continuation of any development projects that had characterized the 1930s.

Tourism under Franco's regime could be roughly divided into three periods: (1) immediate post-war from 1939 to 1950; (2) beginning of the tourist breakthrough starting with the creation of the Ministry of Tourism in 1951; and (3) the tourist boom under Fraga Iribarne's presidency over the Ministry of Tourism (1962–69). The period studied in this book, 1954–64, encomposes both an incipient development of Spanish mass-tourism marked by the foundation of the Ministerio de Información y Turismo in 1951, and its peak years, marked by an unprecedented growth in tourism that started in the mid-1950s. While the years that frame this book do not correspond exactly to the above outlined periods, both 1954 and 1964 are pivotal years within these two developmental cycles, which marked inflections and drastic change to the Spanish economy.

The post-war period is not a story of smooth passage but instead one of tumultuous conflicts embodied in the struggle between different factions within the regime: among the many were the Falange, the military, the monarchists, the Church, the technocrats and the reformists. The discord was reflected in the steady institutional reorganization within the tourist sector: from specific Ministerial decrees and zoning laws to a more broad strategic realignement of various industrial interest groups.

Immediate post-war period (1939–50)

Spain was incapable of meaningful tourism after the war, but nevertheless used tourism as a propagandistic machine. Franco's war-time government established the National Tourism Service (*Servicio Nacional de Turismo*, SNT), then reorganized what was left of various tourism industry institutions. DGT was once again restored to the Ministry of the Interior under the leadership of Luis A. Bolín. Bolín, a journalist with Nationalist loyalties and political aspirations, became a key administrative voice for the tourism industry during this period. However, the real commitment to tourism came at the conclusion of the Second World War, when tourism started to function as a form of international engagement.[4]

In the mid-1940s, Spain had experienced political pressure and economic ostracism from most of its European neighbours due to its fascist past and repressive dictatorship. The country was excluded from most European politico-economic institutions such as OEEC (The Organization for European Economic Cooperation), UNESCO and the United Nations. In addition, the United States had left Spain out of the Marshall Plan, its European Recovery Program vital to reconstruction. Tourism was one of the very few avenues left for Spain to reconnect with the international world as well as one of the few revenue options in a weakened post-war economy.

There were two major issues that informed the Spanish government's outlook on tourism and its development. The first was the belief that international tourism as defined by crossing borders was 'a potential threat to the dictatorship's moral and economic autarky' (Pack 2006: 39). The policing of Spain's borders resulted in setting up very complex and cumbersome regulatory mechanisms such as customs regulations, tourist visas, exit permits, visitor registration requirements and more general control of tourist movement throughout the country. The most cumbersome was a triptych requirement of 'a complicated document to be presented at entry and exit points to demonstrate a clean police record, legitimate purpose for traveling, and prearrangement of all accommodations in the country' (Pack 2006: 53). The border restrictions were tied to external threats from the remnants of the Republican and international forces.

Outside Spain, the exiles still had hopes of contesting Franco's power during the 1940s, and there were several prominent *maquis* operations until as late as 1948.[5] The attempt to control movement was reinforced by other mechanisms detrimental to free tourist flow: monetary protectionism and high currency quotas.

The second trait that marked this period was the government's support for industrial autarky. As Pack has stressed: 'To satisfy his military and industrial constituencies, Franco emphasized industrial autarky throughout that decade [1940s], arguing that Spain could not rely on a hostile outside world for aid in industrialization and national defense' (2006: 40). The main promoter of industrial self-suficiency was Juan Antonio Suanzes who lead Instituto Nacional de Industria (INI) (1941) and became Minister of Industry and Commerce in 1945.[6] Suanzes was a firm believer in industrialist autarkist principles that relegated tourism to secondary place, regarding it only as 'temporary nourishment' (Pack 2006: 42). The nation's need for the foreign currency that tourism provided, however, created tension with these rigid and obsolete principles.

Overall, the important issues and challenges facing Spain at this time were politically motivated: post-war travel restrictions, border security and the rise of the black-market for Spanish currency largely due to unfavourable exchange rates. Despite the political limitations of the period, many important projects were put in motion. Even before 1945, DGT had established a hotel classification system, promoted hotel management through the Professional Hotel School in Madrid, and distributed low interest business loans known as Hotel Credit. A few years later, in 1949, Bolín, supported by INI's capital, created ATESA (Autotransporte Turístico Español). Under Bolín's leadership, DGT also started to look outside for the models of industrialized mass tourism, such as those practiced by the United States and Great Britain.[7] Bolín was a shrewd enterpreneur and politician and as Pack emphasized: 'Bolín…the erstwhile organizer of battlefield tours… quickly adopted an apolitical congeniality after World War II that would define the style of Spanish tourism authorities for the reminder of the dictatorship' (2006: 58).

As seen, propagandistic, xenophobic practices of the immediate post-war and the strict regulations of the early 1940s that accompanied it were slowly giving way to a more conventional business model that was better suited to a more open political climate and an ever-increasing volume of tourist traffic. In this new spirit, Spain concentrated on infrastructural shortcomings and on 'developing transportation and hospitality, leaving the organizing and sales of tour packages to agents in the country of origin. That this directly contradicted the nominally vertical or national-corporatist structure of Spain's tourism sector intervened little in their [planners] thinking…' (Pack 2006: 59). A broader subservience of tourism to industrial autarky was therefore undermined by practices that were directly opposed to it. In sum, while post-war travel restrictions and border security eased in the following years, the denigration of tourism as a source of revenue and tensions and contradictions that surrounded it continued well until Fraga's coming into the Ministry of Tourism in 1962.[8]

The significant shift in tourism came with Cold War politics when Spain was again reincorporated into the—now—Western world owing to its strategic military position. The Cold War geopolitical realignment of international forces favored Spain, which benefited from the Iron Curtain, the erection of the Berlin Wall and the establishment of American military bases throughout Spain in 1953 (in Torrejón near Madrid, Morrón near Sevilla and Rota near Cádiz among others).[9] Thanks to these Cold War dynamics, at the beginning of the 1950s, Spain was finally able to repackage its fascist past and open the door for the economic recovery it had been denied in the 1940s.

The creation of Ministry of Tourism (1951) and the tourist breakthrough

While DGT under Bolín's leadership was instrumental in setting in motion business aspect of tourism and investing into hospitality (hotels and dining) and infrastructure (roads and transportation), most historians agree that the real mass development of a tourism industry took off only after the creation of the Ministry of Information and Tourism in 1951, under the direction of Mariano de Urzáis. Urzáiz replaced Bolín who left DGT to become the government's Press and Information Counselor in Washington. Urzáiz shared Bolín's values and objectives, being both a representative of modern initiatives and a defender of dictatorial interests and values. As Pack observes, Urzáiz was described as 'friendly, pro-British, and favoring more liberal travel and border policies' but he also 'intergrated his office to the mainstream of regime politics, making a *cause célèbre* of the 1954 Holy Year at Santiago de Compostela' (2006: 65).

The Ministry of Information and Tourism was a very peculiar entity. As can be deduced from its ministerial designation, tourism was elevated to a cabinet-level post as well as tacked onto the Ministry of Information—one of the most highly politicized entities in Francoist Spain—encompasing press, theater, cinema and radio. To make matters even more complex, Franco appointed Arias Salgado, one of his most conservative Catholic ministers, as the head of this 'joint' ministry. This strategic appointment together with the incorporation of tourism into the Ministry of Information reflects the ambivalence with which the tourism industry was regarded in general. Tourism, a phenomena of mobility, was enclosed within the Ministry of Information, the regime's most political and intransigent sector. Pack postulates that 'placing tourism under the mandate of Arias Salgado may have served to reign in an activity that, spurred by opening borders, was an uncomfortably liberal force' (2006: 65). The radical reorganization of the tourist sector marked by the creation of the Ministry of Information and Tourism and the formal joining of the two entities points to the industry's hightly complex institutional history, and its extremely political, bureaucratic and volatile nature.

Tourism continued to function as propaganda, but with quite different overtones then in the 1940s, since what was proselytized now was not a greatness of the empire or the evilness of communism but a reinforcement of legitimacy for the Spanish political model, that is, its dictatorship. The tourist boom, enabled by Spain's political *apertura* and stimulated by an economic need for foreign currency, coincided with the post-war prosperity of Western European countries whose newly aquired affluence, spending power and consumerism were preconditions of Spain's tourism industry. Leaving behind a mentality of scarcity that characterized the post-war ravaged Europe, Western Europeans embarked on the search for southern sun and beaches (commodities they lacked) and indulged in the hedonistic spirit of the 1960s. Ironically, Spain was an indirect recepient of the Marshall Plan, which it was denied in its original form. Tourism had a vital impact in both host and guest countries and for Spain, tourism was 'the single most important conduit for the southward redistribution of Europe's wealth in the post-war era' (Pack 2006: 8). Moreover, and as Pack emphasized:

> For industrialized countries of the North, access to mobility and leisure was fundamental to mass participation in the 'incessant movement and displacement' at the center of modern life. For receptor regions, principally Spain, tourism became a significant, if not central, component to the modernization programs that often justified governments' legitimacy. In this sense, Franco's Spain was integral to the construction of postwar Europe's leisure civilization. (2006: 9)[10]

Spain's tourism industry experienced three major trend shifts. The first was a geographical movement from the upscale resorts of Spain's north coast to the more accessible beaches of the south. Within this context, a history of Spanish mass-tourism was also inseparable from the patterns affecting the broader Mediterranean region (Italy, France, Greece, Tunisia, and later Yugoslavia) since 'in 1961, arrivals to Europe's Mediterranean rim accounted for 38 per cent of world border crossing' (Pack 2006: 8). The second one was interlinked with the first, as elite tourism, an exclusive pursuit of the upper classes, was now replaced by its mass variant. Exclusive (American) tourists of Scott Fitzgerald's Mediterranean explorations were now substituted by their common counterpart and their favoured tourist attractions, such as historical tours and sites, were now eclipsed by the beach vacation. That brings us to the third shift in which European tourists replaced Americans, becoming a major force within Europe since 'by 1960, the number of American tourists traveling in Europe had trebled while inter-European tourist movement increased ten-fold' (Pack 2006: 7).[11]

These changing global patterns of travel and leisure that were key to Spain's becoming a tourist destination par excellence were further stimulated by two other post-war phenomena linked to the rise of tourist movement: a general increase in car ownership for the rest of Europe and paid vacation legislated in most European countries by the late 1930s but put massively into practice around the 1950s. Finally, symbolic of Spain's new place on the global tourist map was a suspension of a cumbersome triptych on 1 May 1952 that was 'less the result of tourism industry pressure than of the regime's confidence that anti-Franco guerrilla activity in southern France had subsided' (Pack 2006: 54).[12]

The rise of post-war mass tourism, which stimulated Spain's specialization in low-cost vacation and low-budget tourists, meant that by 1954 Spain had irrevocably entred into the realm of the mass-beach holiday. Three major components of Spain's mass tourism were: (1) 'selling' the country's 'difference' to maintain competitivness in the Mediterranean and later global tourist market; (2) standardization techniques required for decreasing costs of tourist packages and amenities; and (3) modernization programmes that addressed infrastructure needs of mass tourist influx.

Spain's geopolitical location on the southwestern fringe of Europe that contributed to its stigma of otherness began to be used as a marketing ploy in the era of mass tourism. By that time, Spain had already been well ingrained into the European imagination as its 'oriental' counterpart. The orientalist gaze, an essential part of nineteenth-century European Romantic literature and its search for 'authenticity' and 'primitivism' as an antithesis of modern Europe, was still operative. 1950s tourists continued to seek a 'typical' Spain; one of *charanga* (brass band) and *pandereta* (tambourine), with its 'backward' spirit, gypsies and flamenco dance.[13]

The preindustrial way of life, Spain's major appeal, formed the core of the 'Spain is Different' promotional slogan put into circulation in the 1950s by Rafael Calleja, a publicity director under Bolín. Pack writes, 'Though it is not known if Calleja invented the slogan "Spain is Different," it was under his leadership as publicity director that the notion of difference became a central theme of tourist advertising' (2006: 68).[14] Calleja's campain was not a novel concept but at this particular historical juncture it pointed to the confluence of the sunny low-cost destination and a sense of 'authenticity' that was quickly vanishing in industrialized post-war Western Europe. National clichés that symbolized Spain's difference—from the ubiquitous flamenco shows to the bullfight—were transformed into mass-entertainment. Upon his return to Spain from Mexico, Max Aub described this reality as 'algarabía fabricada':

> Sólo borracho puede uno no darse cuenta de esa algarabía fabricada, vinos falseados, música adulterada, comida recalentada....Me da pena, algo de vergüenza. Lo peor es que esta imbecilidad, montada para forasteros, la veo practicada con naturalidad—y gusto—por los nacionales. Puro mariachi. (1995: 433, 434)

But, in his disappointment Aub notes the pleasure that is derived from this performance of Spanishness. In a very short time span, simulacra of the Andalusian village of García Berlanga's 1953 film *¡Bienvenido Mr. Marshall!* multiplied throughout

Spain. As Crumbaugh has pointed out, 'a postmodern fetishization of commercialization itself was not antithetical to Francoism but instead became one of its defining traits' (2009: 11).

The 'Spain is Different' slogan went hand in hand with 'Order and Progress', another key motto of the Francoist Spain. The two mottos of dictatorial Spain were the perfect alchemy to the tourists' yearning for different lands and customs while placating their need for safety and order. There is a strong dose of irony in the Spanish tourist bureau's most memorable promotional slogan since Spain truly was different, but its difference did not rely on the ancient mystery of flamenco, but rather on the country's oppressive dictatorial establishment. The search for an affordable leisure destination by the prosperous West conveniently overlooked the opressive political structure of their impoverished southern host. The post-war tourist flow encompassed a tacit apolitical agreement: '...a country considered the antithesis of postwar European values [became] the epicenter of one of postwar Europe's largest mass rituals, the beach holiday' (Pack 2006: 2).

Besides marketing of difference, a second major factor of rapid tourist development was a drive towards standardization: from food and hotels to organized leisure and entertainment. As early as 1939 DGT recommended to hoteliers to provide tourists 'paella, cocido madrileño, tortilla a la española...and other renowned Spanish dishes that are served abroad with great success' (Pack 2006: 35). Furthermore, it was recommended to avoid "regional concoctions with excessively strange characteristics or strong dressings unknown outside of Spain' (Pack 2006: 35).[15] Another standardization process was noticable in larger costal developments where French Club Méditerranée and second home communities became the model for Spain's own coastal towns. These tourist developments tended to be enclosed, economically self-sufficient enclaves that did little to support the local economy. They evoked the preindustrial way of life that was a hallmark of Spain's underdevelopment, which was paradoxically vanishing under the same forces. Unique and generic, two seemingly mutually exclusive concepts, formed a successful marketing strategy and became a winning formula for Spain's tourism ascent.

The third aspect of mass tourism was the country's path towards modernization. Rapid development, especially rampant in Spain's southeastern and southern Mediterranean littorals, necessitated modernizing the existing infrastructure—roads, water supply, as well as the hospitality industry. Massive investments were required on every scale: private, state, foreign and transnational. The primary goal was development of the hospitality industry (private enterprise) and transportation (state public works domain).[16]

The main problem facing the tourism industry was a disparaging situation between the rapidly increasing demand and inadequate existing accommodation. Pack writes:

> Patterns in private investment gradually began to respond to the pressures of the international travel industry. From 1951 to 1955, total hotel capacity in Spain increased by 34 percent, during which time

> tourist entries doubled. By category, the two extremes of luxury hotels and third-class pensions grew most rapidly, by 77 percent and 80 percent respectively, indicating the Spanish hotel industry's continuing failure to offer much middle ground between luxury and squalor. (2006: 73)

The secondary problem was the quality and regulation of the existing accommodations. The problem ranged from the lack of hot water and substandard plumbing to cleanliness and price-gouging. Limited capacity and resources to oversee and regulate the industry and ever-increasing volume of tourists was at the heart of the problem:

> inspections became increasingly rigorous in principle, especially after rule changes in 1956 made private tourist lodgings subject to the inspection regime hitherto applied only to state-owned establishmets. But the DGT in Madrid lacked the bureaucratic machinery to monitor effectively an industry the main centers of which lay on the Iberian periphery (Pack 2006: 76)

While hotel and coastal resort construction was mostly a private enterprise, transportation was the domain of The Ministry of Public Works whose major focus in the 1950s was the modernization of the roadways. In 1950, the Ministry's plan proposed 'the construction or improvement of over 11,000 km. of roads, mostly major existing routes, and supplementing the traditional radial system emanating from Madrid with a network of peripheral coastal highways' (Pack 2006: 73). Since mass tourism concentrated in the underdeveloped poor fringes of Spain such as the Andalusian Costa del Sol (with the exception of the Catalan Costa Brava), the dramatic growth of road systems benefited what used to be Spain's remote or peripheral destinations. While tourism interests, in this case, fitted well with the proposed transportation policy, tourist development interests did not always coincide with the public works interests, and there was considerable tensions and competition between The Ministry of Public Works and The Ministry of Tourism. Road development was also in sync with the broader transportation trends of the mid-1950s (train travel declined while the car industry massified) and about half of all foreign tourists entered Spain by road.[17]

Besides the explosion of car travel, charter flights, another mass mode of transportation, changed irrevocably travel patterns and international tourism networks. Charter flights replaced regular commercial carriers and were geared to low-budget tourists. Pack points out two key outcomes of this remarkable charter-flight expansion. The first one was 'linking Mediterranean Spain directly with several European cities. Direct flights from northern European airports to Málaga, Valencia, and Majorca challenged the radial network, which for three centuries had required travelers to orient their journeys from Madrid' (Pack 2006: 97). The second one changed the pattern and length of tourist holidays:

Figure 4.1. Barajas Airport Madrid ca. 1955 by Francesc Catalá-Roca.

> Although French motorists formed the largest block of tourists in Spain, British, West German, and Scandinavian package tourists were increasingly visible. These latter groups typically arrived by air and tended to stay in Spain longer than automotive tourists, usually in hotels or rental apartments. (Pack 2006: 96)

These changes gave opportunity for more direct involvement with the industry to, until recently, peripheral cities of the coasts and also changed the quality and quantity of tourist consumption. Most historians agree the charter flight phenomena mostly benefited multinational companies and Northern European tour operators.[18]

The charter flights led to a broader question of foreign investment in Spain as well as debates surrounding questions of economic development and dependancy. On the one hand, the development strategies were seen as neo-colonial models that exploited Spain's natural resources. On the other, they were celebrated as country's opportunity to leave behind autarkic, inefficient economic models. Perceived benefits of development included a move towards more industrial, technological and consumer society. In this sense, modernization was seen positively as the 'Europeanization' of Spain. Development also benefited employment figures through an explosion of temporary service-sector, especially hospitality and construction domains. However, the benefits of seasonal employment had to be juggled with a population jump in summer months alongside the lack of infrastructure to accommodate it. Other detriments consisted of the dramatic transformation of the Spanish landscape and social relations. The benefits and harmful consequences coexisted throughout this period in which Spain's social and cultural geographies were transformed unremittingly.

Fundamental points of inflection in the regime's history was Spain's acceptance into the OEEC Tourism Committee (The Organization for European Economic Cooperation) or 'Europe's most important intergovernmental economic club' (Pack 2006: 91) in 1958. The membership in OEEC pushed in more formal ways for the international border liberalization, elimination of visas and general easing of travelling restrictions. All these changes were accelerated even more with the Stabilization Plan of 1959 (its economic and trade policy reforms) and the substantial increase in foreign investment: 'the regime did not hesitate to exploit the tourism economy to finance inflation and balance its foreign accounts—indeed, by the late 1950s, the tourism economy had emerged as Spain's most valuable collateral for mortgaging sudden and drastic reforms' (Pack 2006: 83).[19] Among these aspects of economic reorientation implemented by the Stabilization Plan, the most far-reaching influence for tourism was a devaluation of the national currency (*peseta*). Subsequent growth of the tourism industry was in direct correlation with the decreasing value of the *peseta*. Spain, already a low-cost market, became even more so after the purchasing power of foreign currency rose.

Most historians agree that the Stabilization Plan of June 1959 was a catalyst for the tourist explosion of the 1960s. But Pack rightfully warns that 'a closer examination of the politics and economics of stabilization reveal that the growth of the tourism industry was among causes of economic reorientation rather then a secondary effect' (2006: 83).[20] In sum, the major shift at the end of this period came with the reevaluation of tourism's role within the national economy. Tourism was no longer considered solely a short-term mechanism that supported more conventional industrial growth. It now became favoured as a long-term economic asset at the forefront of economic growth and foreign currency earnings. The 1959 Stabilization Plan signalled the end of the supremacy of industrial autarkists in decisions regarding tourism policy, irrevocably changing the directions that Spanish tourism industry took in the following decade. All three elements foreshadowed the subsequent role of tourism under Fraga Iribarne's tenure.

Tourist boom: Fraga Iribarne (1962–69)

The year 1962 marks an entirely new period in the history of Spanish tourism. Manuel Fraga Iribarne assumed the post of Minister of Information and Tourism; his tenure lasted from 1962 to 1969. While the 1959 Stabilization Plan curtailed autarkist dominance in tourism planning, Fraga's politics of development continued to clash with technocrats in power. This conflict has been described by Pack as:

Figure 4.2. Beach scene in Las Palmas, Gran Canaria, 1960s with backdrop of the fast paced construction that altered the Spanish coastline.

> a prolonged struggle between the indefatigable reformists of Fraga's ministry, supported by a rising class of tourism interests, and a more conservative set of self-styled technocrats, frequently associated with the lay-Catholic secret society *Opus Dei*, who favored policies supporting conventional industry usually at the expense of tourism development. (2006: 12)

In the 1960s, the technocrats' struggle with Fraga's politics of development was inextricably tied to contemporary discussions and conjecture surrounding what Spain's political future would be after the anticipated death of its dictator.

Besides these inner political struggles, Spain was also facing the consequences of degradation and hazardous overdevelopment of the Spanish coast. Overdevelopment of the coast destroyed the Spanish market's initial and main appeal: undeveloped attractiveness and unspoiled natural beauty. It included reckless construction, land speculation, forest depletion and a general saturation of the coastal areas. It caused posterior abandonment of regions originally targeted for development and the tourism industry's search for new markets. This crises was deepened by the market competition that Spain was facing from other emerging Mediterranean destinations (Greece, Yugoslavia, Tunisia) as well as more established competitors such as France and Italy. A lack of sustainable development was not exclusive to Spain and it affected their competitors as well since it was endemic to the entire Mediterranean region.

Spain's first politics of sustainability was developed in this period since 'only after 1962, when the ambitious and charismatic Manuel Fraga became head of the ministry, would tourism emerge as a more fully holistic and broadly conceived national cause' (Pack 2006: 103). Fraga's holistic approach was both a result of his talent and vision as well as economic pressure for more innovative, sustainable planning for the industry. Fraga professionalized the administrators and administrative sector and radically restructured the industry. He appointed Antonio J. García Rodríguez-Acosta as a Director General of Tourism who, in turn, created Subsecretaría General de Turismo, SGT or Undersecretariat of Tourism. The institution was then divided into two directorates 'one for promotion and another to regulate tourist enterprises and activities' (Pack 2006: 110). The drastic expansion of tourist operations under Rodríguez-Acosta was visible in the DGT expansion: 'The DGT, which in Bolín's day had operated from a cramped office in old Madrid, now occupied an entire floor in a gigantic new building in the city's modern district' (Pack 2006: 110).

Fraga's last legacy was the creation of the Institute of Tourism Studies (*Instituto de Estudios Turísticos*, or IET), 'a new government think-tank…which would serve as an important central clearinghouse of information for the growing class of scholars, students, and entrepreneurs pursuing the tourism sector' (Pack 2006: 110). The 1960s were witness to extraordinary growth and foreign investment as the Mediterranean coastal resorts continued to mushroom along the already overdeveloped Spanish coast.

Fraga left a profound impact on the politics of tourism in this last stage of Francoism.[21] In sum, Fraga's term marked the beginning of the long-term evolution of Franco's authoritarian regime and power struggle for dictatorial ascendancy into which tourist issues were deeply embedded.

Novel and cinema

Tourists brought to Spain their own social, cultural and economic dynamics, which infiltrated the literary and cinematic imagination of the times, while the tourists as protagonists, be they national or foreign, began to inhabit novels and films. This personage was slow to work its way into literary texts, but literally flooded the big screen, even becoming a genre in itself known as *la comedia sexy celtibérica* or *la comedia desarrollista de los años 60*.[22] The literary tourist character makes an early appearance in Juan Goytisolo's two novels *La isla* (1961) and *Fin de fiesta* (1962) and in his essay 'Examen de conciencia' (1963, *El furgón de cola*). The subject was also explored in Juan García Hortelano's *Tormenta de verano* (1962), in Luis Martín-Santos' posthumously published *Condenada belleza del mundo* (1963) while Ignacio Aldecoa wrote about it in *Parte de una historia* in 1967. Although the 'comedies of development' held mass appeal, other films explored the phenomenon of tourism in greater depth. In 1963, Luis García Berlanga directed *El verdugo* and Antonio Eceiza *El próximo otoño* (1963), and a year later Fernando Fernán Gómez shot *El extraño viaje* (1964).[23] These movies explored Spain's problematic entry into modernity through three vital gateways—dictatorial forces (in the last decade of Francoism), emigration and tourism.

Goytisolo's *La isla*, written between 1957 and 1960 and between Torremolinos and Paris, was published in 1961. The 'island' to which the title alludes is Torremolinos, one of the first massive scale developments on the Mediterranean coast of Spain. A sleepy fishing village of Torremolinos turned into cement monster in the 1960s and became emblematic of the early years of Spain's tourism industry. Torremolinos became a commodified 'non-place' in Augé's terms, an archetype for unbridled construction in Spain and a model of the late capitalist mode of conspicuous consumption.[24] Goytisolo's novel is foreboding, since Torremolinos over the years turned into the Las Vegas of Spain along with other cities along the Costa del Sol, attracting hundreds of thousands of tourists a year from northern Europe. For Goytisolo, Torremolinos is a vacation island remote from the mores of the rest of the country, an island of and for foreigners. It is also an island for the Spanish upper-middle class as well as Spanish intellectuals, retreating from Spain's repressive dictatorial regime as well as from their own ineffectiveness in political struggle against it.

A space of entertainment, Torremolinos of Goytisolo's novels, is a space for retreat from routine marriages (bourgeouis institution par excelence), corroded affective life and futile political compromises. Goytisolo's book is prefaced by Jaime Gil de Biedma's

Figure 4.3. Beach on Baleares captured by Francesc Catalá-Roca, ca. 1960.

verses from *Infancia y confesiones*: 'La vida, sin embargo, tenía extraños límites y lo que es más extraño: una cierta tendencia retráctil'.[25] Torremolinos, Goytisolo's coastal village, encarnates that very *tendencia retráctil* or retractile tendency defined by Bonet as 'los mecanismos de autodefensa tan característicos de una clase social, la alta burguesía, conciente de los peligros que la acechan, y que aspira a convertirse en una *isla* hermética, replegada en sí misma' (1994: 176). This hermetic and incestuous class, despite its own decadence, continues to thrive, parasitical of any political or economic system that they are part of, including the fascist dictatorship. The idle foreigners and bored Spanish bourgeoisie are a collective protagonist of the novel, integrated through, as both Goytisolo and Pack point out, the pacific and welcomed invasion of Franco's Spain:

> La pacífica invasión anual de varios millones de turistas ha introducido grandes cambios en su [el burgués español] vida privada. Si el nivel de vida de nuestros visitantes ha abierto los ojos a la clase obrera, el burgués ha descubierto, a su contacto, la posibilidad de divertirse. Hasta hace diez años la burguesía española era una de las más aburridas y convencionales del mundo. La irrupción masiva de los europeos ha trastornado sus hábitos mentales. La proliferación de relatos eróticos y alcohólicos cuya acción se sitúa en el marco dorado de Mallorca, la Costa Brava o Torremolinos, no es producto de una moda pasajera como ha opinado más de un crítico. (Goytisolo, 'Examen de conciencia'; 1976: 260)

La isla takes place during the eleven repetitious days of summer during fiestas de Santiago. The novel's 'non-events' are narrated by Claudia, the first-person narrator who is visiting from Paris while waiting for her husband's job transfer to another European destination. He is a journalist and their marriage crisis forms a loose backdrop to the story that is constructed around the increasing sense of ennui: drinking, driving along the coast, sporadic sex, rekindling of old loves and laying on the beach. As characters sink deeper and deeper into depression and boredom, there is an expansive sentiment of erosion. American tourists intermingle with Spanish ones, participating in their small love dramas and routine infidelities. Central to the text are intellectuals who search for refuge from ennui via drinking and sex; representing a well-to-do middle class who might have been political in their youth but have by now benefited indirectly from the regime or have learned how to incorporate it into their lifestyle. The utilitarian ethos prevails over political beliefs or even libidinal desires echoing Goytisolo's assertion about his class: 'Cuando el burgués habla de los valores del alma, anteriormente piensa en la cotización de sus rentas' ('Examen de conciencia'; 1976: 259). The narrative reliance on repetition and superficiality of characters is an integral part of the work. The formal level of the novel therefore reiterates its content: empty repetition and lack of meaning. Claudia, the novel's narrator, in line with social realist postulates, functions as a film camera and is an 'objective' witness to her class and their alienation. Eleven days of summer seem like an eternity, a non-changing experience and a return to the sameness of their life. In *La isla*, Goytisolo transformes Sartrian existential anguish, of once political group, into a banality of existance. As Claudia leaves her island of forced and meaningless pleasures, she leaves behind her social class and their Biedmian rectractile tendency.

Goytisolo's next novel, *Fin de fiesta* (1962), is a collection of four stories, linked through the theme of tourism and summer vacation. The text is woven through four narrative perspectives: a young boy from the coastal fishing village, a husband in a mid-life crises, a bored middle-class wife and a close friend returning from abroad. The stories are not titled but only numbered as 'Primera', 'Segunda', 'Tercera' and 'Cuarta'. In the first story a young boy-narrator witnesses a crisis of a Scandinavian couple spending their summer vacation in Spain. The second story narrates Álvaro and Ana's marriage, disrupted by an appearance of Loles, a young woman in love with Álvaro. The love triangle is only secondary to the consciousness of the time passing, that the intruder christalized for the troubled couple. The third story is of Marta and Juan, whose weekend on the coast is interupted by a visit of their friends Asun and Jaime, Marta's former lover. Provoked by the incestuousness of the two couples and intensified through their summer ennui, the story centres on friendship and its precariousness as well as the fragility of love. The last story is narrated by Bruno, who visits his old friend Miguel after many years in his country estate near Barcelona. Miguel, now married to Mara, is depressed and fatigued with life. Bruno departs without really having engaged with his old friend.

The four narrations of *Fin de fiesta*, melancholic in tone, are set at end of season; as summer heat and tensions give way to the coolness and calm of the fall. Dissolution of the couple is the background of each story, ambiented in a costal landscape of sea, sand, pines, eucaliptus and bouganvillas. The fragile unity of the stories' couples is disrupted by the intrusion of an outsider, yet everything returns to the same at the end of each narrative. The novel is reminiscent of Pier Paolo Pasolini's *Teorema* but without the shattering element that Terence Stamp's visit provoked in the Milanese family. Goytisolo's materialistic bourgeoisie, unlike Pasolini's, does not benefit from the emotional intensity or transcendental experience of Pasolini's film. The premise of *La isla* and its ambientation continues in *Fin de fiesta*: long repetitious days of summer as a trope for the characters' immobility, the passivity of the middle class, an incapacity for (political) change and the life of routine that eradicates desire. Goytisolo's last story 'Cuarta' ends with warning: 'Hoy por hoy, la fiesta ha terminado' (1962: 141). This last sentence signals not only an end of the *fiesta*—a party, a holiday or an entertainment—but an ending of an epoch and a collapse of the imagined political utopia. *Fin de fiesta*, Goytisolo's last social-realist work, can be read as a lament for the ineffectiveness of anti-Francoist fight, end of comaraderie and the futility of political commitment. Goytisolo and his generation's political utopia collapsed, its remains barely visible in the banality of love triangles and unbearable sense of boredom.

Goytisolo's 1963 essay 'Examen de conciencia' reads well with both *La isla* and *Fin de fiesta*, that are the literary mis-en-scène of Goytisolo's theoretical postulates.[26] 'Examen de conciencia' focuses on tourism as a major force of change in Spain during these tumultuous times and explores the role of intellectual praxis within this changing dictatorial panorama. Goytisolo's ficional intellectual figures, cast as both novels' protagonists, are now the target of his essay. Goytisolo's intellectuals are diseased, suffering from neurasthenia. The psycho-pathological disorder that denotes a condition with symptoms of fatigue, anxiety, headache, neuralgia and depressed mood is the malady of his characters in *La isla* and *Fin de fiesta*.[27] Besides the fatigue that translates into lack of political engagement, they are also unable to assume the modernity and modern lifestyle that they advocate:

> [El intelectual español] unido al mundo burgués por sus costumbres y al pueblo por sus sentimientos, no pertenece verdaderamente a uno ni a otro. El conflicto diario entre las ideas y los hechos, los principios teóricos y los necesarios compromisos con la sociedad en que vive agravan todavía su crisis moral. El intelectual español niega los celos y es celoso, aspira a la libertad y vive bajo la esclavitud de la angustia. Tras repudiar la concepción reaccionaria de la mujer-objeto por la de la compañera igual al hombre en derechos y deberes, se muestra incapaz de asumir las consecuencias prácticas de su elección. Huyendo de la torpe suficiencia viril, cae en la neurastenia. ('Examen de conciencia'; 1976: 263)

Besides tourist development as a major force of economic change and the consequent invasion of Spain by Western Europeans, Goytisolo also focuses on the Spanish intellectuals' inability to accommodate those changes in their practice or political discourse. For Goytisolo, at the heart of the problem is a notion of 'el español eterno', a concept that, with equal blindness, came to dominate both native and foreign conception of Spanishness: 'El español eterno es pobre y orgulloso, sincero y desprendido, apasionado y valiente. Por encima de todo posee un bien de inestimable valor: su alma, que los mercantilizados y vulgares europeos han perdido' ('Examen de conciencia'; 1976: 249). Perceptive and biting, the analysis neither spares foreign guests nor native hosts. Equally coveted as exploited, 'a poor, proud and passionate Spain', is not a virtue for Goytisolo but rather a reflection of Spain's anachronic and backward customs. Goytisolo analysis of developing Spain or *España de desarrollo*, in sharp contrast to the optimism of official development discourses, is linked to what he has denominated *estética de la pobreza* or a false notion of authenticity celebrated indiscriminantely by foreigners coming to Spain.

As the encounter between the two cultures evolves, the 'natives' (*los indígenas*) progress does too, becoming more fond of the utilitarian foreign customs that eventually strip them of their primitive charm:

> Hasta hace pocos años el español desconocía los valores cremásticos. Como la mayoría de los pueblos subdesarrollados, reaccionaba frente al utilitarismo de las sociedades industriales con una mezcla ambigua de envidia y desprecio. Hoy, por fortuna, su mentalidad está sufriendo una completa metamorfosis...Año tras año, los extranjeros que regularmente nos visitan habrán comprobado que, paralelamente a la inevitable subida de precios, las relaciones humanas con los indígenas se 'deterioran'. ('Examen de conciencia'; 1976: 252)

Ironically, the coveted 'authenticity' of Spaniards and their land turns into inauthenticity through this very encounter and Spaniards start to perform their 'Spanishness' for those that seek their genuineness. The performance is encouraged through promise of monetary gain (just like American dollars in *¡Bienvenido Mr. Marshall!*):

> Gracias al turismo y la emigración, el español ha descubierto los valores de las sociedades más avanzadas y los cultiva con celo de neófito. Enriquecerse, ascender, avanzar sin tener en cuenta los obstáculos, tales son las normas de la nueva religión monetaria, que, cada año, gana centenares de miles de adeptos. ('Examen de conciencia'; 1976: 252)

Yet for Goytisolo, progress is not necessarily negative, because he advocates Spain's inevitable metamorphosis:

> Si—demos por caso—el pueblo español ha de transformarse un día, por obra del desarrollo industrial y la elevación del nivel de vida, en un pueblo satisfecho y rollizo como el suizo o el belga, debemos luchar por esta metamorfosis aunque personalmente nos desagrade. Nuestro placer estético no ha de prevalecer sobre los verdaderos intereses del país. ('Examen de conciencia'; 1976: 257)

Acceptance of change and leaving behind the concept of eternal Spain and Spanishness, paradoxically so close to that of official discourse, is precisely the *examen de consciencia* of the essay's title or a call for redefinition of the anti-Francoist struggle (previous ineffective *toma de consciencia*). The year of publication of 'Examen de conciencia', 1963, is also a year of the fictional return to Spain of Álvaro Mendiola, a protagonist of *Señas de identidad* (1966): 'An autobiographically inflicted story of a young intellectual's disenchanting coming of age, *Señas* presents a sobering picture of anti-fascist resistance (in exile) and ends with a view of Francoist Spain's incorporation into Europe through tourism' (Epps 2003: 206). The end of politics proper, explored in both novels and the essay, is a result of disenchantment with the political sphere together with an inability to articulate an alternative political programme. Tourism, as a major force behind late 1950s capitalist development, fits perfectly Goytisolo's analysis since tourist spaces of leisure are seen as overtaking the space of politics. Goytisolo placed his characters into this new space created by tourist development: non-spaces of endless repetition, increased standardization and unlimited leisure. Ironically, this new depoliticized non-space or space of post-politics (abandoning of the anti-Francoist struggle) is a site of desperation, yet perfectly in sync with (intellectual) ennui of those that inhabit them. This is why Goytisolo accused Spain of 'growing fat, but remaining silent' (*España engorda, pero sigue muda*) ('Examen de conciencia'; 1976: 253 n.3) (see p. 29).

Exactly at this historical junction, Goytisolo himself will embark upon radically different literary course involving a destruction of all eternal and sacred: language, territory, landscape, myth and history. As he prophetized in 'Examen de conciencia': 'Una de las paradojas de la época, y no de las menores, consiste en que los intelectuales y artistas peleemos por un mundo que, tal vez, será inhabitable para nosotros' (1976: 257).

Dictatorial Spain's integration into Europe through tourism is also a theme of Juan García Hortelano's second novel *Tormenta de verano* (1962). The novel's protagonist Javier, however, is not an intellectual but a real estate investor whose business is precisely a development of the coastal tourist resorts like the one that is the locus of the novel: Velas Blancas, a summer colony he built on Costa Brava. Hailed as an exemplary novel of social realism, for its use of first-person narrator and objective narration, the book won Prix Formentor a year earlier and was translated and published in thirteen countries simultaneously. The atmosphere in *Tormenta de verano*, not unlike Goytisolo's two novels, is one of apathy and emptiness. García Hortelano himself notes that his novel:

> es un largo relato en primera persona, que narra el proceso de una crisis moral, desencadenada en un hombre de cuartenta y pico años por la aparición en la playa de la colonia donde veranea, del cadáver de una muchacha. Paralela al aludido proceso y a la investigación policíaca de la muerte de la mujer, se extiende la trama de las relaciones del narrador con su familia y sus amigos, de sus formas de vida y pensamiento, mediante el discurrir de sus partys, sus diálogos, sus ocupaciones, sus tedios, de aquella su fatal tendencia egocéntrica. (Yrache 1961: 4)

The event, that shatters an otherwise lazy uneventful summer, is an apparition of a dead, naked body of a women washed ashore in Javier's tourist colony. García Hortelano's now well-known opening sentence, 'Al principio, lo peor fue que la muchacha, además de muerta, apareciese desnuda en la playa' (1989: 67), puts into motion this existentialist detective story in which a woman's stark nakedness is as shocking as her death. The novel's narrator Javier focuses on the naked, dead corpse in great detail:

> La muchacha probablemente había usado en alguna época de su vida un tono claro, casi blanco, para maquillarse los labios. A pesar de las nubes, crecía la luz y la piel de la chica se hizo más amarilla y más tensa. Me hipnotizaba aquella dureza de las comisuras de la boca, levantadas, sin relación con las mejillas, ni con los párpados. Le habían limpiado la arena del pelo y, bajo la sábana, se alzaba la pirámide de sus manos cruzadas sobre el pecho. (García Hortelano 1989: 95)

Significantly, and throughout the novel, the narrator's gaze, in the same detailed mode, lingers on bikini clad women on the beach. The obsession with a dead woman washed ashore is displaced onto tourist bodies. The gaze, like the one examining the dead body, is surgical and anatomical, a microscopic look at legs, thighs and breasts.

The apparition of the woman's dead naked body ties together two central themes of the novel—death and sexuality—the first one connected to the traumas of the civil war and the second one to the emergence of tourism. Death, nakedness and foreignness, the entangled problematics of *Tormenta de verano*, are furthermore connected to an economic realm since the protagonist-narrator's business deals, a background of *Tormenta de verano*, reinforce the linkage between the post-war autarky ('De no haberse producido la Guerra, los negocios no habrían dado el salto', García Hortelano 1989: 351) and the 1960s *apertura* (very specific references to the development years exemplified in El Plan Nacional de la Vivienda).[28] According to one of Javier's business acquaintances,

> Las personas como Javier son las que hacen el mundo…La vida produce dos clases de hombres. Los que hacen las cosas y los sencillos mortales que las contemplamos. Usted ahora maduraba seguramente algún negocio, alguna gran operación financiera que producirá en su día hermosos frutos a la patria. (García Hortelano 1989: 359)

Javier's business, construction and coastal development, is hardly compatible with autarkic principles that *patria* presupposes, yet the two realms prove to be mutually beneficial, reflecting the regime's own passage from God ('Por el Imperio hacía Díos') to Coca-Cola (see 'Introduction').

Javier's capacity to profit from land development is juxtaposed with the immobility of the fishermen and villagers and their incapacity to take advantage of the economic boom. They are also handicaped by the economic insularism of the colony since Javier refuses to grant outsiders permission of economic entry into Velas Blancas: 'En la colonia no puede haber tiendas' (García Hortelano 1989: 269). García Hortelano gives his narrator Javier a brief class consciousness, a notice of those on whose back his economic enterprise is built: 'maleteros, camareros, criados, pescadores' (1989: 156).[29] But this moment of awareness is as temporal and as fickle as the summer weather itself.

The backdrop to *Tormenta de verano* is unbearable boredom, petty affairs and incestuous relationships like those of *La isla* and *Fin de fiesta* but it is also a document of the times; the material history of the Spanish economic ascendency and the moral price it extracted. The history of *desarrollo* years is imprinted on the narrator's life and business trajectory: from the gradual renunciation of autarky from which (according to García Hortelano) Javier's class benefited, to Spain's industrialization and opening up to foreign and large-scale investments. It is not incidental that the point of view is given to the narrator Javier, a target of the author's critique of the middle class who were both winners of the conflict and beneficiaries of its post-war economic opportunities.

Summer storm to which the title of the novel refers, allows briefly for different social configurations, as seen in Javier's liason with the local prostitute, but with fair weather all returns to its original coordinates. It is a return to the same daily routines and business deals that were interrupted by an unexpected event, an appearance of the corpse on the beach. The end marks, once again, a loss of contact with the exterior. Velas Blancas colony is a degenerate island, just like Goytisolo's Torremolinos. It is incestuous and hermetic, symbolic of the class that reproduces itself and its privileges. At the end of the novel, and after a few brief attempts to engage with the outside world, Javier returns to his colony of friends and their incestuous relationships. To ward off future intrusions and protect their insularism symbolized by the coastal development, they put a sign: 'Prohibido el paso, camino particular' (García Hortelano 1989: 422).

Relying on the principle of realism, Goytisolo's and García Hortelano's novels denounce, through objectivist technique, indolent and irresponsible lifestyle of well-established middle class of the 1960s, exacerbated by tourist and economic boom and the consequent prosperity it brings. In 'Questioning the Text' Brad Epps asserts that 'sometimes during the 1960s, the mirror breaks for Spanish narrative' (2003: 193). He refers to mimesis and referentiality that was, as we have seen in the first chapter, highly operative in the mid-century generation. Within this literary tourist corpus we could situate Goytisolo and García Hortelano before the breakage of the mirror and Marín Santos and Aldecoa after 'language, turned into its own object, [became] opaque, restive, polyvalent, and at times even purposeless' (Epps 2003: 193).

Martín-Santos' *Condenada belleza del mundo* (1963) and Aldecoa's *Parte de una historia* (1967) also narrate the violent clash between tradition and modernization and development. *Condenada belleza del mundo*, like *Parte de una historia* are summer stories, set in the rapidly changing landscape of the 1960s. The first on the Costa del Sol and the second on the tiny island of Graciosa (Canary Islands); remote fishing villages (unnamed in the novels) about to be developed into summer colonies like those of García Hortelano's Velas Blancas on Costa Dorada (*Tormenta de verano*) or Goytisolo's Torremolinos (*La isla*). Both writers explore the impact of the encounter between tourists and traditional coastal communities, yet they also focus on the impossibility to grasp or narrate that very 'encounter', which is tied to language, that in its density—betrays any attempt at real and realism. They depart from their generation's efforts to represent accurately, since the 'truth' of the decade becomes paradoxically articulated in a different space; one that 'in its delayed appearance and its belated address, cannot be linked only to what is known, but also what remains unknown in our very actions and our language' (Caruth 1996: 4).

Luis Martín-Santos' *Condenada belleza del mundo* is a little known text, written in 1963 and published more than 40 years later by Seix Barral (2004).[30] In the spring of 1962, Martín-Santos, who just published with great acclaim his first novel *Tiempo de silencio* (Seix Barral, 1961), joined Basque director Antxon Ezeiza in a search for the location of the director's new film *El próximo otoño*. They chose Almuñecar, a tiny fishing village on the Costa del Sol in the province of Granada for the shooting location. The filming was a welcomed distraction from the writer's personal life, the tragic loss of his wife in March of 1962. For Martín-Santos these were tumultous years since he was also detained for political activism—his son Luis Martín-Santos Laffón writes: 'el hecho de encontrarse en esos momentos en libertad provisional añadía un ingrediente más de desasosiego a su situación personal' (2004: x). Ezeiza's film *El próximo otoño*, originally entitled *El último verano*, was filmed in 1963. The title was foreboding since Martín-Santos tragically died the following January and the summer of 1963 was indeed his last one. *Condenada belleza del mundo* was the last text that Martín-Santos wrote before his tragic death.[31] Martín-Santos' novella both recounts the film's plot and documents the filming process itself. Ezeiza and his film crew impacted 1960s film culture as much as Martín-Santos' did literary culture.[32] But while Ezeiza's film pertains to the tradition of realism, exploring an impact of tourism on a traditional fishing community, Martín-Santos story complicates any mimetic (sociological or historical) reading of the film. Martín-Santos' title, a 'condemned beauty of the world', is itself taken from the field of advertising, and foreboding of the 1960s era of the image: 'mi lírico descubrimiento es un slogan publicitario' (Martín-Santos 2004: 4). The story is funny, cruel, ironic and even distanced. As Luis Martín-Santos Laffón, Martín Santos' son, has observed:

> En *Condenada belleza del mundo* se puede encontrar un poco de todo de lo que a mis ojos le caracterizó [a Martín-Santos] como escritor. Un verbo brillante que autoindaga, profundiza y alza el vuelo en las cuatro dimensiones espacio-temporales para describirnos un paisaje. Una fina ironía que de forma constante y disfrazada de objetivismo científico nos arranca carcajadas en algunos momentos. Un ejemplo de análisis dialéctico en la manera en que el ayudante de dirección explica a los actores cómo han de encarar el rodaje de la escena final. (2004: xiv)

But the mood of *Condenada belleze del mundo* is also one of mourning; mourning of the destruction of the landscape and a moribund way of life. It is inevitable yet still a lamented loss. The canto written for the condemned beauty of the world.

Condenada belleze del mundo tells a story of a film director and his crew filming a fleeting summer love tale between a French girl, vacationing on the Spanish coast, and a Spanish boy, a seminarian, on a school break in his native village. It is a summer love story but the pleasure of its reading is interrupted by the writer's ironic rendition of the love encounter that provokes an emotional distance in the reader, and requires a critical engagement with the work that functions as a Brechtian distancing effect:

> El muchacho está absolutamente enajenado por las circumstancias de su familia y de él mismo. Es un débil. No tiene capacidad de cambio. Está resignado a su destino. La francesa se encapricha de él, le ama...Sí, es el topicazo. Ya lo sé. Es lo que todos los españoles estamos esperando, que aparezca la francesa que se enamore de nosotros, que nos redima...El muchacho ama a la francesa. Ella es rubia, alegre, estudiante, emancipada. Ha perdido el tabú de virginidad hace cireto tiempo. Le encuentra a él pintoresco. Procede como una vampiresa, como una chupadora de hombres. Precisamente lo que siempre esperamos y deseamos: que existan mujeres así...(Martín-Santos 2004: 12, 13)[33]

The estrangement effect is reinforced by Martín-Santos' intersecting of this clash between the native culture and foreign tourists with the encounter of the film crew and village inhabitants. The film crew becomes a part of a 'convivencia desencorsetada':

> que conagia a cuantos se aproximan y modifica la existencia total de la pequeña ciudad penetrando en las fiestas de las casas particulares, en los cubículos de los pequeños cabarets, y en los pasillos de los infinitos hoteles improvisados en honor del extranjero que, por una vez, gozan de más divertidas hospitalidades...(Martín-Santos 2004: 24)[34]

Most of the crew appear as characters of the novella, only refered to by their profession (El Director; El Ayudante de Dirección-Guionista) which only complicates further the enmeshing of the various levels of the story:

> Los actores secundarios, graves...miran irónicamente al Director, a la señora del Director, al Cámara 1ero...y piensan para sus adentros en qué porquería de película va a ser ésta...nada les impide a beber una copa de ginebra en una curiosa taberna flamenca en la que se reúnen la colonia extranjera del pueblo y parte de la colonia indígena...(Martín-Santos 2004: 33)

Martín-Santos' novella centres on both tragedy and inevitableness of change. His story is a testimony of tourist destruction, meditation on tradition and modernity, and a perceptive analysis of Spanish underdevelopment and foreign entitlement, with biting and ironic commentary on clichés of supposed Spanish authenticity. The book opens with a detailed description of the destruction of this condemned part of the world:

> Llegó tu hora, virgen: serás profanada. Llegarán las caravanas de europeos para mofarse de ti. Y de nada te valdrá el fantasma del fenicio ni el del griego. Colocarán las telas anaranjadas de sus campings en los plieges de tu falda ocre y cenicienta, poblarán tus aldeas hundidas en la mugre de bares fluorescentes, tus marineros resecos dejarán de pescar sus pececillos para dedicarse a otras navegaciones, tus torreones vigilantes se convertirán en dancings de lujo, las borrachas rubias y altas profanarán con cantos de emoción ilegítima la solemnidad con que acostumbrabas recogerte cada noche, todo quedará lleno de orines y preservativos, de latas vacías y cascaras de huevo, de olor de gasolina quemada, de suecos que se han dejado la barba y de franceses ruines que ahorran también en vacaciones. (Martín-Santos 2004: 9)

Both mythic and post-apocalyptic, Martín-Santos' landscape is as much composed of desecrated earth as of condoms, empty cans and egg shells. Dense poetic language, a mark of his literary style, immediately recognizable to his readers, underscores the gap between world and word-experience.

As much as he destroys the illusory effect of the story itself Martín-Santos also shatters other illusions of authenticity, be it originality of flamenco or imaginary Andalusian soulfulness. The story thus features the clumsy attempts of the film director's wife to learn fandango, the Castilian protagonist pondering nature of his Andalusian character,[35] and pseudo gypsies entertaining ignorant foreigners:

> '...los extranjeros escuchan o hacen como que escuchan el croar de rana de una seudogitana gorda. Los extranjeros dan palmas inadecuadamente' (11) '...el macho...hace del movimiento oscilante del cuero provocación grosera y riéndose al mismo tiempo de hacerlo y del folklore andaluz que es es único superfolklore patrio que invade, cuya frontera asciende siempre hacia el norte' (30) 'la señora del Director tiene interés en aprender el fandango de Huelva...El Director pide al actor número 2, que se llama Andrés y que es vigoroso animal, que cante un fandango de Huelva' (32) 'Cada vez que la gitana gira, suelta un cuesco. Esto no es debido a mala educación de la gitana, sino a la naturaleza impetuosa y comunicativa de su arte...' (Martín-Santos 2004: 33)

The reader's alienation is further underscored by an insistence on the mediated nature of film image, as intrusive as the encounter it narrates: 'El arco voltaico arroja su luz inverosímil (más blanca aún que la del sol) sobre el flanco no achicharrado por el auténtico hacedor de las mediterráneas melaninas. El grupo electrógeno, montado en camioneta, profana el silencio de la playa' (Martín-Santos 2004: 41).

The 2004 edition of *Condenada belleze del mundo* includes Martín-Santos' two dénouments of the story or the two ways of resolving the novella's last scene. The suspensfulness of the ending is woven around the question of the French girl's return home, itself symbolic of an (un)successful encounter of the two radically different cultures. Martín-Santos orchestrates the ending scene in minimalist fashion, with a leading role given to the girl, the girl's suitcase, a bus and the boy. Marín-Santos empties the space from other commotion giving them 'un único plano. Un plano my largo, antonionesco, de los que la cinematografía nacional todavía no ha osado' (Martín-Santos 2004: 51). The boy's and the reader's point of view is conflated. The bus on which the French girl is suppose to leave is in a congealed frame in the midst of the village plaza. These two objects loaded with meaning—the suitcase and the bus—symbolic of movement and nomadism become protagonists themselves. The uncanny suitcase (also embodying a major role in García Berlanga's *El verdugo*) is the leitmotiv of the story and an object around which the ambivalence of the scene is developed. On the one hand, there are the girl's conflicting feelings:

> La francesa se ha planteado un dilema: o irse coincidiendo con la familia hospitalaria, o bien permanecer en el pueblo...la duda ha sido tan intensa que aparece en escena con la maleta significativa de su decisión de realizar viaje que sólo suspenderá en el último momento. (Martín-Santos 2004: 50)

On the other, there is the boy's uncertainty: 'Ella se ha quedado. Para él. Le mira burlona, risueña con la maleta (que es un símbolo sexual) colgando de sus manos, puesta ante su pelvis como ultimo telón protector que no es sino de cartón y que está vacío' (Martín-Santos 2004: 68).[36]

Martín-Santos was a Marxist, a Freudian and an Existentialist. The ending of *Condenada belleze del mundo* reflects his intellectual interests:

> Tienes que hacer sentir al espectador tu miedo...El miedo de poseerla. La deseas. Sufrirás si se fuera en el autobús; pero quedarías tranquilo. Al ver que ella se queda, que es tuya, que te quiere, tú te asustas. Un hombre queda abrumado cuando se entera de que, por fin, ha conquistado a una mujer....Al hombre le da miedo. Cualquier hombre lo comprenderá. Esta película va a tener éxito sobre todo entre los hombres. Entre los hombres que nunca lo hayan conseguido y que se hayan pasado la vida soñando. Precisamente eso: una extranjera, una mujer estupenda; el sueño de los países subdesarrollados...La antítesis es el terror de conseguirla, de caer en el pecado, de ser devorado por ella, de ser criticado por el pueblo entero, de dejar tu mandíbula destructora de la mantis...La

> síntesis es el tercer momento reconciliador. Coges tu maleta. Aceptas la victoria, aunque sabes que va a estar cargada de sufrimientos y de reponsabilidades. Te vas con ella, maleta en mano, atravesando por el medio de la muchedumbre pueblerina que se ríe y te envidia. (Martín-Santos 2004: 60, 61)[37]

The artificiality and 'fictive' qualities of the story are reinforced through the literary techniques, such as the direct address to the characters, as seen in the instructions to the actor/protagonist on how to convey to his public the desire and fear that the ending requires. The narrator's meddling in the story serves a didactic function and shatters any possibility of spectatorial identification. The message of the novella, an affective and economic experience of anxiety produced by an encounter between the two cultures, is directed to the fictional seminarian of the story who does not know what to do with his conquest of the girl; to the spectator who is identified with the boy through point of view and to the collective protagonists of Spain's underdevelopment.[38]

Martín-Santos' dénouements—its Marxist scrutiny, Hegelian synthesis and Freudian psychoanalysis—makes suturing impossible. The suture—the process through which the artificiality of a shot/narrative is naturalized and through which the narrative's illusion is restored—is subverted by Martín-Santos through the 'uncanny poetic effect' created by the subject (character) 'enter[ing] his own picture' (Žižek 2001: 39). This 'impossible' visual perspective of the scene produces a disturbing effect. As in Kieślowski's work, aspects of drab reality are made to operate as the 'door of perception'. Critical interfaces are opened between different realities, through mundane details such as Martín-Santos village plaza frozen in time, the departing bus or the actor/seminarian dragging the symbolic suitcase as the bus leaves. The scene's disconcerting aspects have the effect of making the familiar strange, leaving the reader conscious of the true meaning of the condemned beauty of the world. Martín-Santos' canto, as poetic as historical, is a warning and lament for the destruction the writer prophesied but did not live to see.

Underneath the layers of irony and use of Brechtian alienation techniques, the reader can discern Martín-Santos' existential anguish and sense of loss. That same sensation of mourning is central to *Parte de una historia* (1967), the fourth and last novel written by Ignacio Aldecoa. The plot is quite simple: the novel's unnamed narrator returns to a small fishing village on an unidentified island and his return coincides with an English couple vacationing there and a group of wealthy Americans that shipwrecked on the island's coast while sailing around the unnamed archipelago.[39] The visitors intrude upon the traditional existence as their eccentric habits clash with the inhabitants' way of life. The narrator joins the community of fisherman in their daily labour. Shortly thereafter the island's carnival celebration unleashes a series of excessive and destructive events. One of the Americans drowns and the narrator abandons the island the next day.

Aldecoa's literary life project was a testimonial and he was the witness par excellence of his times. He originally planned to write three testimonial trilogies. The first one, 'La España inmóvil', centred on the representative yet marginal social groups of Spain—the civil guard (*El fulgor y la sangre,* 1954), gypsies (*Con el viento solano,* 1956) and bullfighters (never finished). In his second trilogy 'Los hombres del mar,' Aldecoa, in his words, explored 'the epic of great occupations' or 'la épica de los grandes oficios' (Pittarello 2005: 13). The first novel of the second trilogy, *Gran sol,* 1957, is a powerful exploration of human nature and a tragic rendition of the fisherman's daily struggle with the sea and harsh labour in the fishing industry (deep-sea fishing or *la pesca de altura*). *Parte de una historia* was the second novel in the trilogy, this time centering on coastal fishing or *la pesca de bajura.* The third 'sea epic' as well as the third planned trilogy on iron workers was never written.

Aldecoa's literary projects centre on labour but significantly, his last novel *Parte de una historia* reflects a shift, from politics of labour to that of leisure. The sea, the site of a struggle in Aldecoa's previous opus, was now rendered as the site of enjoyment (beach and tourism). *Parte de una historia* witnesses the encounter of the two worlds that are about to collide:

> Me sonrío pensando en tarjetas postales, en parejas abrazadas en los plenilunios postales, en mujeres que se bañan en los mares postales, en las risas, danzas, terrazas, aperitivos, flores, ferias, escándalos, amores, hazañas y corazones postales. Pero ésta es una isla de trabajo. (Aldecoa 2005: 103)

This thematic shift was accompanied by an aesthetic one, since Aldecoa's language, until then more in line with social-realist postulates, becomes opaque and restive.

Embodied in the individual and collective protagonists of the novel, fishermen, tourists, and the narrator/intellectual meet on this solitary island. The world projects itself, through them, as a tumult of voices, as polyphony. The novel opens with the motif of an unexplained return: 'Ayer, a la caída de la tarde, cuando el gran acantilado es de cinabrio, he vuelto a la isla' but it is the motif of escape that structures the rest of the narrator's experience on the island. Partaking in the fishermen's labour fills the narrator's daily existence. He seems to belong to the island's isolated collective more then the group of tourists, yet he is clearly as foreign:

> He salido descalzo y camino con inseguridad, con aprensión...mi andar entre cauteloso y circense atrae las miradas de todos...me heriré antes de llegar a las piedras del muelle y haré un paso de pirueta que pondrá lágrimas de risa en los ojos de los chiquillos...risas contenidas de las mujeres; risas que serán de alegre tutela en los hombres para el amigo bobo, para el amigo forastero, que cree sentirse de la isla y se desmiente de una manera tan sencilla. (Aldecoa 2005: 85)

The narrator therefore occupies an intermediate space: neither native nor foreign. Moreover, his foreigness is existential as he is a stranger to himself as much as to those around him. While the narrator lives out his existential anguish, the village passes through its life cycles, traditions and rituals: fishing, repairing fishing nets, preserving the fish, preparing for weddings and local festivities, and other daily and yearly labors.

Like in *Tormenta de verano*, the summer storm pushes the narrative forward and announces the conflict between tradition and modernity. The storm is, moreover, prefigured by the narrator's own existential shipwreck:

> Estoy lejos, en mi propio naufragio, siendo una presencia ajena, alguien que no deja compartir lo que pasa. Todos mis riesgos están fuera de esta isla, y aquí en este regazo es donde se desencadenan otros riesgos que no me alcanzan (Aldecoa 2005: 109)

The intrusion of the foreign element becomes embodied by the American tourists—Jerry, Boby, Gary and Beatrice, dispersed and drunk; in their boat and on the beach onto which they shipwrecked. In an anthropological reversal, native fishermen now explore the remnants of their yacht Bloody Mary (Florida):

> Hay un hombre tendido en una litera y el agua y la grasa olean casi a su altura. Paquetes de cigarillos deshechos, papeles, fundas de discos, botellas, revistas que tienen movimientos de rayas, libros, cajas vacías en permanente zozobrar, ropas que se hinchan y recogen como bolsas de pulpo de este extraño y alborotado mar prisionero (Aldecoa 2005: 119)

These objects, indicative of modernity and uselessness, are both contrasted with practical possessions of the villagers such as fishing gear as well as foreboding of a more profound disaster: foreigners wrecking the village traditional ways. Not surprising, central to the conflict are sexual mores and taboos, explored for example through the fisherman Domingo's love interest in his '*americana*'.[40] At that point Aldecoa introduces carnival, as a narrative device that permits further dispersal and transgressions. The natives, as much as the foreigners, become carried away by 'la embriaguez colectiva' or collective drunkeness of the carnival spirit (Aldecoa 2005: 206).

The night climaxes with Jerry's drowning, the novel's second disaster. The event is never described directly and the reader only has access to dispersed comments. The death is witnessed and transmitted by a collective voice: by a *cabildo* (men in municipal council or in this case village tavern that has the same function) and by a *coro* (a choir of women of the island that are unlike men or foreigners excluded from carnivalistic transgressions). Foreigners descried the death in this ancient mode as well: 'De pronto un grito abre el silencio. Jerry…Pero no es una invocación sino una queja' (Aldecoa 2005: 231). Jerry's body, spit out on the shore by a current and found by Roque's search team, is solemnly brought back and it is now a bundle 'pesado y grande, envuelto en una lona' (Aldecoa 2005: 238). The dead body strikingly resembles the woman's corpse in *Tormente de verano*:

> Beatrice se agacha y aparta el pico de lona que cubre la cabeza de Jerry, diseccionada por el arrecife, anquiladas las facciones por rayas y cortes morados, negruzcos y blancos. Un ojo, arrancada la ceja, sin párpado superior, se dispara globular como en una lámina anatómica. (Aldecoa 2005: 239)

Jerry is buried on the island, in its porous ground, sand that is as slippery as the story told:

> Y esperamos, en silencio, a que cadáver desaparezca en la arena y ésta vaya ascendiendo por la fosa con el trabajo de los cuatro improvisados sepultureros...El señor Mateo planta la cruz de limoncillo, que es como un mueble nuevo, lustroso y ambiguo. (Aldecoa 2005: 250)

Unlike Jerry, laid out under layers of sand, and claimed by the natives ['Ya eran como una cosa nuestra' (Aldecoa 2005: 254)[41]] whose lives he disturbed: the narrator leaves the island after the burial: 'Mañana, poco después de que amanezca, dejaré la isla' (Aldecoa 2005: 269). Suspended between two worlds, neither to which he belongs, the narrator is neither punished by death for intrusion (like Jerry) nor reincorporated into the community (like Domingo). He is the embodiment of Goytisolo predicament about intellectuals of their age: impotent witnesses that are about to lose the world they inhabit.

The dead body of an American tourist (Jerry) that functions as narrative closure in *Parte de una historia* returns in Luis García Berlanga's *El verdugo* (1963), also imprinted by the intersection of death and tourism. *El verdugo*, a dark comedy partially set on Spain's island of Palma de Mallorca, the country's prime vacation destination, examines the moral ambiguities of Spain's death-penalty system.[42] Spain, the antithesis of European post-war values, became a tourist destination of choice for those same Europeans that were opposed to the country's politics. The opening music sequence references the split between modernity as symbolized by leisure against the dictatorship as symbolized by the death penalty: an uplifting cadence reminiscent of Miguel Asins Arbo's score for *El cochecito*[43] is interlinked with a flamenco lamentation 'a *martinete* (a gypsy prison song) murmured against the dialogue' (Marsh 2006: 138). Emergent modern Spain and Spain's dark past are immediately interlinked through the score.

The first sequence also introduces Amadeo and José Luis, the protagonists of the film and its two executioners. They first cross paths in the prison scene where an execution has just taken place. This sequence introduces other key objects that circulate in the film:

the executioner's briefcase (*maletín*), an envelope containing the executioner's payment and an ominous coffin with an executed body. The executioner briefcase, in particular, functions as the Hitchcockian 'MacGuffin', setting this black comedy in motion.[44] This ubiquitous briefcase colours most every aspect of the film: it is a visual reminder of the death penalty whose actual application is never shown in the film and as José Luis himself witnesses, it is an object that can not be discarded. The briefcase becomes animated (the rattling of the executioner's tools it contains) and foreboding (a sound bridge to off-screen executions).

García Berlanga's comic technique lies in normalizing the death penalty, making the incongruous or outrageous appear as ordinary. The key here is Amadeo's character, good natured and pragmatic, skillfully played by veteran Pepe Isbert. Isbert was an ideal choice for the protagonist, given his outstanding performance and his ability to communicate the dark, critical and biting humour that is so characteristic of Spanish neorealism. Amadeo thus represents his executioner's role only as a slightly cumbersome undertaking: 'la gente debería morir en la cama naturalmente, pero si existe la pena hay que aplicarla' (*El verdugo*; my transcription). In a darkly comic fashion he proves to José Luis, by attempting to stick his fingers into a light socket, a humanness of the Spanish garroting (*garrote vil*) in contrast to the barbaric American system, an electric chair.[45] He gives a demonstration of the death penalty application during an idyllic country picnic while his daughter Carmen and José Luis court each other in the background. When José Luis does not recall his shirt number, Amadeo sizes up his neck as number 41. He proudly wears his executioner suit to his daughter's wedding despite the protest of his son-in-law: 'para la boda de su hija podía haberse puesto otro traje' (*El verdugo*; my transcription). These are only a few examples of García Berlanga's strategy to normalize the executioner's job and instill it with humor. While Amadeo inspires dread in everyone he encounters, they continue to reiterate throughout the film: 'parece una persona normal' (*El verdugo*; my transcription).

The story is as simple as ingenious: the undertaker and the daughter of the executioner are introduced by her father since their social status preclude them from meeting 'normal' partners. This somewhat unusual love story is pushed to its dark extremes when José Luis inherits his father-in-law's position as state executioner in order to keep the apartment allotted to Amadeo by the state. The film is inspired by material necessity and conditions of a still underdeveloped Spain: from a need for less cramped living quarters to more superfluous material gains such as a José Luis' motorcycle, a new mattress or simply an extra paycheck.

Housing problems, illustrated by Amadeo's long-drawn-out wait for the promised apartment, become a turning point of the story. Motivated by a promise of more spacious living arrangements, José Luis reluctantly consents to this dark profession. The deal forces José Luis into a Faustian selling of his soul, except the state is the devil here. Like in Ferreri's 1959 *El pisito* the material gain is a result of the moral transaction. It is the same ethical dilemma posed by Goytisolo in 'Examen de conciencia' that is directed as much to Spaniards as to foreign visitors to Spain:

> Al buscar refugio en el alma española, nuestros visitantes tratan de eludir el problema capital de la sociedad contemporánea...: ¿cómo hallar un ideal humano, una escala de valores válida, una dignidad nueva, en suma, en un universo crematístico en donde moral y progreso económico se confunden hasta identificarse. (Goytisolo, 'Examen de conciencia'; 1976: 256)

The perceived benefit of state housing turns deceptive since the promised space does not live up to Amadeo's fantasy (magnificent views, electric heating and three large rooms) and uncannily resembles their original cramped quarters. The construction site itself, crowded by other apartment buildings in progress, also illustrates the failed promises of modernity. The film reflects the lack of housing available at the time as well as a social critique of corruption, urban land speculation and state-subsidized housing characteristic of other works by Ferreri and Azcona. As José Luis turns to admire views ('vayan las vistas'), he sees a person defecating outside of the window, a testimony to the unremitting invasion of the country by the city. Never was it more true (as Lacan's commentator Žižek asserted) that the consumer paradise—with its promise of capitalist abundance—frequently ended up being the gift of gold that turned to shit.

To become an executioner proves to be both competitive and contingent upon a series of bureaucratic details. Each request for further paperwork is counterweighted by Amadeo—the father-in-law and expert in the matters of the state—producing a missing document. The scene serves as José Luis' entrance into the state system: he becomes caught in its web of bureaucratic demands that eventually lead to his first execution. The black humour arises out of exaggeration (there are already 37 petitions for the job) as well as neverending paperwork required by the job applicant. The scene is important because it transforms the state's most repressive practice (execution) into a matter of bureaucracy and separates it from its larger moral universe (its ethical meaning). It is therefore not surprising that as soon as José Luis becomes the executioner, he also inherits the skill of reading penal codes.[46] Unfortunately, for José Luis, the execution business is not solely a matter of codes and abstract cases since the registered post that summons him to his first execution proves that letters always arrive to its destination (Lacan). It is delivered precisely when José Luis (seen lounging in his underwear) and Carmen are about to enjoy their new possession, a mattress, acquired by the extra pay from his macabre post.[47]

The scenes interlink economic gain and sexual pleasure with moral loss. Underwear, that García Berlanga put in circulation in the beginning of the film, and prominently displayed in this scene, is another object loaded with meaning. Significantly, the first

Figures 4.4–4.6. Scenes from *El verdugo* where the executioners face the realities of their coveted state apartment.

underwear scene (symbolic of consummation of José Luis and Carmen's relationship) originally bound José Luis to Carmen and thus to the executioner's family. Amadeo's insistence on José Luis marrying Carmen is naturally ironic since he does not live in moral universe. Steve Marsh remarks that Amadeo 'employs traditional morality he clearly does not practice' (2006: 141). Significantly, the scene is parallel to Amadeo's receiving notice about their new apartment ('ya tenemos el piso; con vistas, califacción, tres habitaciones'). Moreover, Spanish men in underwear are iconic of both tourist and emigration films. The scene therefore brings to the forefront José Luis's desire to emigrate to Germany, a backdrop of the story throughout the film and an utopian counterpart to his daily struggles. Germany, constructed as an idyllic space, functions above all as a materialist utopia. García Berlanga thus weaves a web of material temptations around his protagonist, who is only too willing to be lured by them.

These material temptations only intensify thereafter, with García Berlanga's choice of Palma de Mallorca—Spain's vacation paradise not accessible to its lower-middle class represented by *verdugo* family—as the setting for José Luis' first execution. This up and coming location is symbolic of Spain of *desarrollo*, as seen in Amadeo's remark: 'Palma de Mallorca, allá no he actuado yo. ¡Qué suerte, yo siempre iba a los sitios tristes!'

(*El verdugo*; my transcription). Palma de Mallorca unites two Spains—an emerging tourist destination (vacation) and out-of-date dictatorial regime (death penalty). The coexistence of the two worlds is reinforced through the juxtaposition of a desperate and worried José Luis with the ominous ministerial letter in his hand and Carmen trying on her bathing suit for their upcoming 'vacation'. But like the country itself they integrate the two seemingly incompatible elements and transform the executioner's journey into their honeymoon (which they never had due to their limited economic resources).

As the setting of the film moves from its narrow local confines to the international destination of Palma de Mallorca, the executioner's personal death penalty conundrums are transposed onto the national and international sphere. The contestants who are invited to the 'Elección de Miss Naciones Unidas' travel on the same boat that brings the executioner's family to Mallorca. There is great irony in the welcome they share: 'Bienvenidos al Festival Mundial de Elegancia y Belleza'. Making note of the international setting, Amadeo observes: 'más facil que llegue el indulto'. Amadeo's universe is not a moral one but rather a calculating-pragmatic view of the world. His statement echoes Pack's belief that

Figures 4.7–4.9. Arrival in Palma de Mallorca where the gruelling task of the executioner is combined with a family vacation.

> In general, the idea of Europe eclipsed that of democracy as a mobilizing agent for change in late Francoist Spain. International tourism, the infrastructure that supported it, and the society that tolerated its challenges were emblematic of the new 'European' Spain, the consummation of which required formal democratization. (2006: 14)

While José Luis is taken to the prison by the civil guard in a military jeep to perform the execution, the Misses and photographers leave in sport cars and motorcycles for their festivities, and Carmen and Amadeo take the horse cart to their pension. These distinct modes of transportation are a visual reminder of the coexistent stages of modernity that collide on the island. Carmen and Amadeo arrive to the boarding-house determined to enjoy fully their stay on this coastal paradise. Amadeo, the real executioner, as José Luis repeatedly refers to him throughout the film, is the one that truly enjoys the family vacation. Amadeo indulges in life and food.[48] He is a hedonist yet also a harbinger of death. Their enjoyment is interrupted by José Luis' return from prison filmed in an extremely long overhead shot (the same take that will be repeated when he is actually dragged through the prison hall to perform his first execution). As José Luis walks up from the beach to the boarding-house, the privileged point of view is clearly Amadeo's and Carmen's as they sit on their balcony enjoying *zarzuela de mariscos*. José Luis is miniscule, like an insect, fully drab in a suit, among carefree sunbathers. He is clearly an incongruous object on the beach, once again a reminder of the coexistence of the two Spains.

Since the prisoner was sick and the execution postponed, José Luis joins in the family fun. He has been promised per diem (*las dietas*) and an indefinite prolongation of his vacation. Spared an execution, José Luis regains a belief that he can benefit from the system without ever paying back. The promise of indefinite credit (Faustian motif) heightens his enjoyment. At this moment the genre of the film seems to change as the neorealist black comedy gives way to a tourist one. As he discards his provincial outfit José Luis becomes a vacationer, a transformation symbolized by his newly acquired colorful shirt and straw hat. The executioner also becomes a summer lover as he exchanges suggestive glances with a group of foreign girls. In a typically tourist manner they take snapshots of each other. García Berlanga brings to the forefront a question of the image, with tourists and an executioner framed within what turns to be less than idyllic vacation. As they exchange addresses to send photos, the apartment—first time in the film materialized in a real address as 'Polígono sur, grupo 4, bloque 17' (*El verdugo*; my transcription)—becomes a reminder of the unpaid debt.

The enjoyment of leisure continues and Carmen and José Luis, visit Palma de Majorca's major tourist attraction: Drach's caves (Cuevas de Drach). It is here, as he descends into the underground caves, that José Luis becomes a spectator of his own role as an executioner. Faustian debt becomes Dantesque hell. Soothing classical music (Offenbach), played for the sightseers, is interrupted by the voice on the megaphone: 'José Luis Rodríguez,

Figures 4.10–4.13. The stay of execution allows the executioner and family to indulge in being tourists.

José Luis Rodríguez, baje al embarcadero' (*El verdugo*; my transcription). Althusserian interpellation effectively produces José Luis as the subject proper, the real executioner, heir to his father-in-law's profession.

In the last scene of the film, located in the prison itself José Luis finally recognizes his social role as executioner as others already see him. The prison staff treat him with scorn, as they had treated Amadeo in the first scene of the film. His coffee is not handed to him directly but just left on the table and when he shows a photo of his family, a prison functionary remarks: 'Miren, la mujer y el hijo del verdugo' (*El verdugo*; my transcription). García Berlanga emphasizes the need of performing execution in a death penalty state as remarked by Amadeo in the beginning of the film or as repeated in the prison: 'la sociedad siempre necesitará un ejecutor de la justicia bien sea usted o el otro' (*El verdugo*; my transcription). Even when he wants to resign the state bureaucracy is taken as an impediment to his resignation: 'trámites oficiales, el trabajo se acumula, pasa un día, dos, una semana, dos…' or 'el condenado no puede esperar; se ha confesado; ha comulgado' (*El verdugo*; my transcription). The vacated seat of power, materialized in the figure of the executioner, is now filled by José Luis. Significantly, this is the moment in which José Luis appears as 'himself', leaving behind the disguise he wore throughout the film such as: pseudo-aristocratic outfits, white wigs, tourist garb or dark sunglasses.

García Berlanga cleverly focuses on the details surrounding the execution rather than the execution itself. One of the film's key scenes, an assembling of garrote, was originally a lengthy take, but was cut by censors. Despite the cut, García Berlanga still managed to convey that the death penalty is a performance of power, state apparatus at its most barbaric as well as most abstract level. The scene focuses on details surrounding the execution, its technical intricacies, like Amadeo's advice: 'no te olvides de la palomilla de la derecha porque si no, los hierros resbalarían en el palo' (*El verdugo*; my transcription). This last prison scene is a repetition of the very first sequence of *El verdugo*, when, as we realize, José Luis was already positioned to take the 'real' verdugo's place (crossing of paths between the two verdugos, *maletín* that puts the story in motion, the envelope containing Amadeo's payment that economically motivates both, the execution itself). The formal structure of the scene reiterates the thematic one: the first sequence of the film strikingly resembling the last one (prison location, minimalist frame, white walls symbolic of abstract space of power). The film opens and closes with death. Moreover, García Berlanga's idea of the film parted from this last scene to which the director remarked, 'he and Azcona had to add one and half hour of the story' (*El verdugo*, Extras: Interview with García Berlanga; my transcription). García Berlanga was inspired by his friend's anecdote of an execution in which an unwilling executioner had to be dragged to an execution, strikingly resembling the prisoner about to be executed. Parting from the story, García Berlanga envisioned a huge minimalist white space through which the executioner and victim, in striking parallelism, are dragged by: prison bureaucrats, priests and guards. This became the most powerful sequence of the film, resembling a Kafkian universe, intensified through the existence of a tiny door at the far end of scene's abstract space. The black humour is intensified through José Luis' inappropriate outfit: his tourist garb. José Luis' straw hat, a symbol of tourist enjoyment, falls of his head and rolls off the floor, at the threshold of death. This incongruous object becomes a reminder of the two discourses that mark the entire film: imbrication of tourism and dictatorship.

Nothing is what it seems in this universe in radical transition: Germany, constructed as an idyllic space, is really an escape route from paternal responsibility; apartment is an unreal space in construction and its comforts or views are only imagined; and finally Mallorca, a tourist utopia is a deadly dystopia. It is a mirage of development, as Goytisolo has implied in 'Examen de conciencia': 'En lo moral, como en lo económico, pretendemos quemar las etapas sin caer en la cuenta que ni las estructuras ni las costumbres pueden improvisarse de la mañana a la noche' (1976: 255).

Figure 4.14. Executioner and family depart from tourist paradise having accomplished his task.

Manuel Vázquez-Montalbán points to the same problem through his notion of 'portable morality': 'El turismo masivo creó inmediatamente su mitología…De hecho, en las costas se creó una vida portátil, portátil como el verano. Una moralidad portátil que al llegar el otoño se sustituía otra vez por calconcillos de felpa y la contención' (1986: 188). This portable morality is as applicable to the European visitors whose political stance was capricious and self-serving. As Pack writes:

> The notion that Europe's thirst for meridional holiday was extending to the Soviet block indicated how strikingly apolitical resort tourists of the 1960s were in their preference. Rodríguez-Acosta [undersecretary of tourism] explicitly rejected the idea held by some Francoists that 'unfavorable political conditions' formed a disadvantage for Spanish tourism. International manifestations of anti-Francoist opinion, though numerous and loud, produced minimal impact on the tourist trade. Oslo's socialdemocratic daily ran the headline, 'Don't travel to Spain,' … yet the measurable effects on tourism were limited to Scandinavia and were only temporary. (2006: 111, 112)[49]

The coexistence of the two worlds is seen both in *El verdugo* and other texts of the period. Tourism proved to be one of the key instruments of socio-economic and political change in Spain of the 1960s. As Pack makes clear in the subtitle of his study, dictatorship and tourism combined to facilitate 'Europe's Peaceful Invasion of Franco's Spain'.

Notes

1. 'La actualidad de Larra' [*El furgón de cola*], p. 35.

2. Goytisolo gives these examples in 'Examen de conciencia' [*El furgón de cola*] (1976: 255).

3. Pack is citing from a document produced by Patronato Nacional de Turismo, 'Nota sobre el Fomento del Turismo Español', 1928, AHN FC-PRESID-GOB-PRIMERO-DE-RIVERA, p. 140.

4. Pack's terms (2006). See his chapter 'Tourism and International Engagement'.

5. *Maquisards* (*maquis*): a french guerrilla fighters against the Nazis in the Second World War. Paul Preston writes that 'the defeat of the Axis had allowed many of the Spanish maquisards who had played a key role in the French resistance to return to Spain. By the end of 1945, a full-scale guerrilla war against the regime was beginning to build up in the north and east. Dominated by Communists, but including also Socialists and anarchists, the so-called Spanish maquis would threaten the regime until 1947' (1994: 549).

6. Instituto Nacional de Industria (INI) or National Industrial Institute was a product of Franco's protectionist policies and a high level of direct state intervention in the economy. It was founded in 1941 and intended to create or to subsidize industries in key sectors of the economy where private enterprise alone was insufficient to achieve self-sufficiency.

7. Nevertheless, Bolín's agency (DGT) was limited in their scope of operations since they had solely 31 functionaries, a small office, and not sufficient resources to face rapidly growing industry. See Pack (2006).

8. 'British and American demands that group travel be unrestricted, along with the influx of French motorists, undermined the regime's attempts to control and monitor the itineraries of foreign visitors' (Pack 2006: 56).

9. In 1950, US Congress approved 62.5 million dollars economic aid to Spain, and 1953 was a year that saw the signing an economic treaty with the United States. For more information, see Pardo Sanz (2009).

10. See Koshar (2000: 186).

11. Pack writes that 'Americans dominated the initial wave of tourism in postwar Europe, their number rising from 286,000 in 1950 to 861,000 in 1960' (2006: 7).

12. Pack points out that the triptych was still required for automobiles, a requirement that was annuled only in February of 1961.

13. Antonio Machado used the term in 'El mañana efímero poem', refering to antiquated Spain. In general, the term is used in derrogatory fashion. *Charanga* is a brass band and *pandereta* is a folk tambourine.

14. As Eugenia Afinoguénova and Jaume Marti-Olivella have noted, the slogan dates back to 1929, when the Patronato Nacional de Turismo inscribed it on promotional posters. See Afinoguénova and Marti-Olivella (2008: xi–xxxvii).

15. Pack quotes from DGT's 1939 circular to hoteliers. 'Instrucciones y Recomendaciones de la Dirección General del Turismo a los Señores Dueños o Directores de los Establecimientos Hoteleros de España', DGT circular, 8 August 1939, AGA 3: 49.02/14415.

16. For more information, see Pack (2006: 72–78).

17. 'As annual tourist entries to Spain by road more than doubled from 1951 to 1956 to 1.3 million (about half the total), the number of those entering by train stagnated in absolute terms at roughly 250,00 per year' (Pack 2006: 73, 74).

18. See Pack (2006: 98).

19. 'From $5.5 million in 1957 to $82.6 million in 1960' (Pack 2006: 100).

20. Pack outlines in great detail tourist economy relationship to economic stabilization including questions of the black market effect on inflation, erratic pattern of revenue, foreign tour operators skirting of commission fees and American and European pressures for monetary liberalization. See Pack (2006: 82–103).

21. For more detailed account on Fraga's period in office, see Pack (2006: 105–135) and Fraga (1963, 1980).

22. Also known as *cine de destape, destete, cine de reprimidos* or *las comedias de conquistadores y paletos*. A few films from this genre are: *El turismo es un gran invento* (1967), '*Pero…¡En qué país vivimos!*' (1968), *Verano 70* (1969), *Ser hippy una*

vez al año no hace daño (1969), *El hombre abominable de la Costa del Sol* (1970), '*En un lugar de La Manga*' (1970), *Los días de Cabirio* (1971). On the 'comedies of development', see Crumbaugh (2009) and Afinoguénova and Marti-Olivella (2008).

23. *El próximo otoño* was filmed in 1963 but first shown in theaters in 1967.

24. In an essay and book of the same title, *Non-Places: Introduction to an Anthropology of Supermodernity* (1995) Marc Augé coined the phrase 'non-place' to refer to places of transience such as a motorway, a hotel room, an airport or a supermarket.

25. It is significant that the verse is taken from Gil de Biedma, another writer from Escuela de Barcelona and fervent critic of bourgeois values (the very class that both him and Goytisolo were born into). Bonet remarks that algunos escritores de la Escuela de Barcelona: 'hijos rebeldes de su clase (estripe, familia) y cuya literatura semeja un *asesinato* ritual de dicha clase, si bien repito, las armas estéticas en tal destrucción hayan sido proporcionadas por ese entorno sociológico, a la par refinado y decrépito' (1994: 178).

26. See 'Examen de conciencia' (Goytisolo 1976: 243–270).

27. George Miller Beard, U.S. neurologist, coined the term in 1869.

28. El Plan Nacional de la Vivienda: 1961–1976 against which protagonist and his associates are complaining ('Pero ¿Por qué tienen que dar una ley o lo que sea? ¿Para arruinarnos?' (García Hortelano 1989: 308).

29. Javier: 'Antes veía a las personas y no pensaba en ellas. A cierta clase de personas. Maleteros, camareros, criados, pescadores. Gente de ésa. No sé por qué ahora pienso con frecuancia en ellos. Me parece que están vivos' (García Hortelano 1989: 156).

30. *Condenada belleza del mundo* was among the inedited writings that were entrusted to Pepa Rezola and Mario Camus after Martín-Santos' death. Before 2004 publication that includes a fascimile, the story was published twice, but only in fragments. The first publication focused on story's film sequences and came out in the film journal *Griffith*, numbers 3 and 4, in December of 1964 and January of 1965. The second publication came about much later in *El Urogallo* on 1 May 1986.

31. Martín-Santos was writing *Tiempo de destrucción*, a celebrated sequel of *Tiempo de silencio*, at the same time. The novel was posthumously published by Barral in 1975; in a critical edition by literary critic José Carlos Mainer.

32. The producer of *El próximo otoño*, Elías Querejeta, changed the direction of Spanish cinema in the 1960s; Víctor Erice, assistant director and co-scriptwriter, was one of the rising stars of the times; and assistant camera operator Luis Cuadrado and director of photography Luis Enrique Torán were skilled professionals.

33. Moreover, the narrator addresses the French girl ironically: 'Te gusta España. Sí, tienes una cierta idea de que España es romántica, pero sin exageración. Las exageraciones te fastidian. Los toros te fastidian. Se trata de una fiesta sádica y cruel. Tú quieres algo más original' (Martín-Santos 2004: 15).

34. 'Convivencia desencorsetada' is a term coined by Luis Martín-Santos Laffón (2004: xi).

35. The protagonist worries: 'Me siento inquieto. Es un personaje increíble. Me gustaría haber leído algo respecto a la psicología de los chicos andaluces, porque como soy castellano, no me la imagino bien' (Martín-Santos 2004: 26).

36. Suitcase is a leitmotif of the film: '…la maleta será utilizada otra vez como símbolo para que empuñada por José Luis y, transportada a lo largo de la calle, nos informe del "tomar a su cargo," del "comprometerse"' (Martín-Santos 2004: 50, 51).

37. Martín-Santos also offers 'Final alternativo' to his readers. This double ending of *Condenada belleza del mundo*, becomes even more disconcerting because the scenes are almost identical: '*Tesis* es la angustia del deseo insatisfecho, el temor de haberla perdido para siempre. El primer actor teme que ella le ha dejado caer, que se ha ido tras haberlo rozado, tras haber inducido su excitación y su deseo. Esta angustia se expresa en su carrera hasta el autobús que se va sin que él sepa aún lo que va a pasar. *Antítesis* es el terror que le invade en el momento que se hace cargo que es suya. Ella se ha quedado. Para él. Le mira burlona, risueña con la maleta (que es un símbolo sexual) colgando de sus manos, puesta ante su pelvis como último telón protector que no es sino de cartón y que está vacío. La antítesis muestra el terror en la victoria que aparece en lugar de la pura alegría pagana, de la alegría dionisíaca que no es posible en los países subdesarrollados. *La síntesis* resulta del tercer movimiento completador. El varón acepta su victoria, carga con ella y con las dificultades inherentes. Carga con la sonrisa del pueblo, con el runrún que llegará hasta su madre, con la burla, con la envidia, coge la maleta. Se aleja con ella sintéticamente reconciliando las contradicciones, aunque la reconciliación será precaria y transitoria' (Martín-Santos 2004: 68, 69).

38. Martín-Santos' final message *avant la lettre* deconstructs *comedia desarrollista* that flooded Spanish screens in the 1960s and even 1970s: 'El mensaje de esta película va dirigido al varón frustrado. El varón de los países subdesarrollados está crónicamente frustrado. Intenta conseguir una hembra fácil que le satisfaga. Intenta conseguirla pero sin dar él nada a cambio, ni compromiso, ni apasionamiento. Intenta que su libertad abstracta tome forma en el encuentro amoroso. Pretende que ella se le entregue y que considere el acto como una simple experiencia enriquecedora. Pero conseguirla, en realidad, le asusta. Cree que no puede acercarse a la mujer porque el coro de viejas del pueblo se lo impide, porque hay una serie de tabús sociales que están en contra. Pero no son tabús sociales. Es él mismo quien se lo prohíbe. Por ello, junto con la expectación violenta del deseo hay un obscuro temor de la victoria. El varón que se empeña en una conquista se sentirá derrotado si no la logra. Pero si la logra, en el momento de haberla conseguido, se aterrorizará. El terror sagrado ante la hembra, el terror a la vagina dentata, el terror a ser descabezado le dominará ante la dominada. Sabe que la hembra es la más fuerte. Cree en el mito de la *mantis*' (Martín-Santos 2004: 67).

39. From Aldecoa's autobiographical notes we know that the novel's location is a tiny island of Graciosa, north of Lanzarote in Canary archipelago.

40. There are several other examples, such as Roque prohibiting village children from going to certain beaches because foreigners 'se bañan en cueros vivos' (Aldecoa 2005: 93).

41. The full quote reads: 'Ya eran como una cosa nuestra, ¿no es verdad?, y ahora se van. ¿Dondé irán?...Los ricos como éstos no saben dónde van. Son todos náufragos. Miren el Jerry dónde ha encontrado su descanso' (Aldecoa 2005: 254).

42. *El verdugo* was released in 1963, the year of the execution of Communist operative Julián Grimau.

43. Marsha Kinder points out that 'the bouncy Italian-style music by Miguel Asins Arbó (*El cochecito*) is evocative of Nino Rota's scores for Fellini' (1993: 120).

44. MacGuffin is an argumental decoy Hitchcock throws in to divert attention from the real plot. Žižek explains: 'We all know what the Hitchcockian "MacGuffin" means: the empty pretext which just serves to set in motion the story, but has no value in itself'; in order to illustrate it, Hitchcock often quoted the following story: 'Two gentlemen meet on a train, and the one is struck by the extraordinary package being carried by the other. He asks his companion, "What is in that unusual

package you are carrying there?" The other man replies, "That is a MacGuffin." "What is a MacGuffin?" asks the first. The second says, "A MacGuffin is a device used for killing leopards in the Scottish highlands." Naturally the first man says, "But there are no leopards in the Scottish highlands." "Well," says the second, "then that's not a MacGuffin, is it?"' (2003: 1).

45. *Garrote vil* is a method of execution in which a tightened iron collar is used to strangle or break the neck of a condemned person.

46. Annabel Martín has pointed out that 'tras meses de espera, José Luis ya se encuentra familiarizado lo suficientemente bien con el Código Penal como para saber tipificar el castigo correspondiente a los crímenes de la página de sucesos del periódico' (2005: 150).

47. Annabel Martín writes: 'Otro de los subtextos del filme es la constante frustración de una sexualidad más abierta, disfrutada placenteramente, menos escondida y sucia que la puesta en práctica en el apartamento oscuro y desvencijado de Amadeo al comienzo de la película' (2005: n. 70, p. 150).

48. For example, a simple *zarzuela de pescado* or fish stew served in the boarding-house for Amadeo becomes progressively 'zarzuela de mariscos' then 'zarzuela de mariscos con sus gambas' and finally 'zarzuela de mariscos con sus gambas, sus trocitos de mero, langostinos y todo con una salsa picante. Qué te chupes los dedos' (*El verdugo*; my transcription).

49. Pack gives an example of Italy where 'leftist opposition to the Franco regime coincided with the interests of the local tourist trade, which faced rising competition from less expensive, more exotic Spain' (2006: 112). Pack furthermore suggests that sporadic boycotts might have been a result of convenience such as "vendors" attempts to promote package holidays to other destinations' (2006: 112).

Chapter V

Mobile subjects: *La vida sobre ruedas*
SEAT: la Sociedad Española de Automóviles de Turismo

In addition to tourism and emigration, another major force of change during the times was the nascent car industry.[1] Without mass transport, the dawn of mass tourism and emigration would have been unimaginable. Tourists and emigrants crossed Spain's borders in cars, a novel mode of transportation that changed the patterns of travel, affected forms of communication, and dislocated the balance between Spain's centre and its peripheries. Although Spain's car industry had a relatively long history, mass car production was a 1950s phenomenon. The SEAT (la Sociedad Española de Automóviles de Turismo) was established in 1949, Franco inaugurated its first factory in Zona Franca outside of Barcelona in October of 1955, and in June of 1957 SEAT put the 'seiscientos' (FIAT 600), its mass model, into circulation.

SEAT was a product of a joint business enterprise between Spain's INI (Instituto Nacional de Industria or National Industrial Institute) and Italian FIAT (Fabbrica Italiana Automobili Torino).[2] The National Industrial Institute (INI), established in 1941, was a holding company, also inspired by an Italian industrial business model IRI (Istituto per la Ricostruzione Industriale; 1933). INI's president, Juan Antonio Suanzes Fernández was a firm believer in autarkist economic principles and industrial models. He had already put various industrial projects in motion—transport, iron and steel industry, and carbon mining—before focusing on the car industry in 1949.

As Eulàlia Solé has claimed, Spain's car industry grew out of autarkic industrial principles:

> En la ley de su creación, el concepto de autarquía se hallaba presente en varios de sus artículos, manifestándose en términos como el… 'desenvolvimiento de nuestra autarquía económica, ofreciendo al ahorro español una inversión segura y atractiva', o como el '…control absoluto de los negocios en que por razones militares o autárquicas esté interesado (el INI)'. (1994: 13)

Thus, unlike the tourist sector that was regarded by the regime as a soft income bearer, the car industry was a major part of INI's business goals.[3] Suanzes, a voice of opposition to the tourism industry, was a major force behind the SEAT enterprise, one of the most sucessful businesses under the INI umbrella, which, as Solé points out, 'figuró en los primeros puestos en el *ranking* de rentabilidad de las empresas del INI hasta 1975' (1994: 15).

An official agreement between SEAT and FIAT took place in May of 1950. FIAT entered the deal with 7 per cent capital, INI was a major stock holder with 51 per cent capital, and the rest was financed by private capital, through Spain's largest banks: Hispano Americano, Central, Banesto, Bilbao and Vizcaya y Urquijo.[4] Solé points out that despite the strong investment of INI and Spanish private capital, 'los porcentajes no pueden ocultar la sujeción de SEAT a las patentes de la fábrica de Turín, ni la dependencia técnica con que se trabajaba' (1994: 22). Viewed within the context of the SEAT formation and production, the enterprise was a product of autarky and autarkist politics of the 1950s. On the one hand, it was an exemplary company of the Francoist Dictatorship: 'Empresa, por ende, rígida y autoritaria, en perfecta simbiosis con el sistema político y social en que se hallaba inmerso el conjunto de la sociedad española' (Solé 1994: 25). But on the other hand,

> En pleno aislamento del régimen, una empresa extranjera y prestigiosa invertía capital, maquinaria, técnica y diseño en una España que se hallaba en la cola de Europa. Se configuraba así no sólo una incipiente presencia multinacional que iría adquiriendo volumen con el paso de tiempo, sino la consiguiente apertura del franquismo hacia el exterior. (Solé 1994: 25)

The paradoxes of SEAT's business configuration reveal the limits and contradictions at the heart of Franco's regime. They highlight the conflict between the fast industrial modernization of that time (Spain's so-called 'economic miracle') and the persistently outdated structure of the Franco dictatorship.

SEAT 600

In May of 1953, SEAT's first car—the SEAT 1400, based on the FIAT 1400—came out on the market.[5] SEAT 1400 was the first car made on a large scale, which was especially significant in a post-war climate of scarcity with only one car for every 3000 Spaniards (Solé 1994: 33). In 1953, 959 SEAT 1400s were produced and only 3 years later, the production reached 10,590 cars annualy. Solé points out that

> Simultáneamente, y mientras el modelo 1400 se iba introduciendo en el mercado, la empresa acariciaba la idea de conseguir un utilitario capaz de ser adquirido de forma masiva por las clases medias que aún con tímidez, estaban emergiendo en las áreas urbanas. (1994: 34)

The goal was aligned with the general European project of mass motorization. Before the Second World War, for example, France and the United Kingdom had approximately

Figure 5.1. 1960s beach scene depicting newfound mobile tourism. ©akg-images/Album/Oronoz

two million cars and Italy 300,000, in comparison with 30 million cars circulating in the United States. While the Second World War interrupted the development of utilitarian models, by the beginning of the 1950s, Europe, now in recovery, was a prime market for the mass car industry. Already in 1936, Volkswagen launched their 'people's car' (the 'bug') and one year later, FIAT launched its counterpart FIAT 500 (the 'Topolino').[6] The production of both models was interrupted by the war but was firmly back on track by the late 1940s. Spain's goal of making its first *automóviles de turismo de tipo utilitario* belonged to this trend, and by the time the first SEAT 600 was produced in 1957, the Spanish market was ripe for its reception.

Like other SEAT models, the SEAT 600 was fabricated in Spain under an Italian licence and engineering team.[7] The year of the first FIAT 600, 1957, was also the year of the entrance into government of the Opus technocrats: Ullastres, Navaro Rubio and López Rodó. Several other factors contributed to the rise of the car industry, such as the devaluation and stabilization of the *peseta* in 1959, broad-spectrum reduction of state intervention, and Spain's joining the OCDE (la Organización Europea de Cooperación y Desarrollo).[8] The launching of the SEAT 600 also coincided with the inauguration of Spanish television in 1956 and the advent of the advertising age. Spain's first mass car model was timely, since all the new products were, owing to television publicity, presented seductively to the masses ready for consumption. The SEAT 600 lasted 17 years in production and became known as 'el automóvil al alcance de todos los españoles' (Solé 1994: 36).[9]

Novel and cinema

The car 'within reach of all Spaniards' became all the rage; it was featured in pop songs and films of the era, and was the popular cultural icon par excellence. Furthermore, in July 1962, 'Franco premiaría a SEAT con la denominación de "Empresa Ejemplar", cuando nadie disputaba a SEAT el mérito de haber puesto a los españoles sobre cuatro ruedas' (Solé 1994: 37). Symbol of Spain's economic miracle, the SEAT 600 was a modern phenomenon that seemed to guarantee unlimited personal and familial mobility, a dream-turned-commodity of freedom. Echoing Franco himself, Waldo de Mier wrote 'una población con automóviles sin rasponazos ni abolladuras es una población subdesarrollada' (1964: 122). Now that Spaniards had discovered the pleasure of driving, he claimed, 'caminar se hace como dura obligación o deporte' (De Mier 1964: 122).

It was a moment in Spanish modernity when space came to be defined more by mobility than by dwelling. The automobile industry, the symbol of a new Spain in motion, was also tied to the politics of the dictatorship and the economic boom of the early 1960s. The automobile captured popular imagination; it brought excitement and thrills but also revealed a darker side, such as a fear of technology in general. As García Hortelano's novel *Nuevas amistades*

Figure 5.2. Julio Salvador's *Ya tenemos coche* (1958).

Figure 5.3. Fernando Fernán Gómez's *La vida por delante* (1958) depicting the biscúter before the advent of the SEAT 600.

(1959) illustrates, mass leisure and personal mobility took precedent over other forms of living in ways that were both celebrated and disturbing. García Hortelano's story describes the bored youth of 1950s Madrid over the course of a long and monotonous summer. The story's catalyst event is the unnecessary abortion surgery of the well-to-do Julia (who falsely believes she is pregnant). When Julia is apparently near death from the illegal abortion, the frightened peer-group attempts a cover-up by murder: a preplanned car crash. The novel's protagonists Gregorio and Jacinto discuss the murder scheme. Gregorio:

> A Julia le gusta conducir. Julia conduce mal. Coge el coche y el coche se le desmanda en una curva y se estrella. El automóvil, naturalmente, arde. Cuando nosotros llegamos, la están destruyendo las llamas...Ahora se trata de suponer que, en un momento cualquiera, muere. Primero es necesario hallar un lugar adecuado. Empujar el coche, con el cadáver dentro...(García Hortelano 1959: 200)

Jacinto responds:

> Desde la época de los grandes negocios, me ha quedado la costumbre de considerar cualquier majadería que se me proponga. Por si acaso. Existen dos o tres barrancos que servirían para escenario de tu novela policíaca. ¿Por qué no la titulas 'Incendio en la noche'? (García Hortelano 1959: 200)

Although Gregorio corrects him: 'Sería por el día. A pleno sol'—the plan turns out to be unnecessary because Julia recovers from her traumatic 'abortion' wounds (García Hortelano 1959: 201). But García Hortelano's protagonists' somewhat bizarre car-crash fantasy, replete with accident corpses, became a veritable topos in Spanish literature of the times.

Two common threads between the novels and films which incorporate new mobile phenomena are the conflict between society and the individual on the one hand, and the friction between old social models and the new consumer society on the other. Most of these print and celluloid fictions have deadly outcomes.[10] José Suárez Carreño's *Las últimas horas* (1950), about a wealthy businessman who flirts with prostitution in seedy Madrid, ends with a fatal car crash.[11] Alfonso Grosso's *La zanja* (1961) includes a fatal accident in which one of the characters is run over by a Spanish immigrant working in France for Citroën. In Ferreri and Azcona's *Cochecito* (1960), Don Anselmo poisons his entire family in order to obtain a coveted motorized wheelchair or *cochecito* which they had denied him.[12] In *El jardín de las delicias* (1970), Carlos Saura presents Antonio, a car-crash victim in a wheelchair, as a witness of the rapidly changing society of the 1950s and 1960s.

The automotive corpses of *Las últimas horas* (1950), *La zanja* (1961) and *Cochecito* (1960) have their counterparts in novels about tourism. We have referred to García

Figures 5.4–5.9. Key scenes from *Cochecito* depicting tension between modernity and mobility.

Hortelano's *Tormenta de verano* (1962) with its naked cadaver of a woman believed to be a tourist, as well as Aldecoa's *Parte de una historia* (1967) where the intoxicated American merrymaker drowns off the Canaries. Another movie of reference, García Berlanga's *El verdugo* (1963) shows how the pull of the sweet life can turn a normal person into a reluctant garrotter for the regime. To these we can add the repulsive image of two dead bodies on the beach in Fernando Fernán Gómez's movie *El extraño viaje* (1964). As Almodóvar vividly described them:

> …a partir de este momento [el inicio del boom económico] el cine español produjo un montón de comedias playeras, con suecas y playboys españoles y se enfadó mucho con *El extraño viaje*, donde la única playa que aparece exhibe en sus arenas los cadáveres de dos hermanos gordos, feos y borrachos. (2001: 55)

It is not by chance that death haunts these 'genres' tied to tourism and the automotive industry. The death and violence in these texts may be read as an ineluctable return of the trauma of the Civil War, which the 1950s generation of writers and cineasts had not experienced directly (an event that for toddlers and pre-teens was 'experienced too soon, too unexpectedly, to be fully known') (Caruth 1996: 4). Or these mayhems of fiction may be construed as another type of traumatic loss, that of politics proper and the end of the Left-wing struggle that informed the earlier literary production of these intellectuals. Max Aub, one of the most prominent Republican writers, captured it well upon his return to Spain in 1969 from his exile in Mexico:

> En este desconcierto, España es un remanso: auténticamente, la paz de los cementerios; no los de Franco (¿quién se acuerda ya de eso?) sino los de las playas donde yacen, quemados por el sol millares de cadáveres de todas especies y edades. (1995: 450)

He denounced all-conquering soccer as 'the great opium poppy', the opiate of the masses, and called television a monster, observing that for Spain it was no longer a question of *panem et circenses*, but of 'bread and television' (Aub 1995: 417; 307).

As memorably epitomized by Manuel Aznar Soler in his Introduction to Aub's *La gallina ciega*, the emigré's despair over Spain was a lament in much the same key over what the latter perceived as a loss of engaged activism and the beginnings of what were apolitical times:

> La España de 1969, un país sin justicia, libertad ni democracia, se resume para [Aub] en un 'desarrollo' económico propio de una sociedad consumista—paz, sol, turismo…habitado por españoles sumisos

Figures 5.10–5.15. Scenes from *El extraño viaje* showing the dark downside to tourism and modernity.

> y desinformados; desideologizados y despolitizados; ignorantes y resignados, que adoptan una actitud conformista y acomodaticia ante el silencio y el olvido impuestos por el régimen franquista...una sociedad en que la televisión es el instrumento fundamental de la alienación popular y de la subcultura de masas. (1995: 48, 49)

This was what prompted Aub's ironic call: '¡Vacacionistas de todos los países, uníos!' (1995: 450). After spending over 30 years in informed exile, however, Aub was still unable to imagine a different mode of politics that—despite the country's sea change—would be effective in the struggle against the dictatorship. As the 1950s generation who had stayed behind understood only too well, Aub's revolutionary politics of the 1930s were outmoded and impossible in the current climate of consumerism and large-scale, socio-economic transformation.

The country had begun to imagine more innovative modes of political resistance. As the Spanish historian Miguel Ángel Ruiz Carnicer points out, the new economic conditions presented new avenues for political renaissance:

> De alguna manera, la sociedad de masas, de consumo fue emergiendo como parte también de un proceso de renacimiento de la sociedad civil, apoyada por las nuevas condiciones económicas, pero no creada por éstas; el régimen se limitó a 'desencadenar,' es decir, literalmente a romper las cadenas autárquicas que lastraban la producción; y el desarrollo y la propia población, su memoria histórica y el desgaste de los viejos eslóganes de la dictadura hicieron el resto. A pesar del intento de apropriación de este desarrollo y proceso de cambio por parte del régimen (en parte logrado a través de medios masivos de comunicación como la televisión), hubo un vaciamiento progresivo del régimen en cuanto a ideas que hará que la distancia entre la sociedad española y el régimen, entre la España real y la oficial, como entonces se decía, tienda a hacerse cada vez más grande. (2001: 274)

Corpses, literary corpus and *corps politique* are thus hard to disentangle during this transitory, but volatile 'hinge decade' (*decenio bisagra*). In a rare caprice of fate, Martín-Santos, the author of *Tiempo de silencio* (which marked the break between Spanish social-realism and the New novel), died in a car crash in Vitoria on 21 January 1964 after spending his last summer filming a documentary about Spain's coastal tourist development. But Martín-Santos' grotesque demise at the end of our staggered decade, inextricable from tourism and the advent of the automobile, marked a rebirth as well: the consolidation of Spain's new literary and filmic corpus, contemporaneous with the grip of television, global markets and that neo-liberalism which eventually contributed to 'the end of literature and the end of the [sovereign] state' (Levinson 2001: 1, 2).[13]

Paradoxically, the times brought not only movement and dispersion, but also the annihilation of political space and a prior anti-Franco discourse. In the long run, a new configuration took place and the long-promised constitutional monarchy was duly installed. The phenomena discussed in this book—the savvy publishing industry, the expansion of Spain's television network, the making of the child-star system, the development of mass tourism and the national automobile industry—heralded the new era and its inner convulsions. As Goytisolo asserted, the same phenomena foreshadowed the end of dictatorship:

> Poco a poco, gracias a la doble corriente de forasteros y emigrantes, expatriados y turistas, en España y fuera de ella, el español ha aprendido, por primera vez en la historia, a trabajar, comer, viajar, explotar comercialmente sus virtudes y defectos, asimilar los valores crematísticos de las sociedades industriales, mercantilizarse, prostituirse, y todo ello—paradoja extrema de una tierra singularmente fértil en burlas sangrientas y feroces contrastes—bajo un sistema originariamente creado para impedirlo. ('Examen de conciencia'; 1976: 261)

To paraphrase Boyd, the tendencies enumerated by Goytisolo also signalled the end of any credible reality concerning so-called Spanish 'difference', the coddled myth of Spanish ineptitude for modern political and economic life which had helped legitimize the Francoist dictatorship (Boyd 1997: 304).[14] And, to paraphrase both Shakespeare and our eccentric De Mier, Spain had finally shuffled off its mortal coil—or skin—of torpid repression.

Notes

1. *La vida sobre ruedas* was the motto of the Spanish television guide *TeleDiario* that was giving away a car (Dauphine) in a raffle for their subscribers: 'Para él o ella, que en esto de la suerte no caben distinciones de sexo, 1959 hará realidad el lema de 'la vida sobre ruedas' (January 1959, # 54).

2. Giovanni Agnelli's FIAT was created in 1899. FIAT, an extremely sucessful car company, was established four years before American Ford Motor Company.

3. Solé writes that 'En el contexto autárquico, la creación de INI respondió a la necesidad de fomentar, por parte del Estado, un desarrollo industrial para el que

no estaba capacitado el sector privado. Un empuje a la industrialización que se dirigiría con especial énfasis al sector militar, a fin de garantizar la defensa del régimen, interesándose asimismo en la producción de abonos para la agricultura, industria química y automoción' (1994: 12).

4. See Solé (1994: 21, 22).

5. Until 1969 SEAT did not have its unique model that differed from the Italian original: '…toda la producción de automóviles se basaba no solo en proyectos previamente aprobados en Italia, sino lanzados al Mercado por FIAT en primer lugar…los modelos fabricados en España salían al Mercado con unos dos años de retraso respecto a sus homónimos turineses' (Solé 1994: 28).

6. Topolino, FIAT 500, was produced in Italy from 1936 until 1955 and known as 'il Topolino' or little mouse.

7. The Italian original, FIAT 600 (Italian: Seicento), hit the market in 1955. It was a rear-engine model, intended to be more utilitarian and accessible but better then Topolino (FIAT 500).

8. Spain was an indirect recepient of Marshall Plan benefits since FIAT Torino factory, partially destroyed during the war, was rebuilt and put back on track by 1948 with Marshall Plan aid.

9. The first year saw 2500 units of SEAT 600 produced, within the next year the number rose to 12,000 and output reached its pinnacle in 1970 with 78,000 units.

10. Sánchez Ferlosio's *El Jarama* (1955) features another floating and disturbing corpse tied to dictatorship, and as Epps points out: 'After all, the anodyne conversations take place by a river once, and not that long ago, bloodied by battle. The relation between the book and the world, textuality and topography, is fraught with oblivion' (2003: 197). Epps adds: 'Without the drowning, the story would sink into the anonymity of daily life. But with the drowning, literariness is retained, or rescued' (2003: 198).

11. *Las últimas horas* won Premio Eugenio Nadal in 1949.

12. The screenplay for *Cochecito*, was written by Azcona, based on his novella *Pobre, paralítico y muerto*.

13. As clarified in our Introduction, Brett Levinson indicates that the end of a nation state does not refer to its disappearance but 'alludes to the demise of the *sovereign* state, which now must compete with other domains such as the global market and international political organizations' and the end of literature 'signifies that literature, which once occupied a privileged position within the state itself, must now battle for that rank and legitimacy with other forms of creation, above all, mass and popular culture' (2001: 1, 2).

14. Boyd echoes Goytisolo's assertion that 'si España no es aún Europa, para bien y para mal ha dejado de ser España' ('Examen de conciencia'; 1976: 263).

Bibliography

Abella, R. (1996), *La vida cotidiana bajo el régimen de Franco*, Madrid: Temas de Hoy, S.A.

Afinoguénova, E. and Marti-Olivella, J., (eds) (2008), *Spain Is (Still) Different: Tourism and Discourse in Spanish Identity*, Lexington, MA: Lexington Books.

Aldecoa, I. (2005), *Parte de una historia*, Madrid: Clásicos Castalia.

Allen, R. C. (1992), 'Audience-oriented Criticism', in R. C. Allen (ed.), *Channels of Discourse, Reassembled*, Chapel Hill: University of North Carolina Press, pp. 101–37.

Almodóvar, P. (2001), 'Una sórdida comedia neosurrealista', in F. Strauss (ed.), *Conversaciones con Pedro Almodóvar*, Madrid: Ediciones Akal, S.A., p. 55.

Alonso, D. (1986), *Hijos de la ira*, Madrid: Editorial Castalia.

Aragones, J. E. (1959), 'Turismo en zapatillas', *TeleDiario*, 80: 3.

Aub, M. (1995), *La gallina ciega. Diario español*, Barcelona: Alba Editorial.

Augé, M. (1995), *Non-Places: Introduction to an Anthropology of Supermodernity*, London and New York: Verso.

Ayucar, Á. R. (1958), 'Soledad habitada', *TeleDiario*, 17: 9.

——— (1959), 'Yo ante las cámaras', *TeleDiario*, 88: 3.

Azcona, R. and Sánchez, B. (1991), *Otra vuelta en el cochecito*, Logroño: Cultura Riojana, Gobierno de la Rioja, Ayuntamiento de Logroño.

Baget i Herms, J. M. (1992), *Historia de la televisión en España 1956–1975*, Barcelona: Feed-Back.

Ballesteros, I. (1999), 'Mujer y Nación en el cine español de posguerra: los años 40', *Arizona Journal of Hispanic Cultural Studies*, 3, pp. 51–70.

Barciela, C., López, I., Melgarejo J., and Miranda J., (eds) (2001), *La España de Franco (1939–1975). Economía*, Madrid: Editorial Síntesis.

Barral, C. (1975), *Años de penitencia*, Madrid: Alianza Editorial.

——— (1978), *Los años sin excusa*, Barcelona: Barral Editores.

——— (1983), *Penúltimos castigos*, Barcelona: Seix Barral.

——— (1988), *Cuando las horas veloces*, Barcelona: Tusquets Editores.

——— (2000), *Almanaque*, Barcelona: Cuatro Ediciones.

Barreiro, J. (1999), *Marisol frente a Pepa Flores*, Barcelona: Plaza & Janés.

Barroso, J. and Tranche, R. R. (1996), 'La historia de la televisión en España', *Archivos de la Filmoteca*, 23–24, pp. 5–10.

Barthes, R. (1981), *Camera Lucida: Reflections on Photography*, NewYork: Hill and Wang.

Ben-Amí, S. (1980), *La revolución desde arriba: España 1936–1979*, Barcelona: Ríopiedras Ediciones.

Benet, J. (1976), 'Una época troyana', in *En ciernes*, Madrid: Taurus, pp. 85–102.

Benjamin, W. (1969), 'Theses on the Philosophy of History', in *Illuminations: Essays and Reflections*, New York: Schocken, pp. 253–264.

Biedma, J. G. (1974), *Diario del artista seriamente enfermo*, Barcelona: Lumen.

Black, S. (2001), *Juan Goytisolo and the Poetics of Contagion: the Evolution of a Radical Aesthetic in the Later Novels*, Liverpool: Liverpool University Press.

Bloom, H. (1997), *The Anxiety of Influence: A Theory of Poetry*, Oxford: Oxford University Press.

Boltanski, L. (1987), *The Making of a Class: Cadres in French Society*, London: Cambridge University Press.

Bonet, L. (1988), *La revista 'Laye.' Estudio y antología*, Barcelona: Peninsula.

——— (1994), *El jardín quebrado. La Escuela de Barcelona y la cultura del medio siglo*, Barcelona: Peninsula.

Bordieu, P. (1993), *The Field of Cultural Production*, New York: Columbia University Press.

Bousoño, C. (1952), *Teoría de la expresión poética*, Madrid: Gredos.

Boyd, C. P. (1997), *Historia Patria: Politics, History and National Identity in Spain, 1875–1975*, Princeton: Princeton University Press.

Brunsdon, C. (1998), 'What is the "Television" of Television Studies', in C. Geraghty and D. Lusted (eds), *The Television Studies Book*, London: Arnold, pp. 95–113.

Calvo Serer, R. (1949), *España sin problema*, Madrid: Ediciones Rialp.

Campbell, F. (1994), 'José María Castellet o la crítica simultánea', in *Infame Turba: entrevistas a pensadores poetas y novelistas en la España de 1970*, Barcelona: Lumen, p. 298.

Camporesi, V. (1999), 'Imágenes de la televisión en el cine español de los sesenta', *Archivos de la Filmoteca*, 32, pp. 149–162.

(1958) 'Caras nuevas,' *TeleDiario*, 23: 8.

Carr, R. and Fusi, J. P. (1981), *Spain: Dictatorship to Democracy*, London: Allen & Unwin.

Caruth, C. (1996), *Unclaimed Experience: Trauma, Narrative, and History*, Baltimore: The Johns Hopkins University Press.

Castellet, J. M. (1951), 'Las técnicas de la literatura sin autor', *Laye*, 12, pp. 39–46.

——— (1952a), '*La colmena.* (Notas con estrambote)', *Laye*, 18, pp. 51–58.

——— (1952b), 'Notas sobre la situación actual del escritor en España', *Laye*, 20, pp. 10–17.

——— (1953a), 'El tiempo del lector', *Laye*, 23, pp. 39–45.

——— (1953b), 'Faulkner y el lector', *Revista*, 85, p. 10.

——— (1953c), 'Notas sobre la situación actual del escritor catalán', *Ínsula*, 95, p. 10.

——— (1954a), 'Cuatro características de la novela norteamericana actual', *Revista*, 102, p. 6.

——— (1954b), 'En vez de letras, números', *Revista*, 108, p. 10.

——— (1954c), 'Hemingway, Premio Nobel 1954', *Revista*, 134, p. 1.

——— (1955a), 'La técnica objetiva de narración en la novela norteamericana', *Ateneo*, 76, pp. 79–80.

——— (1955b), *Notas sobre literatura española contemporánea*, Barcelona: Laye.

——— (1955c), 'Prólogo para lectores europeos', in a prologue to F. J. Hoffman (ed.), *La novela moderna en Norteamérica*, Barcelona: Seix Barral , pp. 5–11.

——— (1957a), *La hora del lector. Notas para una iniciación a la literatura narrativa de nuestros días*, Barcelona: Seix Barral.

——— (1957b), 'M. Coindreau y la novela española actual', *Revista*, 256, p. 14.

——— (1957c), 'Notas para una iniciación a la obra de John Steinbeck', in L. Caralt (ed.), *Obras completas*, John Steinbeck (vol. I) Barcelona: Piel Editorial, pp. IX–XXIX.

——— (1958a), 'La novela española, quince años después (1942–1957)', *Cuadernos del Congreso por la Libertad de la Cultura*, 33, pp. 48–52.

——— (1958b), 'The Present Situation of the Novel in Spain', *Instituto de Estudios Norteamericanos, American Club*, pp. 54–5.

——— (1959), 'El primer Coloquio Internacional sobre Novela', *Ínsula*, 152–3, pp. 19–32.

——— (1960a), 'El Segundo Coloquio Internacional de Novela en Formentor', *Ínsula*, 163, p. 4.

——— (1960b), *Veinte años de poesía española (1939–1959)*, Barcelona: Seix Barral.

——— (1961), 'Juan Goytisolo y la novela española actual', *La Torre*, 33, pp. 131–40.

——— (1963a), 'La joven novela española', *Sur*, 284.

——— (1963b), 'Veinte años de novela española (1942–1962)', *Cuadernos americanos*, XXII, pp. 290–295.

——— (1965a), *Poesia, realisme, història*. Barcelona: Edicions 62.

——— (1965)b, *Un cuarto de siglo de poesía española (1939–1964)*, Barcelona: Seix Barral.

——— (1970), *Nueve novísimos poetas españoles*, Barcelona: Barral Editores.

——— (1971), 'La actual literatura latinoamericana vista desde España', in *Panorama de la actual literatura latinoamericana*, Madrid: Fundamentos.

——— (1976), 'Tiempo de destrucción para la literatura española', in *Literatura, ideología y política*, Barcelona: Anagrama, pp. 135–156.

——— (1988), *Los escenarios de la memoria*, Barcelona: Anagrama.

——— (1990), 'Una imagen que se aleja', *La Vanguardia. Cultural.*

Celaya, G. (1979), *Poesía y verdad. Papeles para un proceso*, Barcelona: Planeta.

Chicharro, A. (1989), *La teoría y crítica literaria de Gabriel Celaya*, Granada: Universidad de Granada.

Chion, M. (1999), *The Voice in Cinema*, New York: Columbia University Press.

Corner, J. (1999), *Critical Ideas in Television Studies*, Oxford: Oxford University Press.

Crespo MacLennan, J. (2000), *Spain and the Process of European Integration*, Basingstoke and New York: Palgrave Macmillan.

Crumbaugh, J. (2009), *Destination Dictatorship: The Spectacle of Spain's Tourist Boom and the Reinvention of Difference*, Albany: State University of New York Press.

D'Lugo, M. (1997), *Guide to the Cinema of Spain*, Westport: Greenwood Press.

De las Casas, E. (1958), 'Amistad y popularidad', *TeleDiario*, 36: 7.

——— (1958), 'La intimidad', *Telediario*, 33: 3+.

De Mier, W. (1954), *España cambia de piel*, Madrid: Ediciones Cultura Hispánica.

——— (1964), *España cambia de piel* (*Nuevo viaje por la 'España del Milagro'*), Madrid: Editora Nacional.

Derrida, J. (1994), *Specters of Marx*, New York: Routledge.

Díaz, E. (1995), 'The Left and the Legacy of Francoism: Political Culture in Opposition and Transition', in H. Graham and J. Labanyi (eds), *Spanish Cultural Studies*, Oxford: Oxford University Press, pp. 283–290.

Díez Medrano, J. (2003), *Framing Europe: Attitudes to European Integration in Germany, Spain, and the United Kingdom*, Princeton: Princeton University Press.

Dolar, M. (1996), 'The Object Voice', in R. Salecl and S. Zizek (eds), *Gaze and Voice as Love Objects*, Durham: Duke University Press, pp. 7–31.

Elena, A. (2001), 'El cantor del cine Rex. Una revisión del cine de Joselito', *Archivos de la Filmoteca*, 38, pp. 49–61.

(1958), '*En marcha hacia el* futuro', *TeleDiario*, 13: 8.

Epps, B. (1995), 'Figuring Hysteria: Disorder and Desire in Three Films of Pedro Almodóvar', in K. Vernon and B. Morris (eds), *Post-Franco, Postmodern: The Films of Pedro Almodóvar*, Connecticut: Greenwood Press, pp. 99–124.

——— (1996), *Significant Violence: Oppression and Resistance in the Narrative of Juan Goytisolo, 1970–1990*, Oxford: Oxford University Press.

——— (2003), 'Questioning the Text', in H. Turner and A. López de Martínez (eds), *The Cambridge Companion to the Spanish Novel*, Cambridge: Cambridge University Press, pp. 193–211.

(1959), '¿Eres una chica moderna?', *TeleDiario*, 60: 10+.

Faulkner, S. (2006), *A Cinema of Contradiction. Spanish Film in the 1960s*, Edinburgh: Edinburgh University Press.

Fernández de la Mora, G. (1965), *El crepúsculo de las ideologías*, Madrid: Ediciones Rialp, S.A.

Fish, S. (1980), *Is there a Text in this Class? The Authority of Interpretive Communities*, Cambridge: Harvard University Press.

Fortes, J. A. (1988), 'Gallimard y la Novela Española de Postguerra. Años 1957–1968', *Letras Peninsulares*, 1: 2, pp. 183–199.

Foucault, M. (1994), *The Order of Things: An Archaeology of the Human Sciences*, New York: Vintage.

Fox, I. E. (1999), 'Spain as Castile: Nationalism and National Identity', in D. T. Gies (ed.), *The Cambridge Companion to Modern Spanish Culture*, Cambridge: Cambridge University Press, pp. 21–36.

Fraga Iribarne, M. (1952), *How Spain is Governed*, Madrid: Oficina de Información Diplomática.

——— (1955), *La crisis del Estado*, Madrid: Aguilar.

——— (1963), *El turismo en España: balanza y perspectiva*, Madrid: Ministerio de Información y Turismo.

——— (1965), *Horizonte español*, Madrid: Editora Nacional.

——— (1971), *El desarrollo político*, Barcelona-México: Ediciones Grijalbo.

——— (1980), *Memoria breve de una vida pública*, Barcelona: Planeta.

Fragoso del Toro, J. (1958), 'La antena solitaria', *TeleDiario*, 36: 3.

Fusi, J. P. and Palafox, J., (eds) (1997), *España (1808–1996): El desafío de la modernidad*, Madrid: Espasa Calpe.

García Delgado, J. L. (1986), 'Estancamiento industrial e intervencionismo económico durante el primer franquismo', in J. Fontana (ed.), *España bajo el franquismo*, Barcelona: Editorial Crítica.

García Hortelano, J. (1959), *Nuevas amistades*, Barcelona: Seix Barral.

——— (1989), *Tormenta de verano*, Madrid: Editorial Castalia.

García Serrano, R. (1964), 'Prologue', in W. De Mier, *España cambia de piel*, Madrid: Ediciones Cultura Hispánica, pp. ix–xiii.

Gies, D. T. (ed.) (1999), *The Cambridge Companion to Modern Spanish Culture*, Cambridge: Cambridge University Press.

Gil de Biedma, J. (1959), *Infancia y confesiones, Compañeros de viaje*, Barcelona: J. Horta.

Gilmour, J. (1999), *Manuel Fraga Iribarne and the Rebirth of Spanish Conservatism in Post-Franco Polictics 1939–1990*, New York: Edwin Mellen Press.

Gimferrer, P. (1977), 'El pensamiento literario (1939–1976)', in C. Castilla del Pino (ed.), *La cultura bajo el franquismo*, Barcelona: Anagrama.

Gónzales Ruano, C. (1958), 'La televisión', *TeleDiario*, 28: 7.

Gould Levine, L. (1976), *Juan Goytisolo, la destrucción creadora*, México: J. Mortiz.

Goux, J. J. (1990), *Symbolic Economies: After Marx and Freud*, Ithaca: Cornel University Press.

Goytisolo, J. (1954), *Juegos de manos*, Barcelona: Ediciones Destino.

——— (1955), *Duelo en el Paraíso*, Barcelona: Planeta.

——— (1957), *El circo*, Barcelona: Destino.

——— (1958a), *Fiestas*, Barcelona: Destino.

——— (1958b), *La resaca*, París: Club del Libro Español.

——— (1959), *Problemas de la novela*, Barcelona: Seix Barral..

——— (1960a), *Campos de Níjar*, Barcelona: Seix Barral.

——— (1960b), *Para vivir aquí*. Buenos Aires: Sur.

——— (1961), *La isla*. Barcelona: Seix Barral.

——— (1962), *Fin de fiesta*. Barcelona: Narrativa Mondadori.

——— (1976), *El furgón de cola*, Barcelona: Seix Barral.

——— (1981), *La Chanca*, Barcelona: Seix Barral.

——— (1985), *Contracorrientes*, Barcelona: Ediciones Montesinos.

——— (1986), *En los reinos de Taifa*, Barcelona: Seix Barral.

——— (2005a), *Obras completas I. Novelas y ensayo (1954–1959)*, Barcelona: Círculo de Lectores, S.A.

——— (2005b), 'Para una literatura nacional popular', in J. Goytisolo, *Obras completas I. Novelas y ensayo (1954–1959)*, Barcelona: Círculo de Lectores, S.A., pp. 905–916.

Gracia García, J. and Ruiz Carnicer, M.A., (eds) (2001), *La España de Franco (1939–1975). Cultura y vida cotidiana*, Madrid: Editorial Síntesis.

(1958) 'Gracias a la televisión', *TeleDiario*, 7: 1.

Graham, H. (1995), 'Gender and State: Women in the 1940s', in H. Graham and J. Labanyi (eds), *Spanish Cultural Studies*, Oxford: Oxford University Press, pp. 182–195.

Graham, H. and Labanyi, J. (1995), 'Editors' Preface', in H. Graham and J. Labanyi (eds), *Spanish Cultural Studies*, Oxford: Oxford University Press, v–viii.

Graham, H. and Labanyi, J. (1995), 'Introduction. Culture and Modernity: The Case of Spain', in H. Graham and J. Labanyi (eds), *Spanish Cultural Studies*, Oxford: Oxford University Press, pp. 1–19.

Gubern, R. (2001), 'Teoría y práctica del star-system infantil', *Archivos de la Filmoteca*, 38, pp. 9–15.

Guillory, J. (1993), *Cultural Capital: The Problem of Literary Canon Formation*, Chicago: The University of Chicago Press.

Harrison, J. (1978), *An Economic History of Modern Spain*, Manchester: Manchester University Press.

Harrison, J. (1995), *The Spanish Economy from the Civil War to the European Community (Studies in Economic and Social History)*, Cambridge: Cambridge University Press.

Heredero, C. F. (1993), *Las huellas del tiempo: cine español 1951–61*, Madrid: Filmoteca.

Herrero-Olaizola, A. (2007), *The Censorship Files: Latin American Writers and Franco's Spain*, Albany: State University of New York Press.

Herzberger, D. (1991), 'Social Realism and the Contingencies of History in the Contemporary Spanish Novel', *Hispanic Review*, 59: 2, pp. 153–173.

——— (1995), *Narrating the Past: Fiction and Historiography in Post-war Spain*, Durham, NC: Duke University Press.

Hobsbawm, E. (1994), *Age of Extremes: The Short Twentieth Century, 1914–91*, London: Penguin.

Horkheimer, M. and Adorno, T. (1976), *The Dialectic of Enlightenment*, London: Continuum International Publishing Group.

Huyssen, A. (1986), *After the Great Divide: Modernism, Mass Culture, Postmodernism*, Bloomington: Indiana University Press.

Ibáñez, J. C. (2001), 'Televisión y cambio social en la España de los años 50. Apuntes sobre el proceso de legitimación del medio televisivo en la dictadura de Franco', *Secuencias: Revista de historia del cine*, 13, pp. 48–67.

Járegui, F. and Vega, P., *Crónica del antifraquismo: El nacimiento de una nueva clase política (1963–1970)*, Barcelona: Editorial Planeta.

Jiménez, J. R. (1919), *Piedra y cielo (1917–1918)*, Madrid: Fortanet.

Jordan, B. (1990a), *Writing and politics in Franco's Spain*, New York: Routledge.

——— (1990b), 'Sartre, *Engagement* and the Spanish Realist Novel of the 1950s', *Journal of European Studies*, 20: 4, pp. 299–323.

——— (1990c), 'At the Margins of Social Realism: The Early Goytisolo', *Symposium: A Quarterly Journal in Modern Literatures*, 44: 2, pp. 88–101.

Julía, S. (2004), *Historia de las dos Españas*, Madrid: Santillana Ediciones Generales.

Kinder, M. (1993), *Blood Cinema: Reconstruction of National Identity in Spain*, Berkeley: University of California Press.

Koshar, R. (2000), *German Travel Cultures. Leisure, Consumption and Culture*, Oxford: Berg Publishers.

(1957), 'La televisión en el hogar', *TeleDiario*, 1: 2.

Labanyi, J. (1989), *Myth and History in the Contemporary Spanish Novel*, Cambridge: Cambridge University Press.

——— (1997), 'Race, gender and disavowal in Spanish cinema of the early Franco period: the missionary film and the folkloric musical', *Screen*, 38: 3, pp. 215–227.

——— (2000), *Gender and Modernization in the Spanish Realist Novel*, Oxford: Oxford University Press.

——— (2002), 'Musical Battles: Populism and Hegemony in the Early Francoist Folkloric Film Musical', in J. Labanyi (ed.), *Constructing Identity in Contemporary Spain*, Oxford: Oxford University Press, pp. 206–221.

Labanyi, J., Marsh, S., Martin-Márquez, S., Sánchez Biosca, V., Vernon, K. and E. Woods, (forthcoming), *The Mediation of Everyday Life: Remembering Cinema in 1940s and 1950s Spain*.

Laín Entralgo, P. (1948), *España como problema*, Madrid: Seminario de Problemas Hispanoamericanos.

Landy, M. (1998), *The Folklore of Consensus*, Albany: State University of New York Press.

Lázaro-Reboll, A. and Willis, A. (2004), 'Introduction: film studies, Spanish cinema and question of the popular', in A. Lázaro-Reboll and A. Willis (eds), *Spanish Popular Cinema*, Manchester: Manchester University Press, pp. 1–23.

Levinson, B. (2001), *The Ends of Literature*, Stanford: Stanford University Press.

Longhurst, A. (2000), 'Culture and Development: The Impact of 1960s "Desarrollismo" ', in B. Jordan and R. Morgan-Tamasunas (eds), *Contemporary Spanish Cultural Studies*, London: Arnold, pp. 18–28.

López, A. M. (1997), 'Of Rhythms and Borders', in D. Fraser and J. E. Muñoz (eds), *Everynight Life. Culture and Dance in Latin/o America*, Durham: Duke University Press, pp. 310–344.

López Ibor, J. J. (1951), *El español y su complejo de inferioridad*, Madrid: Ediciones Rialp.

MacCannell, D. (1999), *The Tourist: A New Theory of the Leisure Class*, Berkeley: University of California Press.

Mangini, S. (1987), *Rojos y rebeldes. La cultura de la disidencia durante el franquismo*, Barcelona: Anthropos.

Marías, J. (1949), 'El método histórico de las generaciones', Madrid: *Revista de Occidente*.

Marsal, J. F. (1979), *Pensar bajo el franquismo: intelectuales y política en la generación de los años cincuenta*, Barcelona: Ediciones Peninsula.

Marsh, S. (2006), *Popular Spanish Film under Franco. Comedy and the Weakening of the State*, Basingstoke and New York: Palgrave Macmillan.

Martín, A. (2005), *La gramática de la felicidad. Relecturas franquistas y posmodernas del melodrama*, Madrid: Ediciones Libertarias.

Martín Abril, F. J. (1958), 'La ventana maravillosa', *TeleDiario*, 3.

——— (1959), 'Epítomes de cultura', *TeleDiario*, 73: 3.

Martín Gaite, C. (1987), *Usos amorosos de la postguerra española*, Barcelona: Editorial Anagrama.

Martín-Santos, L. (1975), *Tiempo de destrucción*, Barcelona: Seix Barral.

——— (1995), *Tiempo de silencio*, Barcelona: Seix Barral.

——— (2004), *Condenada belleza del mundo*, Barcelona: Seix Barral.

Martín-Santos Laffón, L. (2004), 'Prólogo', in L. Martín-Santos, *Condenada belleza del mundo*, Barcelona: Seix Barral, pp. ix–xiv.

Martínez Uceda, J. and Rodríguez Márquez, I. (1992), *La televisión: historia y desarrollo (los pioneros de la televisión)*, Madrid: Mitre/RTVE.

Marx, K. (1976), *Capital*, vol. 1, London: Verso.

Maxwell, R. (1995), *The Spectacle of Democracy. Spanish Television, Nationalism, and Political Transition*, Minneapolis: University of Minnesota Press.

McCarthy, A. (2001), *Ambient Television*, Durham: Duke University Press.

Melero Melero, J. (1958), 'Cartas a *TeleDiario*', *TeleDiario*, 25: 16.

Mesquida, B. and Panero, L. M. (1977), 'Gil de Biedma o la palabra sentida, sufrida y gozada', *El Viejo Topo*, 7, pp. 41–43.

Mitchell, T. (1990), *Passional Culture: Emotion, Religion, and Society in Southern Spain*, Philadelphia: University of Pennsylvania Press.

——— (1994), *Flamenco Deep Song*, New Haven: Yale University Press.

Moix, T. (1993), *Suspiros de España: la copla y el cine de nuestro recuerdo*, Barcelona: Plaza y Janés.

Morales, J. L. (1979a), 'Marisol nos cuenta su vida (1)', *Interviu*, 169, pp. 25-28.

_____ (1979b), 'Marisol nos cuenta su vida (2)', *Interviu*, 170, pp. 28-31.

Morán, F. (1971), *Novela y semidesarrollo: una interpretación de la novela hispanoamericana y española*, Madrid: Taurus.

Nancy, J. L. (1993), 'Finite History', in J. L. Nancy, *The Birth to Presence*, Stanford: Stanford University Press, pp. 143–166.

Ortega y Gasset, J. (1921), *España invertebrada*, Madrid: *Revista de Occidente.*

——— (1971), *Historia como sistema*, Madrid: Espasa-Calpe.

——— (1982), *Ideas sobre el teatro y la novela*, Madrid: Alizanza Editorial.

Pack, S. (2006), *Tourism and Dictatorship: Europe's Peaceful Invasion of Franco's Spain*, Basingstoke and New York: Palgrave Macmillan.

Palacio, M. (1992), *Una historia de la televisión en España. Arqueología y Modernidad*, Madrid: Consorcio de Madrid Capital Europea de la Cultura.

——— (2001), *Historia de la televisión en España*, Barcelona: Editorial Gedisa.

Pardo Sanz, R. (2009), 'US Bases in Spain since 1953', in L. Rodrigues and S. Glebov (eds), *Military Bases: Historical Perspectives, Contemporary Challenges*, Amsterdam: IOS Press, pp. 56–67.

Pavlović, T. (2003), *Despotic Bodies and Transgressive Bodies: Spanish Culture from Francisco Franco to Jesús Franco*, Albany: State University of New York Press.

——— (2004), '*España cambia de piel*: The Mobile Nation (1954–1964)', *Journal of Spanish Cultural Studies*, 5: 2, pp. 213–226.

——— (2007), 'Television (Hi)stories: *Un escaparate en cada hogar*', *Journal of Spanish Cultural Studies*, 8: 1, pp. 5–21.

Payne, S. G. (1987), *The Franco Regime, 1936–1975*, Wisconsin: University of Wisconsin Press.

——— (1988), 'Spanish Fascism', *Salmagundi*, 76–77 (Fall 1987–Winter 1988), pp. 101–112.

Perlado, J. J. (1959), 'La aventura de la televisión', *TeleDiario*, 84: 3.

Pittarello, E. (2005), 'Edición, introducción y notas', in I. Aldecoa, *Parte de una historia*, Madrid: Clásicos Castalia, pp. 7–68.

Plonowska Ziarek, E. (1998), 'The Scar of the Foreigner and the Fold of the Baroque: National Affiliations and Homosexuality in Gombrowicz's Trans-Atlantyk', in E. Plonowska Ziarek (ed.), *Gombrowicz' Grimaces: Modernism, Gender, Nationality*, Albany: State University of New York Press, pp. 213–244.

Pope, R. D. (1995), *Understanding Juan Goytisolo*, Columbia: University of South Carolina Press.

Prados de la Escosura, L. (1999), 'Economic Growth and Backwardness, 1780–1930', in J. Alvarez Junco and A. Shubert (eds), *Spanish History Since 1808*, London: Arnold Press, pp. 179–190.

——— (2003), *El progreso económico de España*, Madrid: Fundación BBVA.

Preston, P. (1994), *Franco: A Biography*, NY: BasicBooks.

Primo de Rivera, J. A. (1962), *Obras completas*, Madrid: Editora Nacional.

(1958), 'Publicidad', *TeleDiario*, 33: 8.

Rama, Á. (1981), 'El "boom" en perspectiva', in Á. Rama, *Más allá del boom: literatura y mercado*, Mexico: Marcha, pp. 51–110.

Riera, C. (1988), *La Escuela de Barcelona. Barral, Gil de Biedma, Goytisolo: el núcleo poético de la generación de los 50*, Barcelona: Anagrama.

Robbe-Grillet, A. (1963), *Pour un nouveau roman*, Paris: Éditions de Minuit.

——— (1965), *For a New Novel: Essays on Fiction*, New York: Grove Press.

Rodríguez-Puértolas, J. (1987), *Literatura fascista española*, Volume I & II, Madrid: Ediciones Akal.

Ross, K. (1996), *Fast Cars, Clean Bodies: Decolonization and the Reordering of French Culture*, The MIT Press, Cambridge, Massachusetts.

Ruiz Carnicer, M. A. (2001), 'La España desarrollista. Nueva sociedad, viejo régimen', in J. Gracia García and M. A. Ruiz Carnicer (eds), *La España de Franco (1939–1975). Cultura y vida cotidiana*, Madrid: Editorial Síntesis, pp. 271–282.

Salas Romo, E. A. (2003), *El pensamiento literario de J.M. Castellet*, Granada: Editorial Universidad de Granada.

Salisbury, W. and Theberge, J. (eds) (1976), *Spain in the 1970s: Economics, Social Structure, and Foreign Policy*, NewYork and London: Praeger.

Salmon, K. (1995), *The Modern Spanish Economy: Transformation and Integration into Europe*, London and NewYork: Pinter.

Sánchez Vidal, A. (1990), *Sol y sombra*, Barcelona: Editorial Planeta.

Santana, M. (2000), *Foreigners in the Homeland: The Spanish American New Novel in Spain, 1962–1974*, Lewisburg: Bucknell University Press.

Sanz Villanueva S. (1980), *Historia de la novela social española (1942–75)*, Madrid: Alhambra.

Sartre, J. P. (1946), 'American Novelists in French Eyes', *Atlantic*, Concord: N.H. 178: 2, pp. 114–118.

——— (1957), *¿Qué es la literatura?*, 2nd edn., Buenos Aires: Losada, 1957.

——— (1988), *What is Literature? And Other Essays*, Cambridge: Harvard University Press.

Scannell, P. (2000), 'For-anyone-as-someone structures', *Media, Culture & Society*, 22, pp. 5–24.

Seguin, J. C. (1990), *Joselito: la voix inhumaine. Du genre au corpus, du corpus à l'acteur*, Ph.D. Diss., University of Bordeaux.

Serrano, E., 'El rostro de los escritores', *TeleDiario*, 70: 3.

Servià, J. M. (1975), 'Josep M. Castellet', in J. M. Servià, *Catalunya, 3 generaciones*, Barcelona: Ediciones Martínez Roca, 1975.

Sieburth, S. A. (1994), *Inventing High and Low: Literature, Mass Culture, and Uneven Modernity in Spain*, Durham: Duke University Press.

Smith, P. J. (1992), *Laws of Desire: Questions of Homosexuality in Spanish Writing and Film, 1960–1990*, Oxford: Oxford University Press.

——— (2000), *The Moderns: Time, Space, and Subjectivity in Contemporary Spanish Culture*, Oxford: Oxford University Press.

——— (2002), 'Spanish Quality TV? The *Periodistas* Notebook', in J. Labanyi (ed.), *Constructing Identity in Contemporary Spain*, Oxford: Oxford University Press, pp. 311–333.

——— (2003), *Contemporary Spanish Culture. TV, Fashion, Art and Film*. Cambridge: Polity Press.

——— (2006a), *Spanish Visual Culture. Cinema, Television, Internet*, Manchester: Manchester University Press.

——— (2006b), *Television in Spain. From Franco to Almodóvar*, Woodbridge: Tamesis.

——— (ed.) (2007a), 'New Approaches to Spanish Television', *Journal of Spanish Cultural Studies*, 8: 1.

——— (2007b), 'Introduction: New Approaches to Spanish Television', *Journal of Spanish Cultural Studies*, 8: 1, pp. 1–4.

——— (2009), *Spanish Screen Fiction. Between Cinema and Television*, Liverpool: Liverpool University Press.

Sobejano, G. (1975a), *Novela española de nuestro tiempo: en busca del pueblo perdido*, Madrid: Prensa Española.

——— (1975b), *Juan Goytisolo*, Madrid: Editorial Fundamentos.

——— (2003) 'The Testimonial Novel and the Novel of Memory', in H. Turner and A. López de Martínez (eds), *The Cambridge Companion to the Spanish Novel*, Cambridge: Cambridge University Press, pp.172–192.

Solé, E. (1994), *SEAT 1950–1993*, Barcelona: Ediciones de la Tempestad.

Soler, M. A. (1995), 'Max Aub en el laberinto español', in M. Aub, *La gallina ciega. Diario español*, Barcelona: Alba Editorial, pp. 7–95.

Spigel, L. (1992), *Make Room for TV: Television and the Family Ideal in Postwar America*, Chicago: University of Chicago Press.

Sueiro, D. (1959), 'La visita de Ike', *TeleDiario*, 105: 6: 7.

Suleiman, S. (1983), *Authoritarian Fictions: The Ideological Novel as a Literary Genre*, New York: Columbia University Press.

Tamames, R. (1961), *La lucha contra los monopolios*, Madrid: Tecnos.

——— (1967), *Los monopolios en España*, Madrid: ZYX.

Tortella, G. (2000), *The Development of Modern Spain: An Economic History of the Nineteenth and Twentieth Centuries*, Cambridge: Harvard University Press.

Townson, N., (ed.) (2007), *Spain Transformed: The Late Franco Dictatorship, 1959–75*, Basingstoke and New York: Palgrave Macmillan.

(1958), '¡TVE presenta!: La hora de la mujer', *TeleDiario*, 40: 5.

Ugarte, M. (1982), *Trilogy of Treason: an Intertextual Study of Juan Goytisolo*, Columbia: University of Missouri Press.

Umbral, F. (1991), 'Marisol: sociología de una ninfa', in F. Umbral, *Crónica de esa guapa gente. Memorias de la jet*, Barcelona: Planeta.

Urry, J. (2000), *The Tourist Gaze*, London: Sage.

Vattimo, G. (1992), *The Transparent Society*, Baltimore: Johns Hopkins University Press.

Vázquez Montalbán, M. (1986), *Crónica sentimental de España*, Madrid: Espasa-Calipe.

——— (1988), 'Literatura y transición', in Aurora Egido (ed.), *Política y literatura*, Zaragoza: Caja de Ahorros y Monte de Piedad de Zaragoza, Aragón y Rioja.

Vernon, K. M. (1997), 'Reading Hollywood in/and Spanish Cinema: From Trade Wars to Transculturation', in M. Kinder (ed.), *Refiguring Spain: Cinema, Media, Representation*, Durham: Duke University Press, pp. 35–64.

——— (1999), 'Culture and Cinema to 1975', in D. T. Gies (ed.), *The Cambridge Companion to Modern Spanish Culture*, Cambridge: Cambridge University Press, pp. 248–266.

Vicent, M. (1981), 'La artista Marisol: Nancy levanta el puño', *Retratos de la transición*, Madrid: Penthalon.

Vidal Estévez, M. (1999), '*Convenciones y devenires*', in J. L. Castro de Paz, José Luis, and J. Pérez Perucha, Julio, (eds), *El cine de Manuel Mur Oti*, Ourense: Actas del IV Festival de Cine de Ourense, pp. 75–91.

Yrache, L. (1961), '3 preguntas a Juan García Hortelano', *Índice de Artes y Letras*, 150–151, p. 4.

Zielinski, S. (1999), *Audiovisions. Cinema and Television as Entr'Actes in History*, Amsterdam: Amsterdam University Press.

Žižek, S. (1991), *Looking Awry. An Introduction to Jacques Lacan through Popular Culture*, Cambridge: MIT Press.

——— (1992), *Enjoy your Symptom*, New York: Routledge.

——— (2001), *The Fright of Real Tears: Krzysztof Kieślowski Between Theory and Post-Theory*, London: BFI Publishing.

——— (2009), 'The Iraqi MacGuffin', (11/04/2003), http://www.lacan.com/iraq1.htm.

Index